ADVANCES IN THE SPATIAL THEORY OF VOTING

ADVANCES IN THE SPATIAL THEORY OF VOTING

Edited by
JAMES M. ENELOW
and
MELVIN J. HINICH

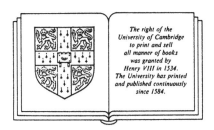

The right of the
University of Cambridge
to print and sell
all manner of books
was granted by
Henry VIII in 1534.
The University has printed
and published continuously
since 1584.

CAMBRIDGE UNIVERSITY PRESS
Cambridge
New York   Port Chester   Melbourne   Sydney

CAMBRIDGE UNIVERSITY PRESS
Cambridge, New York, Melbourne, Madrid, Cape Town, Singapore, São Paulo, Delhi

Cambridge University Press
The Edinburgh Building, Cambridge CB2 8RU, UK

Published in the United States of America by Cambridge University Press, New York

www.cambridge.org
Information on this title: www.cambridge.org/9780521352840

© Cambridge University Press 1990

First published 1990
This digitally printed version 2008

A catalogue record for this publication is available from the British Library

Library of Congress Cataloguing in Publication data

Advances in the spatial theory of voting / edited by James Enelow and
Melvin Hinich.
p.   cm.
Includes bibliographical references.
ISBN 0-521-35284-3
1. Voting.   2. Elections.   3. Social choice.   I. Enelow, James M.
II. Hinich, Melvin J.
JF1001.R37   1990
324.9-dc20   89-17313
                              CIP

ISBN 978-0-521-35284-0 hardback
ISBN 978-0-521-08453-6 paperback

We dedicate this book in grateful appreciation
to Duncan Black.

Contents

Foreword   ix

1   Introduction   1
    James M. Enelow and Melvin J. Hinich

2   Multiparty Competition, Entry, and Entry Deterrence in Spatial
    Models of Elections   12
    Kenneth A. Shepsle and Ronald N. Cohen

3   Heresthetic and Rhetoric in the Spatial Model   46
    William H. Riker

4   Spatial Strategies When Candidates Have Policy Preferences   66
    Donald Wittman

5   A Decade of Experimental Research on Spatial Models of
    Elections and Committees   99
    Richard D. McKelvey and Peter C. Ordeshook

6   Candidate Uncertainty and Electoral Equilibria   145
    Peter J. Coughlin

7   The Theory of Predictive Mappings   167
    James M. Enelow and Melvin J. Hinich

8   Multicandidate Spatial Competition   179
    Gary W. Cox

9   The Setter Model   199
    Howard Rosenthal

Author Index   235

Subject Index   238

Foreword

KENNETH J. ARROW

Stanford University

In an early paper (1929), Harold Hotelling studied the equilibrium of spatial economic competition between two firms that first chose locations and then price. His conclusion was that the firms would locate right next to each other, since each could gain by moving in the direction of the other and thereby increasing market share. It was assumed that consumers were uniformly distributed over an interval and paid the cost of transportation, so that each one would buy from the least-cost source, taking account of both price and transportation. Under these assumptions, the common equilibrium location would, he asserted, be found at the center of the interval, which is, in this case, the location of the median consumer.

Hotelling was especially concerned about this outcome because, as can easily be seen, the optimal locations of the two firms would be at the two quartile points, that is, at one-quarter of the interval length from each end. Hence, the competitive system led to a suboptimal outcome.

At the end of his paper, Hotelling argued that the tendency of competitors to become identical is applicable more generally. Spatial differentiation can be a metaphor for quality differentiation of products and for differences of political programs. Hence, Hotelling concluded, political parties tend to offer programs that resemble each other closely, instead of offering clearly separated alternatives, the latter, he thought, leading to superior outcomes.

The Hotelling argument has been show to be fallacious in its original application (d'Aspremont, Gabszewicz, and Thisse 1979); the problem is that in the second stage, where locations are given, if the firms are sufficiently close to each other, a best response by one firm to a price chosen by the other may be to undercut the latter at its own location and therefore in the entire market area beyond it. For a fixed pair of locations, there is *no* equilibrium in pure strategies. But this difficulty does *not* affect the analogous equilibrium for differentiated political parties, for there is no equivalent of the price competition.

Foreword

The Hotelling paper started a considerable interest in spatial competition. To my knowledge, the only author who referred to the political implications was Smithies (1941). Smithies introduced the elasticity of demand into the story. The political interpretation of elasticity in a two-party world was the possibility that the extremists would abstain if the party closer to their views moved too far away in an effort to get moderate votes.

An unusual and isolated paper was Bowen (1943). He considered each voter as choosing an optimal level of government expenditures, on the assumption that the tax-sharing rules were given. Under standard economic assumptions on each individual's indifference map between collective and private consumption, preferences would be single-peaked, and Bowen did indeed derive the existence of what we might now call a Condorcet majority level of government expenditures. The conclusions were stated in a way that obscured the general line of reasoning.

It was in this somewhat tentative groping that Black's (1948a) paper came as a revelatory light. My personal reaction was that the formulation there was precisely the appropriate one for considering the problem of voting under more general assumptions. I had had a fitful concern with voting as analogous to economic choice and had stumbled (about 1946) on what I now know to be the Condorcet paradox, although I was sure that someone must have anticipated me. I was therefore ready to appreciate Black's precise formulation (developed further in 1948b–d). What was especially remarkable was the achievement of a *positive* result. If one makes the spatial assumption, not dissimilar to Hotelling's and Bowen's, that the alternatives can be located on a line and that preferences are representable by a quasi-concave utility function, then the median most preferred point will have a majority against any other. Indeed, further, pairwise majority voting among the alternatives will actually produce a complete order.

The very fact that such a strong assumption as single-peakedness seemed to be used essentially suggested a general impossibility theorem. Indeed, simultaneous with my own work, Black and Newing (1951) showed that if the alternatives are represented in two dimensions rather than one, even quasi-concavity does not guarantee the existence of a Condorcet candidate, much less an ordering. But the positive results have indeed given rise to a very significant literature in which special assumptions about the structure of preferences over a spatial representation of alternatives have given rise to strong conclusions about existence and properties of equilibria in political competition. The stimulus and power of Black's contributions are permanently recorded in the subsequent literature, and we are all grateful.

Foreword

REFERENCES

Black, D. 1948a. On the rationale of group decision-making. *Journal of Political Economy* 56: 23–34.

———. 1948b. The decisions of a committee using a special majority. *Econometrica* 16: 262–327.

———. 1948c. The elasticity of committee decisions with altering size of majority. *Econometrica* 16: 262–70.

———. 1948d. Un approccio alla teoria delle decisioni di comitato. *Giornale degli economisti e annali di economia* 7(N.S.): 262–84.

Black, D., and A. S. Newing. 1951. *Committee Decisions with Complementary Valuation*. London, Edinburgh, and Glasgow: W. Hodge

Bowen, H. R. 1943. The interpretation of voting in the allocation of resources. *Quarterly Journal of Economics* 58: 27–48.

d'Aspremont, C., J.-J. Gabszewicz, and J. Thisse. 1979. On Hotelling's "Stability in Competition." *Econmetrica* 47: 1145–58.

Hotelling, H. 1929. Stability in competition. *Economic Journal* 39: 41–57.

Smithies, A. 1941. Optimal location in spatial competition. *Journal of Political Economy* 99: 423–39.

ADVANCES IN THE SPATIAL THEORY OF VOTING

I

Introduction

JAMES M. ENELOW
*University of Texas
at Austin*

MELVIN J. HINICH
*University of Texas
at Austin*

The spatial theory of voting continues to be a growth industry in political science. From its modest beginnings in the papers of Hotelling (1929) and Smithies (1941), through the pioneer work of Black (1948, 1958) and Downs (1957) and the early work of Davis and Hinich (1966), spatial voting theory has mushroomed to the point where it can now be broken down into subfields, such as agenda theory and probabilistic election theory. While this growth is a healthy sign, it has made it difficult for the outside observer to obtain a good grasp of recent developments and areas of current research interest. This volume of eight essays by recognized scholars is intended to provide just such an overview of important topics in the spatial theory of voting. These essays are specially written for this book and have never before appeared in print.

It is useful to divide the spatial theory of voting into the spatial theory of committees and the spatial theory of elections. Duncan Black originally analyzed these two social choice problems with a single model, but these two areas of spatial theory are now quite distinct. In the spatial theory of committees, the voters are the key actors, voting over different policy alternatives, each of which is usually represented as a point in a Euclidean space. In contrast, the spatial theory of elections treats the candidates as the key actors, with the voters playing a fixed role. Results in the spatial theory of elections have analogues in the spatial theory of committees. For example, the absence of a pure strategy equilibrium in two-candidate contests is equivalent to the absence of a policy alternative that is undefeated in pairwise committee voting. Still, one must proceed with caution when translating results that obtain in election theory into results in committee theory.

Initially, given Black's formulation, candidates were interpreted as nothing more than policy alternatives. That is, the voters perceived a candidate simply as a vector of positions on the policy issues of the campaign. Voters were assumed to vote strictly according to their preferences over policy alternatives, and the resulting model bore no essential difference to that of a committee deciding which policy alternative to select.

Downs (1957) was the first to begin construction of a spatial theory explicitly designed for elections, but Davis and Hinich (1966) built the mathematical foundations for such a theory. From that point on, election theory and committee theory have taken a very different course. With the introduction of sophisticated voting, committee theory received a game-theoretic foundation, providing voters with a strategic theory of behavior appropriate for small groups (Farquharson 1969). Election theory, on the other hand, with its focus on large electorates, had no reason to abandon the assumption of nonstrategic voting behavior (at least in two-candidate elections). Instead, election theory during the initial period of the late '60s to early '70s was aimed at generalizing the model's key assumptions, while retaining the basic framework of strategic candidates and nonstrategic voters.

The best description of spatial election theory in the early '70s is contained in Riker and Ordeshook (1973). Their summary lists a range of assumptions about voters and candidates and specifies the combinations of assumptions that imply the existence of a pure strategy equilibrium for the candidates. In the 1973 election model, voters are permitted to have different-shaped utility functions; they are allowed to abstain from alienation or indifference; ideal point distributions are no longer required to be unimodal and symmetric. As for the candidates, the goal of winning is generalized to include expected plurality maximization, expected vote maximization, the maximization of the probability of winning, and other definitions.

It is unfortunate that once the assumption of a symmetric ideal point distribution is relaxed, under simple preference-based voting, a pure strategy equilibrium for the candidates becomes quite rare when the election concerns two or more issues (Plott 1967; Davis, DeGroot, and Hinich 1972; Kramer 1973). In most cases, no matter what set of policy positions a candidate adopts, his opponent can defeat him in a majority contest by adopting a different set of positions. This disheartening conclusion is echoed in the committee-voting literature by the equivalent discovery that when a committee votes over multidimensional policy alternatives, a policy alternative rarely exists that cannot be defeated in a majority vote.

The disappointment over the scarcity of majority rule equilibrium in electoral contests and committee voting was made worse by the discovery that in the absence of such an equilibrium, the majority preference relation engulfs the entire outcome space in one gigantic cycle (McKelvey 1976, 1979). This discovery caused some theorists to despair of ever being able to predict candidate behavior or committee-voting outcomes (Riker 1980).

This bleak result prompted several constructive responses. In the area of committee voting, much time was spent looking at solution concepts for n-person cooperative games that could predict the outcome of committee voting in the absence of an undominated outcome. While general existence results were not found, ideas such as the "bargaining set" (Aumann and Maschler 1964), the "main-simple V-set" (Wilson 1971), and the "competitive solution" (McKelvey, Ordeshook, and Winer 1978) were explored, premised on weaker forms of outcome stability. On the noncooperative side, Shepsle (1979), by emphasizing the role of structures and procedures in shaping outcomes, originated a "neo-institutionalist" approach to committee voting. In a vein similar to Shepsle's, Romer and Rosenthal (1978) introduced the field of positive models based on agenda theory, which opened up such subjects as how outcomes are affected by the power to determine: which policies get voted on, the order in which policies are voted on, and the method of dividing the policies that are voted on.

On the question of outcome stability in noncooperative committee voting, results are mixed. In the case of one-issue-at-a-time voting, for example, sincere voting leads to an equilibrium majority outcome, but if voters are sophisticated, an equilibrium outcome may not exist (Ordeshook 1986). Still, noncooperative equilibria in committee-voting games are often numerous, and the challenge is to identify those equilibria that correspond to fully rational behavior on the part of the players. Sophisticated equilibrium is one example of what is termed a "subgame perfect equilibrium," which meets this criterion.

In the field of election theory, a very different set of developments took place, exploiting the crucial distinction that in elections the objects of choice are candidates rather than policies. Beginning in 1972 (Hinich, Ledyard, and Ordeshook 1972), but not picking up speed until the late '70s (Hinich 1977) and early '80s (Coughlin and Nitzan 1981), probabilistic theories of voter behavior were developed. Viewing the vote as a nondegenerate random variable, instead of as strictly determined by policy preference, marked a fundamental departure in election theory. Modeling the vote in this fashion is justified by several different features of election contests: abstention from alienation and indifference, nonpolicy candidate characteristics, measurement error, omitted variables, and other factors. Whether viewed from the perspective of a candidate uncertain about individual voting decisions, or of a voter uncertain about the relevant qualities of the candidate, probabilistic spatial theories seemed ideally suited to the low information environment of elections. Furthermore, sufficient conditions for equilibrium in two-candidate multidimensional contests are much less restrictive than for "deterministic" spatial models (Coughlin in press; Enelow and Hinich 1989).

The early '80s saw two alternative approaches to modeling elections that were designed not to answer the question of missing equilibrium but to incorporate additional realism into spatial election theory. Both approaches include the low information environment of mass elections. The first is McKelvey and Ordeshook's (1985) rational expectations model. In their model, an uninformed voter learns which candidate he is closer to by following public opinion polls. Rather than predicting candidate behavior, the research question McKelvey and Ordeshook pose is whether voters can extract sufficient information to behave as they would in a model with complete information. Under relatively weak conditions, the authors find that the uninformed voters eventually infer the correct midpoint between the locations of two candidates competing for office.

The question of how voters use shorthand devices, such as opinion polls, to save on information costs seems particularly suited to elections. While cue-taking also occurs in legislative bodies, the problem of voters using limited information to reach voting decisions seems especially acute in mass elections. With this thought in mind, Enelow and Hinich (1984) developed a model of predictive dimensions, which allowed the voter to infer a candidate's issue positions from a shorthand label, such as the candidate's political ideology.

While equilibrium results can be obtained, the justification for the predictive dimensions model is largely empirical. By postulating a smaller space of predictive labels that underlies the standard issue space of spatial theory, and by building a theoretical linkage between those two spaces, Enelow and Hinich provide a theoretical foundation for multidimensional scaling analysis that reduces voter opinions about the candidates to a small space in which candidates and voters can be located. In addition, the Enelow-Hinich model answers the question of how a voter, faced with disincentives to investing time in information gathering, can cast a policy-based vote.

As the 1980s progressed, there were some attempts to construct solution theories designed to treat elections and committee voting simultaneously. Perhaps the best-known of these concepts is the uncovered set. As McKelvey (1986) shows, this set of outcomes can be justified as a solution to a certain class of committee and election games. The uncovered set is a subset of the pareto set, its size being determined by the degree of asymmetry of voter ideal points (Cox 1987). While not built on a behavioral theory about the actors, a *post hoc* theoretical justification can sometimes be constructed for this concept. Under amendment agendas, for example, sophisticated voting does narrow the set of possible outcomes to those that are uncovered (Shepsle and Weingast 1984). In elections, if candidates eliminate dominated strategies, they must select strategies from the uncovered set (Miller 1980; Cox 1985).

Another line of research, relevant to both committee and election theory, is taken by Greenberg (1979), Schofield (1986), and Caplin and Nalebuff (1988). This work examines the effect on the existence of equilibrium of enlarging the size of a winning vote from a simple majority to a larger-sized majority. It is not surprising that as majority size increases, equilibrium becomes more plentiful. Although it is more a normative than a descriptive exercise, these results increase our understanding of institutional construction. The strategic implications of increasing the dimensionality of the policy space for a fixed majority size are explored by Riker (1986, this volume).

Other efforts to find electoral equilibrium led to such concepts as mixed minimax strategy solutions (McKelvey and Ordeshook 1976; Kramer 1978), stochastic equilibrium (Ferejohn, Fiorina, and Packel 1978), and dynamical stability (Kramer 1977). Skepticism about the propriety of mixed minimax strategy solutions to election contests dampened interest in the first subject. The somewhat mechanistic nature of the solution concept has perhaps been responsible for the limited interest in the second subject. The inability to generalize initial results in the third area put that subject on a back burner.

While candidate or policy equilibrium remains a primary concern in the spatial voting literature, theorists have expanded the purview of the theory to include electoral and committee phenomena previously unanalyzed. A growing literature concerns electoral competition between three or more candidates with or without the possibility that new candidates may join the race. Spatial modeling of proportional representation systems is also a recent area of inquiry. The two essays in this volume by Cox and Shepsle and Cohen address these subjects.

Another new topic is spatial games of incomplete information, in which players form beliefs about the parameters that are relevant to other players' strategic decisions. In equilibrium, both beliefs and strategies are stable. Such games present simultaneous maximization problems of great complexity and are often limited to a small number of players (Ledyard 1984; Palfrey and Rosenthal 1985). Models of endogenous agenda formation, with and without complete information, are also currently receiving much attention (Austen-Smith 1987; Banks and Gasmi 1987).

It is impossible in this short space to do justice to all the significant work in election and committee voting theory in the last twenty years. As mentioned earlier, this volume is intended to bring the reader up to date with respect to some of the more important research areas in the spatial theory of voting. The following section will briefly describe where these essays fit into the overall theory.

THE ESSAYS IN THIS BOOK

The eight essays in this book are almost evenly divided between the spatial theory of committees and the spatial theory of elections.

In the first essay, Kenneth Shepsle and Ronald Cohen analyze elections in which new candidates are allowed to enter the competition. An entry equilibrium is a location for the existing candidates in the race such that no new location exists that an entrant can profitably adopt.

James M. Enelow and Melvin J. Hinich

Shepsle and Cohen summarize several key articles that are relevant to election models with entry. Beginning with Hotelling's (1929) original duopoly model of spatial competition along a single dimension, Shepsle and Cohen describe Eaton and Lipsey's (1975) expansion of the model to three or more competitors, with actors who anticipate strategic reactions to their own behavior, and electorates that are not described by a uniform distribution. With a fixed number of candidates, this is the single-member, plurality-based election system analyzed by Gary Cox in Chapter 8.

Shepsle and Cohen then deal with the question of entry. Starting with Palfrey (1984), Shepsle and Cohen move to a discussion of Greenberg and Shepsle (1987), who analyze the entry problem in plurality-based, multi-member systems. The general absence of entry equilibrium is the central conclusion of this work. For certain voter distributions, however, existence can be established for two-member districts.

William Riker's essay, directed at both the spatial theories of committees and elections, is perhaps more relevant to committee theory. In the first part of his essay, Riker reviews the main topics in what he has termed the theory of "heresthetics." Briefly put, heresthetics means the art (and science) of manipulating vote outcomes. Three major types of heresthetical maneuver are identified, each designed to change a predicted vote outcome in a desired direction. Strategic voting of both the noncooperative variety (of which sophisticated voting is an example) and the cooperative type (best exemplified by vote trading) are tools by which voters can induce more desired vote outcomes. Examples of both are readily found in legislative settings.

Agenda control, extending beyond the Romer-Rosenthal model, is another type of heresthetic. A committee chairman who selects the method of dividing the alternatives that are voted on or who has the power to recognize a voter who wishes to offer a proposal may have enormous power over the final outcome of the committee's deliberations. In a finite alternative setting, the Plott-Levine flying club experiments (Plott and Levine 1978) are an impressive demonstration of this power.

Increasing the dimensionality of the policy space is the third major type of heresthetic described by Riker. Other things being equal, as the dimensionality of the space increases, equilibrium becomes less likely (Greenberg 1979). Thus, adding a new dimension to a policy debate may destabilize group decision making in a way that promotes an individual's objective.

Riker then turns to a related, but different, method by which an individual may try to get his way: rhetoric. The purpose of this technique is to modify individual preferences or, in the language of spatial theory, to move voter ideal points. Here Riker explores largely uncharted territory but uncovers one rhetorical rule that is supported by experimental and historical evidence: the tactic of exaggerating the probability of a dreaded event.

Donald Wittman's essay analyzes a spatial election model that alters a key

6

assumption about candidate behavior. A standard assumption in spatial models of electoral competition is that candidate motivation is described by one word: winning. In Wittman's model, each candidate maximizes a different objective: the expected utility of the winning set of policies. As Wittman demonstrates, this modification leads to different predictions about candidate behavior. In the one-dimensional, two-candidate spatial model, Wittman shows that in equilibrium, the candidates will adopt divergent policies instead of converging to the median. This result also applies to multidimensional contests.

Wittman analyzes the effect on candidate equilibrium positions of changes in two exogenous variables: voter bias for or against one of the candidates and voter sensitivity to the candidates' policy positions. His results are, again, different from those of the simple Black-Downs model.

In the remainder of his essay, Wittman extends his model to incorporate several additional phenomena, including credible commitments, multicandidate elections, and perfect information. He also discusses related work in macro-level policy models of elections with rational expectations. Throughout the essay, Wittman mentions empirical studies supporting the results he cites.

In the fourth essay, Richard McKelvey and Peter Ordeshook summarize ten years of experimental research on elections and committee voting. Their main conclusion is that if a majority rule equilibrium exists in either a cooperative committee game or a two-candidate election, the players in an experiment eventually select it or come very close. Predictions are harder to make in the absence of an undominated outcome, or pure strategy electoral equilibrium. None of the n-person cooperative solution concepts used to predict outcomes in the absence of an undominated outcome (or "core") performs exceptionally better than the others. Still, outcomes remain centrally located, although with broader dispersion, so one cannot say that "anything goes."

In the realm of noncooperative committee voting, McKelvey and Ordeshook find that institutional restrictions, such as issue-at-a-time voting, are important in affecting outcomes, but not nearly as important as whether the subjects are allowed to communicate with each other during experimental trials. As communication among subjects increases and coalitions find ways to circumvent rules and procedures, institutional restrictions become less important to the final outcome.

All in all, McKelvey and Ordeshook find that the solution concepts of spatial theory do not distort reality. Experimental evidence is most difficult to interpret in games where solution theory is fuzziest. On the other hand, in games with undominated outcomes or a pure strategy candidate equilibrium, experimental evidence strongly supports the theory's predictions.

Turning to election theory, Peter Coughlin summarizes work in the probabilistic theory of elections referred to above. Focusing on two-candidate, expected plurality-maximizing elections, Coughlin shows that stability conditions are basically the same in one-dimensional and multidimensional elections. This result is in stark contrast to deterministic election theory, in which one-dimensional contests are, in Hinich's (1977) description, a "Garden of Eden."

Coughlin goes on to describe the major equilibrium results in probabilistic election theory. He specifies sufficient conditions for equilibrium in several different forms of the probabilistic model. In the binary Luce model, analyzed by Coughlin and Nitzan, the majority equilibrium maximizes a Nash social welfare function.

As Coughlin's essay makes clear, probabilistic election theory is characterized by a fundamentally different set of results from the classical Black-Downs model, in addition to being easier to justify from a statistical standpoint.

The sixth essay is also relevant to both election and committee-voting theory. In this essay, James Enelow and Melvin Hinich examine group decision problems that are both one- *and* multidimensional. If voters evaluate candidates by their positions on multiple policy issues, but infer these positions from a one-dimensional set of predictive elements, the election takes place in two different spaces. In legislative voting, congressmen may decide among different deficit levels, but this choice may determine future choices on program-spending levels. Again, the contest is simultaneously one- and multidimensional.

If voter preferences are directly defined on choice elements in the multidimensional space, under what conditions are the derived preferences in the one-dimensional space single-peaked? This is the basic question that Enelow and Hinich answer. Given the satisfaction of these conditions, it follows from Black's median voter theorem that group decision making will be stable even though the voters are evaluating the objects of choice along multiple dimensions.

Gary Cox analyzes an area of spatial election theory whose technical difficulties long deterred spatial theorists: elections with three or more candidates. Cox's essay is broad in scope, covering elections in both single-member and multimember districts under a wide class of election rules. For single-member districts, these election rules include plurality rule, "scoring" rules, approval voting, and Condorcet procedures. For multimember districts, plurality-based and proportional representation systems are analyzed.

Cox's primary focus is on convergent and divergent candidate equilibrium. Under deterministic voting, equilibrium in elections with more than two candidates is rare, even when the election concerns a single dimension. Nevertheless, Cox finds an important connection between election rules and candidate incentives to converge or disperse. Under election rules such as plurality rule, which gives each voter one vote, candidate dispersion is encouraged. Under rules such as approval voting, which allows each voter to vote for any number of candidates, candidates are encouraged to converge to a central location.

In the final essay, Howard Rosenthal summarizes results in the Romer-Rosenthal agenda-setter model. Beginning with the simplest form of committee theory, in which a monopoly setter with complete information about voter preferences offers the voters a fixed choice between one exogenously and one endogenously determined policy, Rosenthal expands the theory to incorporate setter uncertainty, voter uncertainty, endogenous reversion levels, sequential referenda, and sophisticated voting. The incorporation of these phenomena leads to a much richer theory of agenda setting as well as unexpected and insightful results about agenda-setting behavior.

Rosenthal also ties his setter model into the neo-institutionalist literature originated by Shepsle. Legislative committees play a role in the policy formation process much like that of a public school board with budget-proposing power, the institution that originally inspired the Romer-Rosenthal model. Both have agenda-setting powers. It is not surprising, therefore, that spatial models of legislative choice are closely related to the Romer-Rosenthal model.

In the final section of his essay, Rosenthal reviews the empirical literature that uses data from school budget referenda and data about school spending levels to test the setter model. Looking at budget proposals, expenditure levels, and aggregate voting data in Oregon and New York school districts, Rosenthal summarizes the evidence that supports the setter model.

CONCLUSION

The main purpose of this volume is to apprise readers of major theoretical developments in the spatial theory of voting in the last ten years. This literature continues to grow exponentially, so that any volume is "dated" as soon as it appears. Still, we believe that these essays provide a comprehensive overview of work in spatial theory in the 1980s.

REFERENCES

Aumann, R., and M. Maschler. 1964. "The Bargaining Set for Cooperative Games." In *Advances in Game Theory*, ed. M. Dresher, L. Shapley, and A. Tucker. Princeton: Princeton University Press.

Austen-Smith, D. 1987. "Sophisticated Sincerity: Voting Over Endogenous Agendas." *American Political Science Review* 81:1323–30.

Banks, J., and F. Gasmi. 1987. "Endogenous Agenda Formation in Three-Person Committees." *Social Choice and Welfare* 4:1–20.

Black, D. 1948. "On the Rationale of Group Decision-Making." *Journal of Political Economy* 56:23–34.

———. 1958. *Theory of Committees and Elections*. Cambridge University Press.

James M. Enelow and Melvin J. Hinich

Caplin, A., and B. Nalebuff. 1988. "On 64% Majority Rule." *Econometrica* 56:787–814.

Coughlin, P. In press. *Probabilistic Voting Theory.* Cambridge: Cambridge University Press.

Coughlin, P., and S. Nitzan. 1981. "Electoral Outcomes with Probabilistic Voting and Nash Social Welfare Maxima." *Journal of Public Economics* 15:113–22.

Cox, G. 1985. "Undominated Candidate Strategies Under Alternative Voting Rules." Washington University (unpublished).

———. 1987. "The Uncovered Set and the Core." *American Journal of Political Science* 31:408–22.

Davis, O., M. DeGroot, and M. Hinich. 1972. "Social Preference Orderings and Majority Rule." *Econometrica* 40:147–57.

Davis, O., and M. Hinich. 1966. "A Mathematical Model of Policy Formation in a Democratic Society." In *Mathematical Applications in Political Science, II,* ed. J. Bernd. Dallas: Southern Methodist University Press, pp. 175–208.

Downs, A. 1957. *An Economic Theory of Democracy.* New York: Harper & Row.

Eaton, B., and R. Lipsey. 1975. "The Principle of Minimum Differentiation Reconsidered: Some New Developments in the Theory of Spatial Competition." *Review of Economic Studies* 42:27–49.

Enelow, J., and M. Hinich. 1984. *The Spatial Theory of Voting: An Introduction.* Cambridge: Cambridge University Press.

———. 1989. "A General Probabilistic Spatial Theory of Elections." *Public Choice* 61:101–13.

Farquharson, R. 1969. *Theory of Voting.* New Haven: Yale University Press.

Ferejohn, J., M. Fiorina, and E. Packel. 1980. "Nonequilibrium Solutions for Legislative Systems." *Behavioral Science* 25:140–8.

Greenberg, J. 1979. "Consistent Majority Rules Over Compact Sets of Alternatives." *Econometrica* 47:627–36.

Greenberg, J., and K. Shepsle. 1987. "The Efffect of Electoral Rewards in Multiparty Competition with Entry." *American Political Science Review* 81:525–37.

Hinich, M. 1977. "Equilibrium in Spatial Voting: The Median Voter Is an Artifact." *Journal of Economic Theory* 16:208–19.

Hinich, M., J. Ledyard, and P. Ordeshook. 1972. "Nonvoting and the Existence of Equilibrium Under Majority Rule." *Journal of Economic Theory* 14:144–53.

Hotelling, H. 1929. "Stability in Competition." *Economic Journal* 39:41–57.

Kramer, G. 1973. "On a Class of Equilibrium Conditions for Majority Rule." *Econometrica* 41:285–97.

———. 1977. "A Dynamical Model of Political Equlibrium." *Journal of Economic Theory* 15:310–34.

———. 1978. "Existence of Electoral Equilibrium." In *Game Theory and Political Science,* P. Ordeshook, New York: New York University Press, pp. 371–89.

Ledyard, J. 1984. "The Pure Theory of Large Two-Candidate Elections." *Public Choice* 44:7–41.

McKelvey, R. 1976. "Intransitivities in Multidimensional Voting Models and Some Implications for Agenda Control." *Journal of Economic Theory* 12:472–82.

———. 1979. "General Conditions for Global Intransitivities in Formal Voting Models." *Econometrica* 47:1085–111.

———. 1986. "Covering, Dominance, and Institution Free Properties of Social Choice." *American Journal of Political Science* 30:283–314.

McKelvey, R., and P. Ordeshook. 1976. "Symmetric Spatial Games Without Majority Rule Equilibria." *American Political Science Review* 70:1172–84.

Introduction

————. 1985. "Elections With Limited Information: A Fulfilled Expectations Model Using Contemporaneous Poll and Endorsement Data as Information Sources." *Journal of Economic Theory* 36:55–85.

McKelvey, R., P. Ordeshook, and M. Winer. 1978. "The Competitive Solution for N-Person Games Without Transferable Utility, with An Application to Committee Games." *American Political Science Review* 72:599–615.

Miller, N. 1980. "A New Solution Set for Tournaments and Majority Voting." *American Journal of Political Science* 24:68–96.

Ordeshook, P. 1986. *Game Theory and Political Theory.* Cambridge University Press.

Palfrey, T. 1984. "Spatial Equilibrium with Entry." *Review of Economic Studies* 51:139–56.

Palfrey, T., and H. Rosenthal. 1985. "Voter Participation and Strategic Uncertainty." *American Political Science Review* 79:62–78.

Plott, C. 1967. "A Notion of Equilibrium and Its Possibility Under Majority Rule." *American Economic Review* 57:787—806.

Plott, C., and M. Levine. 1978. "A Model of Agenda Influence on Committee Decisions." *American Economic Review* 68:146–60.

Riker, W. 1980. "Implications from the Disequilibrium of Majority Rule for the Study of Institutions." *American Political Science Review* 74:432–46.

————. 1986. *The Art of Political Manipulation.* New Haven: Yale University Press.

Riker, W., and P. Ordeshook. 1973. *An Introduction to Positive Political Theory.* Englewood Cliffs: Prentice-Hall.

Romer, T., and H. Rosenthal. 1978. "Political Resource Allocation, Controlled Agendas, and the Status Quo." *Public Choice* 33:27–43.

Schofield, N. 1986. "Existence of a 'Structurally Stable' Equilibrium for a Non-Collegial Voting Rule." *Public Choice* 51:267–84.

Shepsle, K. 1979. "Institutional Arrangements and Equilibrium in Multidimensional Voting Models." *American Journal of Political Science* 23:27–59.

Shepsle, K., and B. Weingast. 1984. "Uncovered Sets and Sophisticated Voting Outcomes with Implications for Agenda Institutions." *American Journal of Political Science* 29:49–74.

Smithies, A. 1941. "Optimum Location in Spatial Competition." *Journal of Political Economy* 49:423–39.

Wilson, R. 1971. "Stable Coalition Proposals in Majority-Rule Voting." *Journal of Economic Theory* 3:254–71.

2

Multiparty Competition, Entry, and Entry Deterrence in Spatial Models of Elections

KENNETH A. SHEPSLE

Harvard University

RONALD N. COHEN

Cornell University Medical School

We cannot have observations of deaths without observations of births.
Riker (1976: 99)

Political theories based on the spatial model have enjoyed a dual existence. As reflected in the title of Duncan Black's (1958) famous volume, the spatial model provides a foundation for the analysis of electoral phenomena and committee decision making. It does this by providing an abstract characterization of the outcomes and preferences common to electoral and committee choice. In each setting, outcomes are represented by points in a Euclidean space. Preferences over outcomes are represented by voter (legislator) utility functions defined on points in this space. Whether an actor is called a "voter" or "legislator," and whether a point in the space is designated a "voter's [legislator's] preferred policy," the "policy of a candidate," or a "legislative bill," is little more than a labeling convention. It indicates the substantive domain of interest to the researcher.

The spatial theory of elections and the spatial theory of committees, however, have followed different paths of development as subfield-specific scholars have charted distinctive research agendas. And yet, a question pursued in one subfield – for example, is there a spatial location for a candidate that cannot be beaten by a candidate at any other location? – typically has a dual in the other subfield – for example, is there a motion that cannot be successfully amended? It is from this perspective that we explore multicandidate competition and entry in spatial models of elections. We see these phenomena as duals to agenda-setting activities in legislatures.

In first-generation models of legislatures, as represented in some of Duncan

Multiparty Competition, Entry, Deterrence

Black's earliest work (Black 1948, 1958; Black and Newing 1951), a set of alternative motions was given exogenously. Legislators voted on these motions according to fixed rules of procedure. The questions that interested Black and others concerned whether some one motion could defeat all others, how the existence of such a motion depended on the configuration of legislator preferences, and how its existence depended upon the decision rule in place. That is, if $N = (1, 2, \ldots, n)$ is the set of legislators, $X = (x_1, x_2, \ldots, x_m)$ is the set of exogenously given motions, and P_i the preference ordering over X of the ith legislator, is there a distinguished alternative x^* in X that beats every other x? How does the existence of such an x^* depend upon the configuration of P_is? How does the existence of x^* depend upon the decision rule (majority rule, two-thirds rule, dictatorship, unanimity)?

All these questions bear on the issue of under what conditions an equilibrium exists in a *given* set of alternatives. This is a perfectly reasonable first-generation question. As a next step, however, one might rightfully ask, "Since alternatives do not fall from the heavens, where do they come from?" In legislatures, the answer is usually straightforward: Institutional arrangements – rules and procedures – govern how an agenda is built. In some settings, legislators may be randomly recognized to make motions. Alternatively, there may be an agenda committee – a subset of legislators – charged with bringing motions to the floor of the legislature. As a final example, there may be one committee (a legislative committee) charged with bringing a motion to the floor, and another committee (a rules committee) charged with determining what other motions will be in order – a procedure common in the U.S. House of Representatives.

Such agenda processes have been modeled in recent work on legislatures in the spatial framework (Romer and Rosenthal 1978; Shepsle 1979; Shepsle and Weingast 1981, 1984; Banks 1985; McKelvey 1986; Ferejohn, Fiorina, and McKelvey 1987). The purpose of these models is to *endogenize* the set X of alternatives. Given agenda-setting rules and procedures, how will rational agents select the contents of X and the order in which alternatives will be considered?

What about on the electoral side? Is there a dual in the electoral realm to agenda setting in the legislative realm? In the second section we formulate the electoral dual to agenda setting, suggesting that a prospective candidate's decision to *enter* an electoral contest is the parallel phenomenon of interest. In subsequent sections of this essay we examine the burgeoning literature on entry in industrial organization and a small complementary literature on entry in political contests. We lay out, in an informal manner, some of the components of these models and some of the insights they provide on when an entrant will throw her hat in the ring (or, alternatively, be deterred from doing so).[1] As shall become evident, a political discussion of entry is inextricably connected to theories of equilibrium in multiparty (multicandidate) settings.

Kenneth A. Shepsle and Ronald N. Cohen

Before beginning this analysis, we note that outside the spatial framework, even outside the modeling tradition altogether, there has been a good deal of interest in candidate entry and party formation. Much of the literature on Duverger's Law (see Riker 1982) attempts to characterize the mechanisms by which small parties are destroyed (or still-born) under some electoral systems while they are encouraged under others. The spatial theory of multiparty competition with entry will contribute to this discussion, providing, as the Riker quote in the headnote suggests, conditions for the birth of new parties and candidacies and the dynamics of positioning.

Another literature – on U.S. congressional elections – is similarly preoccupied by matters involving entry, which our discussion should illuminate. Rohde (1979) and Jacobson and Kernell (1981) have described casually, and Black (1972) and Banks and Kiewiet (1987) have modeled formally, the decision of a prospective candidate to enter a congressional race. Their discussions are not cast in a spatial framework and are essentially decision-theoretic. The strategic orientation of the spatial approach promises to capture an additional layer of complexity. In short, the formal consideration of entry, by endogenizing candidacies, will provide a fuller picture of electoral systems and their equilibrium tendencies.

A PRELIMINARY CONSIDERATION OF ENTRY

In the legislative context, legislators vote directly on outcomes; the alternatives under consideration are motions that would alter an existing policy. In the electoral context, however, voters do not vote directly on outcomes; rather, they vote for candidates or parties that serve as *carriers* of policy outcomes. Candidates and parties compete for election by identifying with particular policies. If candidate promises about future policy are trustworthy (as we shall assume throughout this essay), and if an elected candidate is capable of delivering on his or her promises (see below), then it would appear that the voter's decision problem is exactly the same as the legislator's. Each is effectively voting on future policy. Candidates announcing policy positions are equivalent to legislators making motions.

There are complications, however, that make this equivalence problematical. For instance, candidate policy promises may not be deliverable. Of course, if election confers a policy *monopoly* on a candidate (as when a single, all-powerful, chief executive is being elected), there may be no difficulties. On the other hand, if, as in legislative elections, a *set* of candidates is being elected, the policy positions of the winning candidates have a more ambiguous status. A voter, in casting his vote for a given candidate, cannot assume that the policy position of his winning candidate will be implemented. The winning candidate (and his policy position) is but one of many in the legislature. Thus, in what Austen-Smith (1987b) refers to as "multidistrict electoral systems," the simple association of candidates with policy positions is attenuated: a vote for a winning candidate is *not* necessarily instrumental for that candidate's policy position.

In multidistrict elections, then, in which a separate coalition-building or government-formation process inside a legislature must be taken into account, candidate selection by voters is not equivalent to the simple selection of a motion by legislators. The equivalence may also fail on the basis of the method of conducting the voting process. There are many distinct methods for electing legislators (Wright and Riker 1987), none of which is even remotely similar to the methods by which motions are considered in most legislative processes.

These caveats aside, parallels nevertheless remain between the decision to enter an electoral race and the decision to enter a motion on the agenda of a committee. In each case a decision is predicated on prior, simultaneous, and subsequent decisions made by others. It depends on the preferences of others and the way those preferences are revealed in voting. It depends on the motives of decision makers (in an election an entrant may want to win the most votes, to finish among the top K vote-getters, to affect the behavior of other existing or prospective candidates, and so on). Finally, it depends on information – about the preferences of others, about the sequence of decision making, and so on. Although in what follows we make no explicit analytical use of this dualism in spatial models, it is worth keeping in the back of one's mind. It represents, down the road, a possibility rich approach for comparing decision by election with choice by committee.

HOTELLING AND "MINIMUM DIFFERENTIATION"

In this section we begin our examination of multicandidate competition and entry in the spatial modeling context in which it first arose – Hotelling's (1929) model of a firm's decision to enter a market. Many of the issues that arise in political competition are also present in the original Hotelling formulation – indeed, it was Hotelling's model that first attracted Anthony Downs.

In much of the discussion to follow, we elaborate issues pertaining to entry in a stripped-down spatial model. The space is one-dimensional and in most circumstances it will suffice to talk about the closed unit interval,[2] $[0,1]$, with x a typical point. Individual voters (consumers) either comprise a finite set $N = (1,2, \ldots , n)$, with i a generic voter (consumer), or are described by a distribution function, $F(x)$, on $[0,1]$. Each i has preferences over the alternatives in $[0,1]$ representable by a symmetric, single-peaked utility function, $u_i(x)$. Candidates (or firms) are given by the set $C = (1, 2, \ldots , m)$, and x_j is the location of the jth candidate (firm) in $[0,1]$. Unless otherwise specified, each voter (consumer) votes for (buys from) the candidate (firm) closest to it in Euclidean distance. Since utility functions are symmetric, this is essentially an assumption of sincere preference revelation.

Imagine now the setting for Hotelling's famous discussion of competition between duopolists. The unit interval may be taken to be Main Street, and x_1 and x_2 as the locations for firms 1 and 2, respectively.[3] The consumers are assumed to be uniformly distributed along Main Street and to have inelastic demand for the two firms' (homogenous) product. That is, each consumer purchases one unit per time period at a parametrically given price. In addition to the fixed purchase price, he also pays a transportation cost that is monotonic in distance from the location of purchase. "No customer has any preference for either seller except on the ground of price plus transportation cost" (Hotelling 1929: 45).

To simplify matters let us assume that there is no price difference between the two sellers – indeed, we will normalize it to zero—so that the only thing that distinguishes between them in the eyes of any consumer is the distance between the consumer's address and that of the sellers, that is, the respective transportation costs of purchasing from either seller. In this setting each consumer will have preferences over various locations for either of the sellers. Specifically, Mr. i will prefer a seller to locate a store (essentially) at i's address, in which case i's transportation cost will be reduced to zero. Mr. i's utility function decreases from this maximum symmetrically as the closest store moves farther and farther from his address in either direction. That is, i's utility function is symmetric and single-peaked: If i's address is x_i, then his utility for location x is $u_i(x) = K_i - |x_i - x|c$, where $c > 0$ is the transportation cost per unit of distance and K_i is the reservation value. Thus, Mr. i would not consume if transportation cost exceeded K_i; he obtains "full value" if per unit transport cost is zero ($c = 0$) or distance is zero ($x = x_i$).

Let us simplify further by assuming that the profit of a seller depends only upon the number of sales he makes. The latter, in turn, depends upon the number of consumers to whom he is closest. Under these conditions, Hotelling sought to determine where, in equilibrium, the duopolists would locate.

To get at some underlying principles, suppose first that there were only one seller. Where will he locate? The answer is indeterminate, since his profit would be the same no matter where he located: In all cases he would capture the entire market, since he would be trivially "closest" to each consumer. Now suppose that our initial seller anticipates he will be joined by another seller. *But the first seller has to locate his shop first.* Where will he locate? The location, x, he chooses divides the market into two segments: $[0,x)$ and $(x,1]$. If one segment is larger (and by this we mean that it contains more consumers), then a profit-maximizing second seller will capture that segment by locating in it adjacent to the location of the first seller. If, for example, $(x,1]$ contains more consumers, then by locating slightly to the right of x, the second seller captures the largest segment. In short, the first seller can forecast exactly what a rational second seller will do and knows that he (the first seller) will always get the smaller of the two segments. Thus, from profit maximizing it follows that his objective will be to maximize the size of the smaller segment. And this will be accomplished if he locates at the median of the market. With a uniform distribution of consumers, this will be at $x = 0.5$. If the first seller locates there, the second seller will choose the same location (next door or across the street), and each will share the market equally.

The conclusion a somewhat dejected Hotelling drew from his analysis has come to be known as the *principle of minimum differentiation* (MD)[4] in which competitors are seen to bunch up close to each other, since they are animated by profits and thus wish to capture as large a market segment as possible:

The mathematical analysis thus leads to an observation of wide generality. Buyers are confronted everywhere with an excessive sameness . . . [T]here is an incentive to make the new product very much like the old, applying some slight change which will seem an improvement to as many buyers as possible without ever going far in this direction. The tremendous standardisation of our furniture, our houses, our clothing, our automobiles and our education are due in part to the economies of large-scale production, in part to fashion and imitation. But over and above these forces is the effect we have been discussing, the tendency to make only slight deviations in order to have for the new commodity as many buyers of the old as possible, to get, so to speak, *between* one's competitors and a mass of customers

[Hotelling 1929: 54].

Hotelling clearly believed his analysis applied to a wide range of social phenomena. And Anthony Downs certainly seized upon Hotelling's insights to lay down a spatial foundation for party electoral politics in which *voters* "are confronted everywhere with an excessive sameness." But before turning to the electoral interpretation and the consequences of prospective entry – the main purpose of this essay – let us push the Hotelling model a bit further.

RECONSIDERING MINIMUM DIFFERENTIATION

Eaton and Lipsey (1975), in their fine paper on generalizations of the spatial model, observe that the Hotelling analysis depends on a number of specialized assumptions. Some – for example, the assumption of inelastic demand in which each customer is assumed to purchase one unit per unit time at a parametrically given price plus transportation cost – received early attention. Smithies (1941: 423) observed that

Hotelling's assumption of completely inelastic demand means that neither competitor makes sacrifices at the ends of the market when he invades his rival's territory; thus there is no check on the two competitors' moving together. . . . I suggest, however, that it is important to analyze not only the forces that tend to bring them together but also those that keep them apart.

Kenneth A. Shepsle and Ronald N. Cohen

He demonstrated that a relaxation of the inelasticity assumption, so that the *quantity* purchased by a customer depended (inversely) on the price plus transportation cost, dampened the tendency toward MD. The prospect of losses in the "hinterland," as more distant customers reduce purchases, causes a firm to think twice before competing for that part of the market lying between it and its competitor.[5]

In addition to the inelasticity assumption, Eaton and Lipsey characterize various classes of assumption that also play a role in Hotelling's analysis as well as in subsequent work. We summarize some of them here, suggesting still others when we turn to political application:

1. Alternative Space: Hotelling assumed a closed, bounded continuum isomorphic to the unit interval. Subsequent work has considered (a) an unbounded finite interval (the circumference of a unit circle), (b) an unbounded infinite interval, and (c) multidimensional extensions.

2. Customer distribution: Hotelling assumed a uniform distribution on [0,1]. Subsequent work has allowed for any symmetric, continuous distribution (and some work has dropped the symmetry requirement).

3. Customer "sincerity": Hotelling assumed each customer buys from the firm that sells at the lowest delivered price (mill price plus transport cost). For a parametrically fixed price and utility symmetric in distance, this is equivalent to nonstrategic preference revelation, or sincere consumer behavior. Subsequent work, especially in its political format, has allowed for the possibility of "sophisticated" behavior (see, especially, Austen-Smith 1987a,b; and Austen-Smith and Banks 1987).

4. Relocation costs: Hotelling assumed that firms may reposition themselves costlessly. Subsequent work has entertained the possibility that capital costs (plant and immovable equipment) make relocating costly. In political contexts, concepts like ideological reputation may be given a similar interpretation.[6]

5. Agent conjectures: Hotelling employed a Cournot-Nash hypothesis about conjectures (or what Eaton and Lipsey call "zero conjectural variation"). Accordingly, each firm computes the advantage of relocating on the hypothesis that its competitor will hold to its current location. Subsequent work, more in the spirit of the Stackelberg hypothesis, has permitted an agent to consider, in computing the advantage of relocation, likely reactions from its competitor. An especially prudent version of this assumes maximin expectations: a firm believes a competitor will react to its move by inflicting maximum damage.

6. Number of firms: Hotelling's is a model of duopoly. Subsequent work has sought to generalize to any finite number of firms (limited by the size of the market and the costs of production).[7]

It should be clear that the Hotelling model is but one of a family of spatial models defined by the six classes of assumptions just enumerated (and there are others as well). Eaton and Lipsey explored several important variations on Hotelling.[8]

Version #1

In this version, Eaton and Lipsey accept most of the Hotelling model and seek to determine the effect of a variable number of firms. Thus, (a) the space is [0,1]; (b) customers are uniformly distributed; (c) customers buy from the "closest" seller; (d) sellers may relocate costlessly; (e) firms make Cournot-Nash conjectures; but (f) the number of firms is variable.

For any configuration of firms in [0,1] a firm's *market* is the interval defined by the midpoints of the firm's location and those of its right and left neighbors. If a firm has no left (right) neighbor, then its market is defined by a midpoint on one side (the side that has a neighbor) and a boundary point of the whole space (0 or 1, respectively) on the other side. Such a firm is called *peripheral*. If a firm has neighbors on both sides, it is *interior*. The segment of a firm's market to its left (right) is a *half-market* and, if they are unequal, one may refer to the *long* and *short* sides of its market. Finally, two firms are said to be *paired* if the distance between them is as small as permitted (which we shall take to be zero, that is, when they occupy the same location).

Eaton and Lipsey (1975: 29) state the following necessary and sufficient conditions for *equilibrium*, where the latter is a configuration of locations from which no firm has an incentive to move:

1. No firm's market is smaller than any other firm's half market.
2. The two peripheral firms are paired.

That these conditions are necessary may be demonstrated simply. If, in violation of (1), one firm's market were less than half of another's, then (by the assumption of costless movement) the first could relocate to the latter's location and capture half of that market (which exceeds its entire original market). If, contrary to (2), a peripheral firm were unpaired, it could move toward its (only) neighbor, thereby increasing its market. The proof of sufficiency is lengthier and thus is omitted.

Eaton and Lipsey proceed to examine the effect of these equilibrium conditions on markets with different numbers of firms. In a market with one firm – a degenerate market, if you will – the firm's location is indeterminate and the equilibrium conditions apply trivially to any location.

For two firms, both are peripheral so, by (2), they must be paired. By (1) they must occupy the market median position. This, of course, is the Hotelling MD principle.

For three firms, *there is no equilibrium.* By (2) both peripheral firms must be paired with the one interior firm, that is, all three firms must be minimally differentiated. But then this violates (1), since the interior firm will be left with less than half the market of either of his competitors and thus will have an incentive to "leapfrog."

For four firms, (2) requires that each peripheral firm be paired with an interior firm. (1) requires that their respective locations be at $x = .25$ and $x = .75$, the first and third quartiles, respectively.[9]

For five firms, (2) requires the two peripheral firms be paired, and (1) requires paired locations of $x = \frac{1}{6}$ and $x = \frac{5}{6}$. The unpaired interior firm is located at $x = \frac{1}{2}$. Notice that each of the paired firms captures one-sixth of the market, whereas the interior firm captures one-third. Notice also that in both the four- and five-firm cases, there is "bunching" (among peripheral firms) but not MD. To the contrary, firms are spread throughout the market.

In the six-firm case, there is no longer a unique equilibrium. At one extreme, much like the five-firm case, peripheral firms are paired up at $x = \frac{1}{6}$ and $x = \frac{5}{6}$, and the interior firms are paired at $x = \frac{1}{2}$. All six firms capture one-sixth of the market. At the other extreme, peripheral firms are paired at $x = \frac{1}{8}$ and $x = \frac{7}{8}$, while the interior firms are located at $x = \frac{3}{8}$ and $x = \frac{5}{8}$. In this configuration, the four extreme firms control one-eighth of the market each, and the two interior firms each control one-fourth of the market. It may be seen, however, that for any degree of separation between the interior firms ranging from (essentially) zero (the first limiting case) to one-fourth (the second limiting case), there are pairing locations for the remaining firms that produce an equilibrium. Thus, there is a continuum of equilibrium configurations.

Eaton and Lipsey conclude their analysis of this model by looking at large markets (more than six firms). They are much like the six-firm case, but the equal spreading of firms throughout the market – $[\frac{1}{2}n, \frac{3}{2}n, \ldots, (2n-3)/2n, (2n-1)/2n]$ – is *not* an equilibrium. This latter configuration has some normative interest because it is the one that minimizes transport cost for the entire economy. The equilibrium that comes closest to this ideal is one in which two firms are paired at each end of the market and the remaining $n - 4$ firms are equally spread through the interior.

The Eaton–Lipsey analysis (see also Denzau, Kats, and Slutsky, 1985) demonstrates the limited generalizability of Hotelling's Principle of Minimum Differentiation. Firms ($n > 2$) may "bunch" in pairs, each fighting with an opponent for a submarket, but in equilibrium they need not collectively confront the consumer with "an excessive sameness."

For our purposes, it is important to note the absence of equilibrium in the case of three firms. Many models in the political realm examine the effects of entry on two-party competition. It would appear that, under the assumptions of Version #1 (especially zero conjectural variation and costless mobility), there will be no equilibrium. Yet it would also appear that the disequilibrium of the three-firm case is the exception.

Multiparty Competition, Entry, Deterrence

Version #2

In this version of the Hotelling model, all the features of Version #1 are maintained except the Cournot–Nash hypothesis. Unlike in Hotelling or Version #1, firms are assumed to conjecture about responses to their actions. In particular, Eaton and Lipsey employ the Minimax Hypothesis (MM): Firm i conjectures that, whatever it does, another firm, j, will relocate so as to produce the maximum loss of market to i. Firm j does this by pairing with i on the long side of i's market. As Eaton and Lipsey (1975: 32–33) report:

> Firm i thus adopts a minimax strategy of choosing the location that minimizes the damage that j can do to it—i.e., it maximizes the short side of its market. The firm maximizes its short side by locating in the middle of its own market, and this implies that interior firms locate at the mid-point between their two neighbours, and the peripheral firms locate one-third of the distance from the market boundary to their one neighbour.

That is, an interior firm locates midway between two neighbors so that both its right- and left-hand markets are equal. Similarly, a peripheral firm, by locating one-third of the way between the boundary and its neighbor, equalizes the size of its two half-markets.

In equilibrium, n firms ($n > 2$) will locate at equal intervals – $\frac{1}{2}n$, $\frac{3}{2}n$, $\frac{5}{2}n$, . . . , $(2n - 3)/2n$, $(2n - 2)/2n$ – the social optimum in terms of minimizing total transport cost. Each firm will capture $1/n$th of the market. In equilibrium, the MM hypothesis substitutes for the pairing of peripheral firms: With pairing a peripheral firm is deterred from relocating by the firm paired with it; with the MM hypothesis, a peripheral firm is deterred from approaching its neighbor by its expectation of damage, in other words, that some other firm will move into its larger half-market.

The one exception to the spreading of locations in equilibrium occurs when there are $n = 2$ firms and there is no possibility of entry by a third firm. In this case, as in the Version #1 model, the MM hypothesis produces minimum differentiation as the two firms locate at the median of the market. If entry by a third firm is possible, then the MM conjecture leads to locations at $x = \frac{1}{4}$ and $x = \frac{3}{4}$.

The MM equilibrium has an odd feature. Notice that, in equilibrium, no firm's MM conjecture is confirmed. Consider the case of two firms and a prospective entrant. The MM conjecture by firms 1 and 2 is that the entrant will locate so as to capture one of their long half-markets, that is, just to the left of $x = \frac{3}{4}$ or just to the right of $x = \frac{1}{4}$. But this configuration is not an equilibrium (so the MM conjectures by the existing firms are not confirmed). The entrant will locate at the midpoint of its two prospective neighbors' locations, since it, too, will make the MM conjecture. The MM conjecture sustains this as an equilibrium but, as just noted, paradoxically no firm's conjecture is substantiated at this equilibrium.

Kenneth A. Shepsle and Ronald N. Cohen

Two features of this result should be emphasized. First, except when $n = 2$, the distinction between an existing firm, j, maximizing the harm done to i, and a new firm entering and doing the same, is not relevant. If existing firms employ the MM conjecture, then they are guarding against damage from either source. Second, the fact that the MM conjecture is never realized in equilibrium is bothersome. The reason it is never realized is that an existing firm or new entrant, itself employing the MM conjecture, would never choose to locate so as to do the most damage to an existing firm; rather, it would locate so as to minimize the damage that subsequently could be done to it. A proper equilibrium notion should incorporate not only conjectures about the locations of other firms, but also conjectures about their conjectures, conjectures about conjectures about their conjectures, and so on. And these conjectures should be *realized* in equilibrium. Finally, let us once again note the distinctiveness of the $n = 2$ case.

Version #3

In this model, Eaton and Lipsey return to Version #1, except that they allow the distribution of customers on [0,1] to be nonuniform. As in the first model, the Cournot–Nash hypothesis is employed. Letting $f(x)$ represent the customer density, they establish the following equilibrium conditions:

1. No firm's whole market is less than another's long-side market.
2. Peripheral firms are paired.
3. If i is an unpaired interior firm, then $f(B_L) = f(B_R)$, where B_L and B_R are the left and right boundaries of i's market.
4. If i is a paired firm, then $f(B_{SS}) \geq f(B_{LS})$, where B_{SS} and B_{LS} are the short- and long-side boundaries of i's market.

Conditions (1) and (2) play the same role as analogous conditions in Version #1. Condition (3) falls out as a first-order condition for i to maximize market share. And condition (4) for paired firms gives the requirement for i not to be tempted to move away from its paired partner.

It turns out that equilibrium configurations for a nonuniform $f(x)$ are considerably more problematical than in the uniform distribution case. For $n = 2$ and $n = 3$, the results are the same: In the two-firm case, pairing at the median of $f(x)$ is an equilibrium; in the three-firm case, (1) and (2) are incompatible so there is no equilibrium. For $n \geq 4$, unlike in Version #1, there often will *not* be an equilibrium. Eaton and Lipsey prove that there will be no equilibrium if the number of firms exceeds twice the number of modes of $f(x)$. Thus, for a unimodal distribution of customers, for example, there is no equilibrium for $n > 2$. (The reader is referred to the original source for details.) Suffice it to say here that the uniform distribution, with its many equilibrium configurations,

22

appears to be an exceptional case. Some of the political science modeling of entry is, therefore, doubly limited in generality, both because of the uniform density assumption and the assumption of two existing parties.[10]

Version #4

The final variation, which we mention in passing, combines minimax conjectures (as in version #2) with a nonuniform density function of consumers (as in version #3). Eaton and Lipsey (1975: 36–37) specify equilibrium conditions, from which they conclude that the existence of equilibrium, as in version #3, is idiosyncratic. Again, they remark upon the uncommon qualities of uniform customer distributions.

In concluding their analysis, Eaton and Lipsey concede that they have not explicitly considered entry (although their minimax analysis touched on the equivalence between competition from an entrant and from some other existing firm). Indeed, they note that, since the cost of production has been assumed to be zero so that entry is free, as many firms as consumers would exist, each located at a consumer's address. On the other hand, suppose there were some fixed cost so that a firm would not enter if that cost could not be covered. Let a distribution of locations be an *entry equilibrium* if it is an equilibrium in the sense we have been considering *and* if no new location can be profitably adopted by an entrant. Eaton and Lipsey assert that, for any number of firms, any equilibrium configuration can be made into an entry equilibrium by an appropriately high choice of the fixed cost, that is, one in which existing firms cover costs while no prospective firm could enter and also do so.

Eaton and Lipsey (and Hotelling as well) do not consider two additional features. While focusing on the conditions of equilibrium, they pay only implicit attention to dynamics, yet the division of a market among firms (through price, locational, and product characteristic decisions) takes place in real time, sequentially. In consideration of *sequentiality,* we formally turn to an explicit examination of the decision to enter. Second, these models impose no barriers to relocation; yet the immovability of capital, the irreversibility of product decisions, or the adverse reputational effects of price changes may diminish, if not destroy altogether, the value of relocation. We now turn to these concerns.

SEQUENCE AND COSTLY RELOCATION

In some of the models examined in previous sections, agents are endowed with a capacity to forecast potential reactions to their own strategic choices. In contrast to the Hotelling model, where an agent takes the choices of others as fixed, in some versions of the Eaton-Lipsey generalization, agents make minimax conjectures. As we have noted in passing, however, this kind of conjecture is problematical because it is never realized in equilibrium. If agent i has no incentive to inflict maximum harm on some other agent j, then why should i assume that, whatever he does, some other agent k will inflict maximum harm on him? This sort of conjecture is never fulfilled in equilibrium. It seems to us that unfulfilled expectations make for implausible conjectures.

Some recent efforts have employed a more appropriate hypothesis about conjectures (see Hay 1976; Prescott and Visscher 1977). These more appropriate conjectures derive from a modification of the Hotelling-type model.[11] These papers assume that capital mobility is limited so that once a location is selected, it is prohibitively expensive to alter it. Unlike the ice-cream push-carts on the boardwalk, which can be moved costlessly in response to changes in customer and competitor locations, the locational choices of shops on Main Street or political parties on an ideological spectrum may be more resistant to subsequent change. As a consequence of limited mobility, agent conjectures and ultimate locational choices depend both on their own immobility and, once located, on the immobility of their competitors.

In the models of this section, a firm chooses whether to compete in a market (whether to *enter*), and if so, where, on the basis of (a) the *fixed* locations of existing firms, (b) its own fixed location once it makes a choice, and (c) the prospect of subsequent choices by other firms, which it conjectures are based, in turn, on considerations like (a)–(c). These kinds of considerations will lead to very different calculations than were the case in earlier models.

Recall that in our initial discussion of Hotelling, we suggested a guiding locational principle: Maximize the short side of the market (since a competitor will move into the long side). That principle, in the Hotelling two-firm model, drives the first firm (i) to the median and then the second firm (j) to an adjacent location. Because there are only two firms, j does not need to anticipate subsequent activity and, therefore, does not practice the just-mentioned prescription. That is, in its choice it does *not* maximize the short side of its market. But what if j does need to concern itself with the prospect of subsequent competition? And if j is to take this prospect into account, should not i take it into account as well in order to assess the likely move that j will make?

In particular, following Prescott and Visscher (1977: 381–82), suppose that exactly three firms can profitably enter the market [0,1] on which customers are uniformly distributed.[12] The numbers of firms, and the order of their respective choices, are given exogenously, with i moving first, then j, then k. Recall also that once a firm locates, it cannot relocate. Firms i and j each reason that whatever they do, k, being the last firm, will look to maximize the size of its market conditional on what i and j have done. Specifically, j can forecast exactly what k will do. Given i's choice and its forecast of k's choice, j will then maximize the size of its market. But then i can do the same thing. Knowing j's forecast of k's behavior, and j's optimal response given any prior move by i, i can figure out what move of its own (and subsequent responses by j and k) will maximize the size of its market.

This process, known as "backward induction," of assuming that each agent, in turn, will behave optimally, conditional on prior moves and rational forecasts of subsequent moves, produces an equilibrium locational pattern. Before saying precisely what it is, the reader should appreciate that this determinate result, in contrast to the disequilibrium of Hotelling for three firms, follows from a number of specific assumptions: the fixed number of firms; the exogenously given order of choice; the fact that each firm is required to make a once-and-for-all-times locational choice (immobile capital); and the fact that each firm can make forecasts about the behavior of others (forecasts that are fulfilled in equilibrium, in contrast to Eaton and Lipsey's MM conjecture).

Without loss of generality, assume that $x_i < \frac{1}{2}$ and begin with the choice of the last firm. Firm k will choose conditional on x_i being some point in $[0,\frac{1}{2})$ and x_j being anywhere in $[0,1]$, according to the following decision rule:

$k.1$: If $x_j \leq \frac{1}{2}$, then locate just to the right of max (x_i, x_j).

$k.2$: If $x_j > \frac{1}{2}$ and $x_i > \max \{1 - x_j, (x_j - x_i)/2\}$, then locate just to the left of x_i.

$k.3$: If $x_j > \frac{1}{2}$ and $1 - x_j > \max \{x_i, (x_j - x_i)/2\}$, then locate just to the right of x_j.

$k.4$: If $x_j > \frac{1}{2}$ and $(x_j - x_i)/2 \geq \max \{x_i, 1 - x_j\}$ then locate at $(x_i + x_j)/2$.

The explanation for this decision rule is straightforward. If contingency k.1 holds, then both i and j are to the left of $\frac{1}{2}$ and k will maximize its market size by locating just to the right of its right-most competitor. If contingency k.2 holds, then the market segment $[0, x_i]$ is the largest, which k can capture by locating just to the left of x_i. If k.3 holds, then the market segment $[x_j, 1]$ is the largest, which k can capture by locating just to the right of x_j. Finally, if k.4 holds, then the segment of the market between x_i and x_j is the largest, and k can capture it by locating at the midpoint between its two competitors.[13]

Given this reaction function for k, and i's location already established, firm j's optimal response is characterized by the following decision rule:

$j.1$: If $x_i \leq \frac{1}{4}$, then locate at $x_j = \frac{2}{3} + x_i/3$.[14]

$j.2$: If $\frac{1}{4} < x_i < \frac{1}{2}$, then locate at $x_j = 1 - x_i$.

Kenneth A. Shepsle and Ronald N. Cohen

To see this constitutes the optimal response for firm j, suppose $x_i \leq \frac{1}{4}$. In this circumstance, no matter where j locates, k will never locate to the left of x_i; thus, it will either invade j's left-hand market or its right-hand market. Given this rule for k's response, j will want to locate so that its long and short markets are equal. That is, j will choose x_j so that $(x_j - x_i)/2 = 1 - x_j$. A little algebra produces $j.1$. Similar considerations yield $j.2$.

Given these decision rules for j and k, i's choice is now determined. Firm i will choose to locate at $x_i = \frac{1}{4}$. Firm j will then locate at $x_j = \frac{3}{4}$, according to $j.1$, and k at $x_k = \frac{1}{2}$ by $k.4$ (although k could locate anywhere in $(\frac{1}{4}, \frac{3}{4})$ – see note 13). In this configuration, i and j each capture 37.5 percent of the market, while k receives a 25 percent share. A separate calculation, omitted here, shows that this is the largest market share i could hope to obtain.

What is attractive about this model is that individual agents make conjectures about subsequent choices, which are confirmed in equilibrium. Immobility of location allows for predictability. This result generalizes to any *fixed* number of competitors entering in sequence, although the calculations become ridiculously tedious for numbers much larger than three. Prescott and Visscher, however, generalize their argument even further.

Suppose there is a very large number of potential firms, larger than the number of firms that could profitably be supported by the customer distribution in the market $[0,1]$. Specifically, suppose a firm requires a market of at least size R $(0 < R \leq 1)$ to enjoy a normal return on investment. Thus, in equilibrium there will be no more than $1/R$ firms supported in $[0,1]$. Knowing this permits the deduction of certain locational "principles." For example, if two firms, i and j, are already located so that $|x_i - x_j| \leq 2R$, then no firm will locate between them (since that firm would control a market of less than R). Similarly, if a firm is located at one end or the other of the market such that $x_i \leq R$ or $x_i \geq 1 - R$, then no firm will outflank it. From these principles, a sequence of entry decisions may be derived. Accordingly, the first firm will enter at $x_i = R$, the second at $x_j = 1 - R$, and subsequent firms a distance of $2R$ from an existing firm until this is no longer possible. At this point there will still be room for one last firm, after which no other firm can enter. As Prescott and Visscher (1977: 385) conclude, "Firms [after the first two] locate as far away from their nearest competitor as is possible without inviting entry in between." They further note that firms will be equally spaced as long as the customer distribution is uniform; for nonuniform distributions, the spacing will no longer necessarily be equal, but the locational sequence articulated above will still apply.

ENTRY AND COMPETITION IN ELECTORAL SETTINGS, I

We have devoted considerable attention thus far to the intellectual legacy of Hotelling in the analysis of markets. It is time now to turn to electoral settings.

Many of the same tools and forms of analysis used to study markets may fruitfully be applied here. But there are differences as well.

Perhaps the most significant of these involves payoffs to the participants. In the market setting, in which a firm sells a homogenous product at a parametric price, its objective is fully described in terms of the *size* of the market it controls.[15] It maximizes profit by maximizing size of market. In the electoral setting, the relationship between size of support group and candidate objectives is less clear. In some circumstances (see Austen-Smith and Banks 1987), a party or candidate may actually suffer for having a support group larger than some other party or candidate.[16] Alternatively, in those electoral systems where several candidates are elected, all that a candidate may seek is to be among the top K vote-getters, where K is the number of seats to be filled. Maximizing support group size may not accomplish this objective (see Greenberg and Shepsle 1987). Finally, Downs (1957) devotes some attention to what he calls "influence parties." Such parties care less about winning elections or attracting voters than about influencing other, more electorally viable parties. In a similar vein, some candidates or parties may have policy preferences that compete with, or substitute for, office preferences. They care about the policies enacted by the elected government, and may not care whether they are a part of that government (see Wittman 1983; Calvert 1985). In sum, while none of the market-based models questioned the underlying objectives of the agents they studied – consumers were utility maximizers and firms profit maximizers – agent objectives are less transparent in electoral settings.

This point is given emphasis by Greenberg and Shepsle (1987), who observe that a candidate's utility function is *system-dependent*. Suppose there are n candidates who adopt positions in [0,1] labeled $(x_1, x_2, \ldots, x_n)$. A candidate, say the ith, will evaluate this configuration according to what result it produces. And it is the electoral system that "produces results" by determining how a distribution of electoral support gets translated into a distribution of legislative prizes and policy outcomes. Consider two such systems, identified by the parameter K. For $K = 1$, the n candidates are competing for a single seat, and the candidate with the most votes wins it. For $K = 3$, they compete for three seats: The three highest vote getters win seats, and any two may form a government. Letting u_i^K be i's utility function for electoral system of type K, it is generally the case that $u_i^1 (x_1, x_2, \ldots, x_n)$ and $u_i^3 (x_1, x_2, \ldots, x_n)$ are not equal. The identical distribution of spatial strategies will be differently evaluated by a candidate depending on the electoral system in effect. Even if the spatial locations given by the x_is yield in system 1 the same distribution of voter support as in system 2 for each candidate, candidates will evaluate this n-tuple of spatial locations differently in each system.

Austen-Smith (1987a) takes this argument one step further by suggesting that voters, too, will take system effects into account in determining their rational response to a configuration of announced spatial locations by parties.

Kenneth A. Shepsle and Ronald N. Cohen

He chastises Greenberg and Shepsle, among others, for *assuming* that voters support the candidate closest to them spatially (much like consumers in the Hotelling model). He demonstrates that in many multimember legislative systems, there are incentives for at least some voters not to support the candidate closest to them. Thus, he "argues against the assumption of sincere voting in models of multi-member legislative elections. Instead, the complete legislative game – election rule and legislative outcome function – should first be explicitly defined, and then [rational] individuals' voting behavior deduced" (Austen-Smith 1987a: 9). We comment on this possibility in our concluding section.

It would appear, then, that ambiguity about candidate motives invites a number of different approaches to spatial political competition in multicandidate settings. In order to advance our understanding of entry into political races, we need to flesh out candidate objectives – both existing candidates and prospective entrants. And Austen-Smith's work suggests that the straightforward assumption, that is that candidates maximize votes (the equivalent of market size), may not be the appropriate one. First, however, we look at the cleanest version of the multicandidate spatial model of elections with entry – one for which the familial resemblance to Hotelling's original model is the most transparent.

ENTRY AND ELECTORAL COMPETITION, II: PALFREY

Palfrey (1984) examines the Hotelling–Downs problem of spatial equilibrium but, unlike many of the economic applications reviewed above, he explicitly designs the model to accommodate *political* considerations. In terms of the various assumptions discussed when we considered Eaton and Lipsey (1975), Palfrey's set-up may be described as follows:

1. the space is [0,1];
2. voter ideal points (analogous to consumer addresses) are described on [0,1] by a distribution function, $F(x)$, from the class of distributions with an associated symmetric, unimodal density;
3. voters have symmetric utility functions and vote sincerely – that is, for the closest candidate;
4. candidates have zero "relocation" costs so that, in equilibrium, there must be no incentives to change positions;
5. there are two established candidates and one prospective entrant;
6. established candidates choose locations simultaneously and are vote maximizers;
7. the prospective entrant, also a vote maximizer, chooses her strategy after the established candidates have located;

8. each established candidate makes a Cournot–Nash conjecture about his established opponent and a Stackelberg conjecture about the entrant.[17]

Recall that in Hotelling, with assumptions of uniform customer distribution and Cournot–Nash conjectures, there is no three-actor equilibrium. In Eaton and Lipsey, too, there is no equilibrium for three firms if either Cournot–Nash conjectures are assumed or if there is a departure from the uniform distribution. In Prescott and Visscher, there *is* a three-firm equilibrium if costly mobility and fulfilled expectations (foresight) are assumed.

Palfrey departs from the uniform distribution (as in several of the Eaton-Lipsey models) and assumes fulfilled expectations, but not costly mobility, as in Prescott and Visscher. He is able to establish the following equilibrium (which he calls a *limit equilibrium*). Letting i and j be the established candidates, k the entrant, and $F(x)$ the voter distribution on $[0,1]$, the location of the two established parties, (x_i, x_j), is a limit equilibrium, if and only if

$$F(x_i) = 1 - 2F(\tfrac{1}{4} + x_i/2)$$
$$F(x_j) = 1 - F(x_i).$$

The location of the entrant x_k is the vote-maximizing reaction to (x_i, x_j). Note that k *always* enters. Palfrey's is not a theory of entry or entry-deterrence.

To take a concrete example, if $F(x)$ is uniform, then $x_i = \tfrac{1}{4}$ and $x_j = \tfrac{3}{4}$ is the limit equilibrium. In this equilibrium, $x_k = \tfrac{1}{2}$. That is, given x_i and x_j, the vote-maximizing location for the entrant is at the median.

Notice that the entrant loses. She receives one-fourth of the vote, whereas each of the established candidates receives three-eighths. But she can do no better.

Notice also that neither of the established parties can improve upon his electoral share. Suppose i shifted to the right. He conjectures that j will stay put (Nash–Cournot), but that k may react (Stackelberg). In fact, for any $x_i > \tfrac{1}{4}$, k will switch from the median to a location just to the left of x_i. She will obtain as her vote share all of the votes to the left of x_i, namely $F(x_i)$, which, with the uniform distribution, exceeds one-fourth (since $F(\tfrac{1}{4}) = \tfrac{1}{4}$ and $x_i > \tfrac{1}{4}$). Meanwhile, i will receive half the votes distributed between his location and j's, that is, half of less than half the voters. Established party j will capture the other half of these voters plus all the one-fourth of the voters to the right of $x = \tfrac{3}{4}$. In short, k's vote share increases, as does j's (unless $x_i > \tfrac{1}{2}$), but i will receive a smaller vote share than he would had he stayed put in the first place. This demonstrates that $(\tfrac{1}{4}, \tfrac{3}{4}, \tfrac{1}{2})$ for i, j, and k, respectively, is indeed a limit equilibrium.

Palfrey goes on to establish under fairly general conditions that (a) the established candidates never converge, thus confirming the atypicality of MD in the Hotelling-Downs model; (b) the entrant always enters between the nonconverging established candidates; and (c) the entrant never wins.

Kenneth A. Shepsle and Ronald N. Cohen

How might we assess this model? Taking it on its own terms – that is, accepting all the assumptions – some of the conclusions Palfrey derives are substantively troublesome. First, if the entrant never wins, even though her location is vote-maximizing, then one must wonder why she bothers entering (or why she bothers vote-maximizing). Second, the entrant's vote-maximizing location in the Palfrey model is always *between* the established parties. While the Social Democratic–Liberal Alliance of the 1980s in Great Britain, and Teddy Roosevelt's Bull Moose party of 1912 and the 1980 Anderson candidacy in the United States, are consistent with this result, at least some American experience with third-party entry would seem to contradict it. The Populist Party of the late nineteenth century, the Socialist Party of the early twentieth century, Dixiecrats and Wallacites in 1948, the American Party in the 1960s, and most splinter parties throughout the postwar period tend to be *extremist* parties trying to outflank an established party; they are not moderate parties. Third, much of the rationale for third-party entry is, *contra* Palfrey, the alleged *convergence* of the established parties. Typical of this was George Wallace's refrain: "There's not a dime's worth of difference between [the established parties]."

Our uneasiness about the conclusions of Palfrey's model should be taken principally as an acknowledgment of the need for second-generation work. As Palfrey himself notes,

Undoubtedly, some of the limitations of the Hotelling equilibrium will apply to this model as well. If voter abstention is introduced [the equivalent of elastic demand in the Hotelling setting], the equilibrium may change. If candidates and voters must make decisions without full information the equilibrium may change. . . . Despite these possible difficulties, the model should have some appeal

(Palfrey 1984: 140).

We agree. What Palfrey is suggesting, in effect, is further relaxation of assumptions that drive his limit equilibrium. He has suggested several. First is the possibility of "abstention from alienation," as Davis, Hinich, and Ordeshook (1970) characterized it in the infancy of spatial modeling. In the original Hotelling model, the assumption of inelastic demand meant that, no matter how distant the closest firm got from a customer's address, the customer would still purchase one unit of product per time period. The equivalent assumption in the voting setting, one employed by Palfrey and most others, is that no matter how politically unappealing all the candidates become, each voter will nevertheless vote, if only for the lesser of evils. Allowing voters to abstain, possibly in a probabilistic fashion,[18] may provide an additional reason for nonconvergence. Established candidates will hesitate to desert their respective bases for fear of alienating core constituents in the ideological hinterlands. This force for divergence, in turn, may provide a basis for entry and, moreover, may permit circumstances in which an entrant has a shot at

30

winning (if established candidates diverge "too much" to protect their respective hinterlands).

The second relaxation suggested by Palfrey deals with incomplete and imperfect information. Probabilistic participation, for example, generates imperfect information for candidates as the casting of individual votes takes on the characteristics of a lottery. Incomplete information might be produced by candidate uncertainty about voter preferences, that is, the voter distribution $F(x)$, about the objectives or conjectures of other candidates, or about how much of what he or she knows is common knowledge. Palfrey conjectures (1984: 155) that the relaxation of extreme informational assumptions in his model will destroy the conclusion that the entrant wins with probability zero. Indeed, he suggests that the probability of an entrant winning need not be very high to justify entry (justification we have found lacking in his original model) if the costs of entry are small relative to the benefits of winning office.

A third suggestion Palfrey makes for second-generation work involves sophisticated voting. He is certainly not alone in making the simplifying assumption that voters cast votes for the candidate closest to them in [0,1]. But, as he notes, there may be grounds on which voters fail to observe this behavioral rule. Although Palfrey makes no more than a passing reference to this prospect, we may illustrate it with one of Palfrey's own results. Consider the limit equilibrium above for the uniform distribution on [0,1], $(x_i, x_j, x_k) =$ (¼, ¾, ½). Recall that in this equilibrium the respective vote shares are (⅜, ⅜, ²⁄₈). In this situation, the two established candidates "tie," and some random device is employed to determine a winner. One might well imagine, as Duverger's Law suggests, a number of k's supporters, who are closer to i than j or vice versa, deserting k and voting "strategically" for one of the "viable" candidates.[19]

Finally, Palfrey (1984: 154) mentions that the objective function assumed for each candidate – vote maximization – is key. Were it not for vote maximization, it would be (as we observed above) irrational for a prospective candidate to enter at all, since an entrant cannot win in equilibrium. By assuming vote maximization, Palfrey is able to dodge the criticism of the futility of entry, but this only calls into question the plausibility of vote maximizing as an appropriate objective. Indeed, it raises the possibility that some other objective might serve an entrant better than maximizing votes. We treat this notion next.[20]

ENTRY AND ELECTORAL COMPETITION, III: GREENBERG AND SHEPSLE

Not all multicandidate contests are of the winner-take-all variety. In these circumstances, it is normally quite pleasant for a candidate to receive more votes than any other, but it may well turn out that failing to achieve this

Kenneth A. Shepsle and Ronald N. Cohen

objective is no disadvantage. When electing delegates to a national political convention, for example, a local caucus may send the top K vote-getters. A candidate for delegate might well hope to get more votes than any other, but *any* candidate finishing among the top K wins a spot at the convention. To take another example, a southern gubernatorial primary is typically a multi-stage process. The objective at the first stage is to finish among the top *two* vote-getters (so long as no one receives an outright majority) in order to advance to the runoff. Finally, in some nations the entire legislature is elected from a single "district," with the top K performers winning election to the legislature.[21]

From this discussion it should be clear that $K = 1$, the first-past-the-post method, is a special instance of a more general phenomenon. What is important in the more general case is that the number of prizes is fixed exogenously, performance sufficient for reward is determined endogenously by competition, and success is measured by a relative standard. Greenberg and Shepsle (1987) sought to analyze this problem.

As in the work of Palfrey, Eaton and Lipsey, and others, Greenberg and Shepsle assume that competition occurs on [0,1], that voters have symmetric, single-peaked, utility functions, and that they vote sincerely. Candidates, however, are motivated to finish among the top K vote-getters. Thus, Greenberg and Shepsle make a special point of emphasizing that maximizing the size of one's support group (or market size in the economic context) may not be an appropriate objective. Rank maximizing[22] rather than vote maximizing makes more sense in this context.[23]

Greenberg and Shepsle define a *K-equilibrium* to be a set A of K locations in [0,1], with the property that the support garnered by a politician locating at one of these locations exceeds the support garnered by a politician entering at any other location. Thus, at any location in A a politician will win (be among the top K vote-getters) because he cannot be displaced by a prospective entrant locating at a position not in A.

More formally, let $S(a;A)$ be the set of voters closer to a than to any other point in A; $S(a;A)$ is the *support* of a. For a distribution of voters $F(x)$ on [0,1], the *size* of the support for a is given by

$$s(a;A) = F[(a + a^+)/2] - F[(a + a^-)/2]$$

where a^+ and a^- are the locations of a's right and left neighbors, respectively.[24] A K-equilibrium is a set A such that (1) $|A| = K$ and (2) $s(b; A \cup b) \leq s(a; A \cup b)$ for all a in A and all b not in A.[25]

In effect, Greenberg and Shepsle employ the same conjectural arrangement as Palfrey, but a different motivational hypothesis. Existing candidates employ a Nash conjecture relative to existing rivals and a Stackelberg conjecture with regard to a prospective entrant. Thus, one of the K incumbents, for example, in contemplating a relocation, assumes his $K - 1$ existing rivals will hold to their current locations but that a prospective entrant will optimize relative to the new configuration. The novel motivational hypothesis is that each candidate wishes to ensure he is among the top K vote-getters; this may not entail maximizing the size of his support. A prospective entrant, on the other hand, is deterred from entering if she cannot finish (strictly) among the top K.[26]

The main result of the Greenberg–Shepsle model is an impossibility theorem. For any $K \geq 2$ there are societies (satisfying the definitions and conditions described informally above) for which there is no K-equilibrium.

Consider the following finite electorate example with $K = 2$. Suppose a mini-polity of 15 voters, charged with electing two representatives, is partitioned into three blocs: (a) the Lefties have ideal points at .05, .10, .15, and .20; (b) the Centrists have ideal points at .47, .48, .49, .50, .51, .52, and .53; and (c) the Righties have ideal points at .80, .85, .90, and .95. In this example, for any pair of locations there is always a third location at which the size of support exceeds that of *at least* one of the existing locations. If, for instance, candidates i and j locate at $(x_i, x_j) = (.20, .52)$, then $x_k = .53$ yields

$$s(x_i; x_i, x_j, x_k) = 4$$
$$s(x_j; x_i, x_j, x_k) = 6$$
$$s(x_k; x_i, x_j, x_k) = 5,$$

and k's support exceeds that of i. The reader may convince himself or herself that no location for i and j deters successful entry by k. The impossibility theorem generalizes this example to all values of K.

In the conclusion of their paper, Greenberg and Shepsle note that while the impossibility theorem indicates an entry-deterring equilibrium cannot be *guaranteed,* it does not indicate the voter distributions for which an entry-deterring equilibrium *does* exist. They do, however, suggest a comparison between their K-equilibrium and Palfrey's limit-equilibrium.

ENTRY DETERRENCE: A COMPARISON OF LIMIT-EQUILIBRIUM AND 2-EQUILIBRIUM

In arguing for his limit-equilibrium idea, Palfrey suggests that, in two-party systems, the objective is to be (and to remain) an *established* party. Palfrey's important insight was that, in equilibrium, established parties rotate in office. So it is important to *be* an established party. In Hotelling-like fashion, competing against an established opponent is a force for convergence. But to remain an established party means protecting against prospective entry by unestablished parties seeking to displace a vulnerable established party. This latter concern discourages convergence. The balance of these two opposed forces is a limit-equilibrium.

Greenberg and Shepsle took this intuition a step further by suggesting that if remaining established were indeed the objective of an existing party (and becoming one the objective of a prospective entrant), then vote maximization is the wrong instrumental objective. In a system of two established parties, if a limit-equilibrium is not a 2-equilibrium, then it is possible for an entrant to enter and obtain more support than at least one of the existing candidates (but not by vote maximizing). In short, Greenberg and Shepsle claim that their solution concept of (symmetric) 2-equilibrium captures Palfrey's intuition better than his own limit-equilibrium concept. A (symmetric) 2-equilibrium, like a (symmetric) limit-equilibrium, forces a halt to convergence; it protects against third-party entry, and the established parties both remain established and rotate in office.

Greenberg and Shepsle construct the following example in which both a 2-equilibrium and a limit-equilibrium exist. (Recall that a limit equilibrium always exists but not so for a 2-equilibrium; hence care is required in selecting the example in order to conduct a comparison.) Define $F(x)$ on [0,1] by

$$F(x) = 2x^2 \qquad\qquad 0 \le x \le 1/2$$
$$F(x) = 1 - F(1 - x) \qquad 1/2 \le x \le 1.$$

This distribution of voters satisfies the assumptions made by Palfrey for a limit-equilibrium; it will be recognized by the reader as an S-shaped distribution function with $F(0) = 0$ and $F(1) = 1$. The unique (symmetric) limit-equilibrium (x_1, x_2) and unique (symmetric) 2-equilibrium (y_1, y_2) are:

$$x_1 = (1/6)(\sqrt{10} - 1) = .3604$$
$$x_2 = 1 - x_1 \qquad\qquad = .6396$$

$$y_1 = 1/2\sqrt{2} \qquad\qquad = .3535$$
$$y_2 = 1 - y_1 \qquad\qquad = .6465$$

In the 2-equilibrium, the established parties have converged slightly less toward one another than in the limit-equilibrium because they must not guard only against an entrant winning, but against her finishing second as well.[27] Given its characteristics, the 2-equilibrium will deter the entry of a third party seeking to displace one of the established parties; for no location in [0,1] can an entrant obtain greater support than either established party.[28]

This, however, is not the case for the limit-equilibrium given above. Suppose a left wing third party entered just to the left of x_1. Since $F(x) = .25$ at $x = .3535$ (see footnote 28), a location just adjacent to x_1 (that is, x_3 satisfying $.3535 < x_3 < .3604$) will command more than 25 percent of the vote. The party at x_1 receives less than 25 percent (since the votes in $[x_1, x_2]$, which will be shared by the two established parties, amount to less than 50 percent of the votes), and thus is displaced by the third party. Of course, in the limit-equilibrium, established parties *assume an entrant is a vote maximizer.* Yet, if *an entrant is "merely" content to displace an established party (perhaps*

34

hoping next time to have a shot at governing), then this conjecture will not be fulfilled. In these circumstances the left-most established party will be in for a rude shock.

Cohen (1987) generalizes some of the Greenberg–Shepsle results and further develops the comparison between a limit-equilibrium and a 2-equilibrium. Cohen begins by showing that for the standard normal distribution of voters, a 2-equilibrium always exists at the first and third quartiles of the distribution and is the only such 2-equilibrium. He extends this result to all symmetric unimodal voter distributions (precisely the class employed by Palfrey) as follows. Rescale the unidimensional space of competition so that the mode of the unimodal voter distribution is at zero. Label the third quartile point w (and, since the distribution is symmetric, the first quartile point is $-w$).[29] Then,

THEOREM: If the distribution of voters, $F(x)$, has a continuous, symmetric, unimodal density, $f(x)$, and if $f(0) \leq 2 f(w)$, then $(-w, w)$ is a unique symmetric 2-equilibrium.

The inequality condition requires that not "too many" voters be concentrated near the mode of the distribution relative to the numbers at the first and third quartiles.[30]

In effect, Cohen has shown that 2-equilibria exist for much the same broad class of voter distributions used by Palfrey for limit-equilibria. In doing so, he takes the edge off the negative conclusion of the Greenberg–Shepsle impossibility result. He then suggests a useful class of voter distributions with which to compare the two equilibrium concepts. Let

$$F_n(x) = \begin{cases} 2^{n-1}x^n & 0 \leq x \leq 1/2 \\ 1 - F_n(1 - x) & 1/2 \leq x \leq 1. \end{cases}$$

As n grows large, the slope of $F_n(x)$ becomes steep as x tends toward $\frac{1}{2}$; that is, as n grows large, voters are increasingly concentrated near the mode of the distribution. Notice that $F_1(x)$ is simply the uniform distribution, and that $F_2(x)$ is the distribution in the example of Greenberg and Shepsle. For this family of distributions, Cohen establishes that 2-equilibria exist at the first and third quartiles. He then compares limit- and 2-equilibria for various values of n. For $n = 1$, the uniform distribution, $(\frac{1}{4}, \frac{3}{4})$ is both a limit-equilibrium and a 2-equilibrium. For $n=2$, they diverge, as reported above in our discussion of Greenberg and Shepsle. In general, however, again letting (x_1, x_2) represent the limit equilibrium and (y_1, y_2) the 2-equilibrium, the difference between them, $x_1 - y_1$, tends to zero as n increases. That is, as the voting distribution gets more and more concentrated around its mode, the difference between a vote-maximizing entrant and a rank-maximizing entrant evaporates.[31]

Kenneth A. Shepsle and Ronald N. Cohen

DISCUSSION

In this essay we have surveyed the historical background and some recent developments in the continuing evolution of spatial models of electoral competition. Much of this essay has been concerned with multiagent competition and entry. We have tried to isolate some of the modeling issues without using too many technical details. We have done so by reviewing closely related work in spatial economic competition. As the headnote of this essay emphasizes, we believe it is important to develop spatial equilibrium theories that endogenize the decision to throw one's hat in the ring. In our judgment, this is precisely the sort of second-generation development that has already transpired in the legislative spatial modeling realm under the rubric of agenda setting.

We focus in this concluding section on some theoretical loose ends. We have only a few comments about two of the most basic – the dimensionality of the space and the distribution of voter preferences. Almost all the work to date on multiparty competition and entry have assumed unidimensionality. This is also true in the spatial economic competition literature, although some multidimensional efforts do exist (Losch 1954). Given the complexity of the issues, this is hardly surprising. Unidimensionality is extremely restrictive, and yet we doubt much progress will be made on other issues without the assumption. So we are not particularly troubled at this juncture by it. One cannot attempt to generalize to the multidimensional setting until results are established in more simplified settings.

The same comment applies to assumptions about the distribution of voters. After sixty years, it is apparent that the uniform distribution has some odd features associated with it. During that time, however, a number of important theoretical issues have been clarified, which might otherwise have remained clouded. Contemporary scholars have built their models on slightly more general assumptions (for example, Palfrey's work on symmetric, continuous, unimodal distributions) or have sought results that are "distribution-free" (for example, Eaton and Lipsey's result on the relationship between the number of modes in the distribution and the number of firms in equilibrium). These strike us as entirely sensible developments. As in the matter of dimensionality, we can only commiserate with those who bemoan the specificity of assumptions, yet nevertheless encourage those who must employ them in order to make any headway.

The remainder of this section focuses on three features of multiagent competition models that, in our opinion, deserve priority: agent objectives and preference revelation, agent conjectures, and locational costs.

Multiparty Competition, Entry, Deterrence

Agent objectives and preference revelation

We noted in our discussion of spatial electoral competition, in contrast to spatial economic competition, that the matter of agent objectives cannot be regarded as uncontroversial. In spatial economic competition, agent objectives – profit and utility maximization for firms and consumers, respectively – are quite conventional. Thus, subject to available strategies, conjectures about others, and so on, agent behavioral choices – where to locate, from whom to purchase—may be deduced straightforwardly.

The same can be said about neither agent objectives nor agent behavioral choices in the electoral setting. In the last several sections of this essay we have recounted the potential difficulties produced by a simple assumption like vote maximization for candidates or parties. When there is competition for several prizes (Cohen 1987; Greenberg and Shepsle 1987), or when the "real" objective is to become or remain an established party (Palfrey 1984), or when it is advantageous (in coalition-government settings, for example) to be one of the smaller parties, and hence an attractive coalition partner (Austen-Smith and Banks 1987), then vote maximization is not the appropriate instrumental objective.

This is seen most clearly in a recent paper by Austen-Smith and Banks (1987). They exploit a very significant institutional feature of legislative coalition formation (or at least a stylized version thereof). They assume that if no party commands a legislative majority, and thus cannot organize a government on its own, then the subsequent bargaining to form a governing coalition is specified by a predetermined rule: The largest party has the first opportunity to form a government and, if the "deal" it offers is accepted by the requisite number of legislators (usually a simple majority), then the process ends. If, on the other hand, the deal is rejected, then the second largest party is given the opportunity. This sequence is continued until some majority accepts some deal; failing that, a caretaker (distributionally neutral) government is established until new elections can be called. This predetermined sequence allows each agent to exercise foresight. Knowing the consequences of a caretaker, each agent can forecast what the nth (smallest) party will offer if the deal-making reaches it at the penultimate stage.[32] In turn, they can forecast the deal the $(n-1)^{st}$ party will offer.[33] This form of backward induction can be taken all the way back to the deal that the largest party will offer. Austen-Smith and Banks establish that in a perfect/complete information setting, the optimal offer of the largest party will be accepted so that the process never goes more than one iteration. In the three-party case, the one they develop most fully, this equilibrium offer excludes the second-largest party. That is, if you can't be the largest party, then (in the three-party case) be the smallest one. Rewards are *not* monotonic in voter support, so that vote maximization is not necessarily instrumentally rational.

37

What about voters? In parametric-price models of economic spatial competition, consumers are assumed to behave "sincerely." They purchase from the closest supplier and never have an occasion to do otherwise. Most of the models of electoral spatial competition we have reviewed make a parallel assumption: Voters vote for the most proximate party or candidate (symmetric utility functions and sincere preference revelation). Austen-Smith (1987a,b), however, has shown that this is rarely rational for all voters. Indeed, he proves a general theorem that, for most interesting electoral arrangements, it can never be rational for all voters to vote sincerely.

It should be noted, in partial defense of those (like the present authors) who have invoked the sincerity assumption, that the informational and forecasting demands on voters to enable them to engage in strategic voting are considerable. The Austen-Smith result would be especially compelling if it could be demonstrated under weaker assumptions of this sort. On the other hand, in defense of Austen-Smith, his results do not require *all* voters to vote strategically in equilibrium. In several of his examples, most of the voters cast votes for the closest candidate. The reader should consult his papers for elaboration.

In sum, there is not yet consensus in the literature about agent objectives and strategic behavior. The admonitions by Austen-Smith about voter preference revelation or by, say, Greenberg and Shepsle about candidate objectives should be taken seriously. As contributors to this literature ourselves, however, we are sympathetic to the need to simplify when necessary.

Agent conjectures

The Austen-Smith and Banks procedure, just described, for bargaining inside a legislature to form a governing coalition has a very nice property. The forecasts made by the various agents about the kinds of deals that will be offered at various stages are confirmed. As we have mentioned several times in this essay, equilibrium points sustained by unfulfilled conjectures (for example, Eaton and Lipsey's minimax conjecture) may be found in the literature. This provides an artificial basis for sustaining an equilibrium and, in modern game theory, much effort has been invested in characterizing equilibria that are sustainable both in terms of best-response strategies and *plausible beliefs*.[34]

But what conjectures are plausible? This is not as easy a problem as it may first appear. For one thing, an agent must know the objectives of other agents. Thus, Eaton and Lipsey should have realized that if all agents are trying to maximize their market share (and this is common knowledge), then minimax conjectures are implausible (they are mutually inconsistent with market-share maximizing).

When the objectives of others are ambiguous or unknown, a form of incomplete information, then it is more difficult to specify plausible conjectures. In the Greenberg–Shepsle discussion of the Palfrey paper, for example, we saw that an incorrect conjecture by established parties about the objective of a prospective entrant (that she was a vote maximizer rather than a rank maximizer) would produce nonequilibrium behavior.

Downs (1957) speculated, to take another example, that many prospective entrants are interested neither in vote maximizing nor in rank maximizing. Rather, they regard themselves as "influence-type" parties whose political mission is to cause established parties to shift their locations (toward the location of the entrant). In equilibrium (a point Downs did not appreciate), if established parties maintain correct conjectures about such parties, then one would rarely see them actually enter. The mere threat of entry, coupled with accurate conjectures about their behavior, produces the desired result. Indeed, if the minor party were to enter anyhow (in which case an existing party's conjecture would be disconfirmed), it would do damage to its own cause by siphoning off votes from precisely the party it had (successfully) sought to influence.

The point here is that an appropriate equilibrium for elections with multiple candidacies and prospective entry must allow for best-response strategies (each agent must have no incentive to alter his or her strategy) and plausible beliefs. Part of what keeps an agent from altering strategy is the correct belief, one consistent with the real objectives and incentives of others, that when everyone is finished responding to a prospective alteration, the agent will be worse off than if no alteration in strategy had been made. This point extends to conjectures by candidates about the behavior of voters, a point made by Austen-Smith. Thus, candidate beliefs about the strategic possibilities available to voters must also be factored into the equilibrium.

Locational costs

The original Hotelling model allowed firms to move freely along Main Street, an assumption maintained in most of the literature through Eaton and Lipsey. Both Prescott and Visscher and Hays, however, employed the notion of locational immobility. A firm, once located, cannot costlessly alter its location in response to subsequent competition from new entrants. At best it can desert its current location, at huge cost, and start over again as a new firm. With this assumption a premium is placed on making accurate conjectures about the locational choices of subsequent entrants, since one's own locational choice is essentially irreversible.

The idea of spatial immobility strikes us as an important notion in spatial models of elections. In national election contests among parties with well-developed reputations, or even in primary contests among well-known politicians, the idea of relative immobility seems intuitively plausible. To some extent, Downs took this view in proscribing "leap-frogging." The idea of

39

spatial immobility takes the view a step further. Thus, no matter how much 1988 Democratic presidential contender Michael Dukakis touted the "Massachusetts miracle" and his fiscal prudence, it was most unlikely that he would ever be regarded as ideologically more conservative than Republican George Bush. And had Senator Sam Nunn of Georgia entered the race, it is unimaginable that he would have been perceived as anything but the righthand anchor of the Democratic field. The point here is that, in many circumstances, politicians and parties come to a contest with reputations that can be altered only marginally during the course of a campaign. In contrast, lesser known candidates may be endowed with considerably more spatial mobility. Different assumptions about locational mobility will produce different models of electoral contests with varying implications for prospective entrants.

* * *

We have tried to highlight various features of multicandidate contests in the spatial framework. This concluding section has emphasized specific features that deserve continued attention and development. In large measure one of the limitations of the spatial research agenda since Davis and Hinich's (1966) seminal paper has been its preoccupation with American-style electoral politics: two existing parties competing against one another for votes with little concern for prospective entrants, multipartism, legislative government-formation, and so on. Most of the world democracies deviate in important ways from this formulation. At the heart of these deviations is the birth and death of parties. It is clear that there is a full agenda of spatial research to be pursued on these topics. Such work will display an even broader utility and generality of the spatial approach than has been demonstrated in the last two decades.

ACKNOWLEDGMENTS

The senior author acknowledges the research support of the National Science Foundation (SES-8616372) and the Zentrum fur Interdisziplinare Forschung at the University of Bielefeld, where revisions of an earlier draft of this paper were completed.

NOTES

1 Throughout the essay, prospective entrants are cast as female and existing competitors as male. This helps keep pronouns unambiguous.
2 In some considerations, it matters whether the interval is bounded or not. Unless otherwise indicated, we shall assume it is bounded.
3 This dimension could equally well be some characteristic of a good—quality, color, size, and so on—so that "location" must be taken figuratively.
4 Eaton and Lipsey (1975) attribute the expression to Kenneth Boulding.
5 Momentarily we shall suggest that prospective entry plays a similar role: An

exposed flank caused by convergence toward an existing competitor encourages a new firm to enter.

6 Downs (1957) provided something of a halfway house. He assumed a considerable degree of "costless" spatial mobility, but forbid parties from leapfrogging each other.

7 Downs, too, seeks this sort of generalization in his discussions of multiparty systems. His arguments, however, are casual. A more formal analysis, in which many theoretical issues are framed, is found in Hinich and Ordeshook (1970), section IV. A survey of multiparty models is found in Shepsle (1990).

8 Needless to say, our summary is no substitute for reading Eaton and Lipsey in the original.

9 Eaton and Lipsey apparently assume that minimum differentiation means that paired firms are not precisely identical. Thus, in the four-firm case, the two paired firms "at" $x = .25$ share their market as follows: the left-most of the pair gets the market $[0,.25)$ and the right-most gets $(.25,.50)$. A similar sharing rule applies to the two firms at $x = .75$. For any other location, condition (1) would be violated. Suppose, for example, the two pairs are located at $x = .40$ and $x = .60$. The right-most firm of the left pair and the left-most firm of the right pair would each capture only 10 percent of the market, while their respective pairs each captured 40 percent, a violation of (1).

10 Palfrey (1984) appreciates the distinctiveness of the uniform case and thus examines more general distributions in his work on spatial political competition with entry. But he does devote most of his analytical work to the circumstance of *two* existing parties and a prospective entrant.

11 Actually, in each of these papers there are several models, each of which differs from Hotelling in a number of ways. We shall dwell on the one mentioned in the text, along with its implication for conjectures.

12 Recall that there is no equilibrium in the case of three firms in the Hotelling model.

13 Actually, k could locate at any point in the interval $[x_i, x_j]$ and obtain the same market size (this is a function of the uniform distribution). Prescott and Visscher observe the arbitrariness of putting k at the midpoint.

14 Either a mistake or a typographical error in Prescott and Visscher gives the wrong formula for what we have called condition $j.1$.

15 Many of these market models, following Smithies (1941), have even relaxed the parametric price restriction. Nevertheless, profit (now written in terms of both a price and a market size) is still well defined.

16 In their model of legislative coalition formation, which we will discuss, Austen-Smith and Banks show that, while it is always advantageous to be the largest party, it is generally not an advantage to be larger otherwise. If three parties are represented in the legislature, for example, and none commands a majority, then it will turn out to be better to be the third-largest than the second-largest since, in equilibrium, the second-largest will be excluded from a governing coalition.

17 That is, an established candidate, in contemplating a strategy shift, assumes his established opponent will stick with his existing strategy (Cournot–Nash), but that the entrant will react to the new move, possibly changing her own strategy (Stackelberg).

18 By this we mean that the probability of participation depends upon the utility a voter derives from supporting his preferred candidate. As that utility declines (that is, as the preferred candidate grows more and more unappealing), so, too, does the probability of participation.

19 A nicely developed example illustrating this is found in Austen-Smith (1987a).

20 Brams and Straffin (1982) have an earlier model closely related to that of Palfrey. But as Palfrey notes somewhat elliptically, theirs is not an equilibrium model. Their principal result is what they refer to as "the ⅓ separation obstacle." For a general distribution of voters on [0,1], if the established candidates (*i* and *j*) locate at the ⅓- and ⅔-fractile of the distribution, then there is no spot for a vote-maximizing entrant (*k*) which allows her to win a plurality; her vote-maximizing response is to locate just to the left of the ⅓-fractile or just to the right of the ⅔-fractile, but she is *indifferent* between these options. This is all certainly true enough, but neither *i* nor *j* has an incentive to remain at the location prescribed by Brams and Straffin. If, for example, *i* should move slightly to the left of the ⅓-fractile, then the entrant is no longer indifferent and will have an incentive to enter just to the right of *j* (instead of at the median), thereby elevating *i* from a tie with *j* to an absolute plurality. Thus, the Brams-Straffin theorem does not characterize an equilibrium. Palfrey's theorem establishes the equilibrium result.

   In another related paper, Cox (1987) gives a lovely characterization of Nash equilibrium multiparty competition on [0,1] under alternative voting institutions (scoring rules, Condorcet completion procedures, and multiple vote procedures). It is similar in spirit to some of the models developed in Eaton and Lipsey. It differs from Palfrey in that Palfrey allows existing parties to make Stackelberg conjectures about the entrant, whereas Cox, in focusing on Nash equilibrium, allows zero conjectural variation by the candidates.

21 Of course, many of us in academia are familiar with fellowship contests in which, say, the top three graduate student performers on qualifying examinations are awarded dissertation fellowships.

22 Actually, it is more appropriate to think of rank-"satisficing" with *K* as the "level of aspiration."

23 For a general examination and comparison of market (electoral) share maximizing and rank maximizing, see Denzau, Kats, and Slutsky (1985).

24 The formula is slightly different if *a* is "peripheral." Also the formulas and definitions in the text are in terms of a continuous voter distribution. There are natural analogues for the finite voter case.

25 Two technical features figure prominently in the results of Greenberg and Shepsle. First, they assume that no two candidates may occupy the same location. Second, if a prospective entrant locating at *b* obtains the *same* number of votes as some candidate located at an *a* in *A*, the established candidate wins; for an entrant to win, her support must *strictly* exceed that of some established candidate.

26 In contrast, entry is *never* deterred in Palfrey's model. The entrant always enters at her vote-maximizing location, *even if she has no prospect of winning*. We question this aspect of Palfrey's model and think that an essential feature of a spatial equilibrium with prospective entry is that, in equilibrium, entry is deterred.

27 The cynical reader who suggests that differences in the second or third decimal point are hardly worth theorizing about should note that this depends wholly on the fact that the dimension of competition was normalized to [0,1]. It is nevertheless worth commenting that these equilibrium results are not wildly different. We do so shortly.

28 Greenberg and Shepsle show in an appendix that the 2-equilibrium has the property that $F(y_1) = ¼$ and $F(y_2) = ¾$; that is, that the established parties locate at the quartiles of the distribution. By the formula given in our earlier discussion of Palfrey, this is clearly not the case for limit-equilibria. At this 2-equilibrium, no matter where the third party might enter, it receives the support of no more than 25 percent of the voters, a proportion exceeded by both of the established parties.

29 The point w has the property that 75 percent of the voters are distributed to its left. Similarly, $-w$ is the point to the left of which 25 percent of the voters are distributed.

30 As noted, this inequality is satisfied for all normally distributed collections of voters, and extends to practically the entire class of distributions considered by Palfrey.

31 It is, therefore, somewhat ironic that Greenberg and Shepsle based their discussion on the member of the general family of distributions with the largest difference between 2-equilibrium and limit-equilibrium.

32 In effect, if the process reaches the nth party, then it need only provide a bare improvement over the outcome under the caretaker for a bare majority. That is, the penultimate offer will entail the smallest party taking nearly all the goodies (portfolios, pork barrel projects, and so on). This is what all agents forecast will happen at the penultimate move.

33 As in the logic of the preceding note, all agents may forecast the best deal the $(n - 1)$st party can make for itself, which a bare majority would prefer to what it would get if it let the process reach the nth party. Nonuniqueness may prove troublesome.

34 See Myerson (1985) on Bayesian equilibrium and Kreps and Wilson (1982) on sequential equilibrium.

REFERENCES

Austen-Smith, David. 1987a. "Sincere Voting in Models of Legislative Elections." Social Science Working Paper #637. Pasadena: California Institute of Technology.
———. 1987b. "Electing Legislatures." Presented at Conference on Coalition Theory and Public Choice. Fiesole, Italy.
Austen-Smith, David, and Jeffrey S. Banks. 1987. "Elections, Coalitions, and Legislative Outcomes." Presented at Conference on Coalition Theory and Public Choice. Fiesole, Italy.
Banks, Jeffrey S. 1985. "Sophisticated Voting Outcomes and the Covering Relation." *Social Choice and Welfare* 1:295–306.
Banks, Jeffrey S., and D. Roderick Kiewiet. 1987. "Explaining Patterns of Candidate Competition in Congressional Elections." Presented at annual meeting of the Public Choice Society. Tucson, Arizona.
Black, Duncan. 1948. "On the Rationale of Group Decision Making." *Journal of Political Economy* 56: 23–34.
———. 1958. *The Theory of Committees and Elections.* Cambridge: Cambridge University Press.
Black, Duncan, and R. A. Newing. 1951. *Committee Decisions with Complementary Valuation.* London: William Hodge.
Black, Gordon. 1972. "A Theory of Political Ambition: Career Choices and the Role of Structural Incentives." *American Political Science Review* 66: 144–59.
Brams, Steven J., and Philip D. Straffin, Jr. 1982. "The Entry Problem in a Political Race." In Peter C. Ordeshook and Kenneth A. Shepsle, eds., *Political Equilibrium.* Boston: Kluwer-Nijhoff. Pp. 181–97.
Calvert, Randall L. 1985. "Robustness of the Multidimensional Voting Model: Candidate Motivations, Uncertainty, and Convergence." *American Journal of Political Science* 29: 69–95.
Cohen, Ronald N. 1987. "Symmetric 2-Equilibria of Unimodal Voter Distribution Curves." Harvard University (unpublished).
Cox, Gary. 1987. "Electoral Equilibrium under Alternative Voting Institutions." *American Journal of Political Science* 31: 82–109.

Davis, Otto A., and Melvin J. Hinich. "A Mathematical Model of Policy Formation in a Democratic Society." In J. L. Bernd, ed., *Mathematical Applications in Political Science, II.* Dallas: SMU Press. Pp. 175–208.

Davis, Otto A., Melvin J. Hinich, and Peter C. Ordeshook. 1970. "An Expository Development of a Mathematical Model of the Electoral Process." *American Political Science Review* 64: 426–48.

Denzau, Arthur, Amos Kats, and Steven Slutsky. 1985. "Multi-agent Equilibria with Market Share and Ranking Objectives." *Social Choice and Welfare* 2: 95–117.

Downs, Anthony. 1957. *An Economic Theory of Democracy.* New York: Harper and Row.

Eaton, B. Curtis, and Richard G. Lipsey. 1975. "The Principle of Minimum Differentiation Reconsidered: Some New Developments in the Theory of Spatial Competition." *Review of Economic Studies* 42: 27–49.

Ferejohn, John A., Morris P. Fiorina, and Richard D. McKelvey. 1987. "Sophisticated Voting and Agenda Independence in the Distributive Politics Setting." *American Journal of Political Science* 31: 169–94.

Greenberg, Joseph, and Kenneth A. Shepsle. 1987. "The Effect of Electoral Rewards in Multiparty Competition with Entry." *American Political Science Review* 81: 525–37.

Hay, D. A. 1976. "Sequential Entry and Entry-Deterring Strategies in Spatial Competition." *Oxford Economic Papers* 28: 240–57.

Hinich, Melvin J., and Peter C. Ordeshook. 1970. "Plurality Maximization vs. Vote Maximization: A Spatial Analysis with Variable Participation." *American Political Science Review* 64: 772–91.

Hotelling, Harold. 1929. "Stability in Competition." *Economic Journal* 39: 41–57.

Jacobson, Gary C., and Samuel Kernell. 1981. *Strategy and Choice in Congressional Elections.* New Haven: Yale University Press.

Kreps, David M., and Robert Wilson. 1982. "Sequential Equilibrium." *Econometrica* 50: 863–94.

Losch, August. 1954. *The Economics of Location.* New Haven: Yale University Press.

McKelvey, Richard D. 1986. "Covering, Dominance and Institution-Free Properties of Social Choice." *American Journal of Political Science* 30: 283–314.

Myerson, Roger B. 1985. "Bayesian Equilibrium and Incentive-Compatibility: An Introduction." In Leonid Hurwicz, David Schmeidler, and Hugo Sonnenschein, eds., *Social Goals and Social Organization.* Cambridge: Cambridge University Press. Pp. 229–59.

Palfrey, Thomas R. 1984. "Spatial Equilibrium with Entry." *Review of Economic Studies* 51: 139–56.

Prescott, Edward C., and Michael Visscher. 1977. "Sequential Location Among Firms with Foresight." *Bell Journal of Economics* 8: 378–93.

Riker, William H. 1976. "The Number of Political Parties: A Reexamination of Duverger's Law." *Comparative Politics* 9: 93–106.

———. 1982. "The Two-Party System and Duverger's Law: An Essay on the History of Political Science." *American Political Science Review* 76: 753–67.

Rohde, David W. 1979. "Risk-Bearing and Progressive Ambition: The Case of the United States House of Representatives." *American Journal of Political Science* 23: 1–27.

Romer, Thomas, and Howard Rosenthal. 1978. "Political Resource Allocation, Controlled Agendas, and the Status Quo." *Public Choice* 33: 27–45.

Shepsle, Kenneth A. 1979. "Institutional Arrangements and Equilibrium in Multidimensional Voting Models." *American Journal of Political Science* 23: 27–59.

———. 1990. *Models of Multiparty Electoral Competition* (London: Harwood).

Shepsle, Kenneth A., and Barry W. Weingast. 1981. "Structure-Induced Equilibrium and Legislative Choice." *Public Choice* 36: 221–37.

———. 1984. "Uncovered Sets and Sophisticated Voting Outcomes with Implications for Agenda Institutions." *American Journal of Political Science* 25: 49–75.

Smithies, Arthur. 1941. "Optimum Location in Spatial Competition." *Journal of Political Economy* 49: 423–39.

Wittman, Donald. 1983. "Candidate Motivation: A Synthesis of Alternative Theories." *American Political Science Review* 77: 142–57.

Wright, Stephen G., and William H. Riker. 1987. "Electoral Systems and Numbers of Candidates." University of Rochester (unpublished).

3

Heresthetic and Rhetoric in the Spatial Model

WILLIAM H. RIKER

University of Rochester

What are the moving parts in the spatial model of politics?

The formal theorems about equilibrium reveal nothing about moving parts. Black's median voter theorem simply identifies the equilibrium, given single-peaked utility curves, as the ideal point of the median voter (Black 1948, 1958). Plott's multidimensional extension of this theorem identifies the equilibrium, given convex utility curves, as the ideal point of the voter at the multidimensional median (Plott 1967). These fundamental facts require no moving parts, mainly because they describe outcomes from the black box, not the processes that go on inside it.

But if one wishes to get inside the black box to describe how the process moves toward equilibrium (or not, as the case may be), then it is necessary to assume something about the moving parts. In Downs's informal model of spatial competition, the candidates or parties position and reposition themselves, converging to the ideal of the median voter (Downs 1957). In McKelvey's agenda theorem, the agenda-controller moves motions in a trajectory toward his or her goal (McKelvey 1976, 1979). Something similar, but less well directed, occurs in Kramer's model of convergence to the minmax set (Kramer 1977). In the recent modifications of McKelvey's model (Ferejohn, McKelvey, and Packel 1984), as also in the models of Feld and Grofman (1988), the trajectories are confined to a central portion of the space, but still it is the motions that vary, not the voters.

As far as I know, the candidates (or parties) and their platforms or, alternatively, the motions, are all that anyone has proposed as moving parts. But nothing inherent in the model prevents other parts from moving. At the very minimum, the voters might also move. This means that they might change their tastes, that is, change the location of their ideal points or the shapes of their indifference curves. Alternatively, they might simply pretend to change the location of their ideal points, as in strategic voting. Beyond these actions of voters, participants (either candidates or voters) might change the space itself, distorting it by adding or subtracting dimensions or by expanding

46

dimensions as if they were elastic or elastic in certain distances. (Adding or subtracting dimensions always changes the shape of the space and the distribution of voters. Distorting dimensions need not change the relative position of the voters, but in two dimensions it can easily affect the relative location of the center of the distribution, and in higher dimensions it can significantly change the kinds of coalitions.)

These possibilities, which certainly exist in the real world, ought to be examined in the model in order to describe analogues of real-world events. In this chapter, I look into moving other parts than motions or the candidate's platforms. I concern myself mainly with two processes to induce adjustment by voters: heresthetic and rhetoric. Heresthetic has to do with changing the space or the constraints on the voters in such a way that they are encouraged, even driven, to move themselves to the advantage of the heresthetician. (I coined the word "heresthetic" to describe this process because, while many previous writers have described particular instances of heresthetical manipulation, no one has classified these actions under a rubric suitable for theoretical analysis. I used the Greek word for "choosing" and "voting" both to emphasize the social choice feature of the action and to point out the parallel with rhetoric, which the Greeks should, perhaps, have noticed, but did not.) Rhetoric, on the other hand, has to do with changing the opinion of voters so that they, rather than motions or alternatives, move about in the space. By focusing on these two processes it will be possible to disclose some of the nuances and complications of the spatial model.

HERESTHETIC

Suppose a participant in a decision-making group predicts that, given the voters' tastes and the vote-counting mechanism, he will be on the losing side. What might he do to avoid that unfortunate outcome?

If his tastes are extreme, he might seek to change the constitution, which involves, among other things, changing at least the vote-counting mechanism, and perhaps also the voters. Of course the revolutionary must abandon hope of immediate victory (that is, in the next election), consoling himself with the hope of winning after the revolution. This strategy is arduous, however, and unlikely to succeed—except when the political system displays nearly anarchic instability. Failure is, indeed, almost certain in liberal democratic governments – to which we mean to apply the spatial model – because they minimize the number of extremists. It is also almost certain in cruel despotisms – for which the spatial model is not well suited – because they minimize the formation of revolutionary parties.

Putting aside, therefore, the possibility of revolution, the expectant loser might rhetorically persuade other voters to relocate spatially closer to him, or he might heresthetically restructure the space so that, willy-nilly, they join his

47

spatial neighborhood. The distinction between these strategies is that rhetoric consists of an appeal to the reason or emotion of the auditor, while heresthetic requires no appeal because it consists of a redefinition of the situation. Sometimes, of course, redefinition is rendered salient and palatable by rhetorical flavoring, but for heresthetic maneuvers, the flavoring is only incidental.

Consider, as an explanatory example of heresthetic, a maneuver by Senator Warren Magnuson (Democrat, Washington) in 1970 (Smith 1984; Riker 1986). The Department of Defense, perhaps embarrassed by an accidental release of stored nerve gas in 1969 in Okinawa, Japan, announced a program of repatriation and detoxification of nerve gas weapons. Seattle was to be the port of entry, and the live shells would then be transported by train across Washington to a detoxification center in Oregon. Magnuson immediately objected, in part, no doubt, out of concern for his constituents, and in part, perhaps, to embarrass and discredit the Republican administration. The Department of Defense ultimately changed its proposal from Washington and Oregon to Alaska; but I suspect that the other senator from Washington, Henry Jackson, who was on especially good terms with the Pentagon, had, although he was also a Democrat, far more influence on the change than did Magnuson. Naturally the Alaskan senators objected, and Magnuson espoused their cause, just as they had espoused his.

In his initial opposition, Magnuson's main weapon was rhetoric. He argued that repatriation was unnecessary because, first, Okinawans were, without complaint, currently living with the weapons and, second, detoxification could occur outside the United States. But the more important feature of his rhetorical appeal was an impassioned and dramatic description of the lethal consequences if nerve gas were to be released in Washington or Alaska, either by accident or by terrorists. As I will show later, this type of appeal (the prediction of unlikely disasters) is characteristic of campaigns about policy, and Magnuson behaved as if he believed it was the best argument in his repertoire.

But his rhetoric was not enough. Initially he could count on the thirty or so radical Democrats (mostly from the Northeast) who would be likely to oppose any initiative from the Republican Defense Department. For this ideological support neither rhetoric nor heresthetic was necessary. Beyond that he could win the support of both Republicans and Democrats from the Northwest by the rhetoric of terror – although Henry Jackson, the "senator from Boeing," deserted him as soon as the danger to Washington was averted. These two groups – only about 40 percent of the Senate – were not, however, enough to win. The rhetoric of terror, while effective for the Northwest, had little force elsewhere.

Stymied by the fact that most Republicans and southern Democrats supported the administration, and unable to persuade these senators by rhetorical appeals, Magnuson could win only by an heresthetical maneuver that would drive some opponents to his side. So he invented a clever diversion. He pointed out to the Senate that the president had promised to inform it of the progress of negotiations for a treaty with Japan over Okinawa, and he suggested that the repatriation of nerve gas from Okinawa probably was a part of the negotiations. Yet, he pointed out, the Senate had not been informed. According to Magnuson, the president had ignored the "advice and consent" of the Senate, thus, presumably, depreciating its dignity and its constitutional role in foreign affairs.

Probably every member of the Senate recognized this maneuver for what it was: an effort to transform the repatriation issue from a parochial concern in the Northwest and a matter of Defense expediency into a profound and compelling matter of senatorial dignity. Probably every member also recognized that the allegation about presidential motives was spurious, because the repatriation was occasioned by the previous accident and was worldwide in scope, not limited to Okinawa. Nevertheless, about 10 percent of the Senate (mostly conservative Republicans who might otherwise have been expected to be the administration's strongest supporters) were diverted to Magnuson's side by the maneuver. These senators, for whom the dignity of the Senate was surely a primary concern, believed they were compelled to vote as if the dignity of the Senate were truly at stake, Thus, merely verbalizing the issue rendered it salient. Ten senators provided Magnuson's margin of victory, even though they probably detested Magnuson personally and even though they probably believed that his previous rhetoric about terrorism and trains was the cheapest kind of demagoguery. While recognizing that his heresthetic was as cheap as his rhetoric, they were compelled by their own vision of themselves to defend senatorial dignity, once Magnuson had laid it on the table. So they took his view of the issue at face value and voted on his side.

As illustrated by this example, the distinguishing feature of heresthetic is that voters are induced to change sides, not by persuasion, but by reinterpretation of the issue. What made the voters appear to move, in this incident, was a change in the salient dimensions of the space. So it may properly be said that the shape of the space changed rather than the voters themselves. Thus, one way of distinguishing between heresthetic and rhetoric is to say that heresthetic is aimed at changing the voters' environment, while rhetoric is aimed at changing the voters' opinions.

THE THEORETICAL BASIS OF HERESTHETIC

To understand the reason heresthetic works and is, I believe, a more significant feature of the real world than rhetoric, let us look at the spatial model to see what in the model world permits heresthetical maneuver. A good way to approach this subject is to examine kinds of equilibrium in the model. If tastes or institutions are certain to induce a stable outcome, there is little the prospective loser can do – other than obfuscation – to prevent prospective winners from arriving at the anticipated outcome. But if stable outcomes are difficult to arrive at, or are not obvious, or do not exist, then it is possible for the prospective loser to rearrange politics to his or her advantage. This is what heresthetic is all about.

In the one-dimensional spatial model, using simple majority rule, there is a clearly defined equilibrium: an alternative in the space that can beat any other alternative, which is, of course, the ideal point of the median voter (assuming single-peaked utility curves). In two or more dimensions, the equilibrium under simple majority rule continues to be well-defined, the ideal point of the multidimensional median voter, the Plott equilibrium (Plott 1967). But there is a significant difference between the two equilibria. In one dimension, the equilibrium of the model seems likely to exist often in the real world. Calculations of the expected frequency of a set of single-peaked curves, given random selections of tastes, suggest that real-world equilibria are likely (Niemi 1969), and experience in the real world seems to confirm the likelihood (Poole and Rosenthal 1985; Niemi and Wright 1987). But in two or more dimensions, a real-world analogue of the model's equilibrium seems highly unlikely, because the requirements for a multidimensional median are, in terms of spatial arrangements, extremely restrictive. Nothing in our experience leads us to expect a Plott equilibrium in the real world.

As we turn from simple majority rule, with no other institutions defined, to other methods of summing voters' tastes and other circumstances of summation, the nature of equilibria changes. Increasing the majority required from simple majority to something larger increases the number of alternatives that cannot be beaten by others, so the set of potential equilibria increases (Schofield 1985). Considering the circumstances of the process of summation, numerous constitutional rules and accepted methods of operation impose restrictions on the process, and these restrictions typically increase the number of equilibria. Shepsle has defined "structure-induced equilibria" as outcomes that are stable, given some institution (like a committee system with committees having jurisdiction over different dimensions), but that would not be stable in the absence of these institutions (Shepsle 1979; see also Shepsle and Weingast 1984 and Hammond and Miller 1987 for an appreciation of the wide range of institutional effects on equilibria).

There are heresthetical maneuvers (both to protect the status quo and to induce new outcomes) appropriate for all these equilibria (or nonequilibria). I will not discuss the host of maneuvers unique to particular institutions (maneuvers like gerrymanders, electoral qualifications, many principles of judicial review, constitutional structures like the separation of powers, and so forth) because very few generalizations can be uttered about them in the present state of our knowledge. But for the simpler cases of equilibria of tastes, it is possible to generalize about heresthetic maneuvers. Consider decision by majority rule with no other institutional restrictions on one-dimensional, single-peaked preferences. This is perhaps the most difficult case for the heresthetician, because with reasonably complete information about tastes, the prospective winners know exactly what can occur and have an incentive to move along quickly to the equilibrium they desire. (Indeed, given complete information, there is some evidence that in the real world, as in the model, nothing can keep the winners from arriving at the equilibrium [Plott and Levine 1978].)

Prospective losers are not without defenses. They can withhold information about relevant matters (Austen-Smith and Riker 1987); they can obfuscate, thus forcing other participants to estimate probabilities about their preference orders (Shepsle 1972). Their simplest defense is delay, in the hope of rhetorically inducing changes in tastes or of heresthetically inducing changes in the dimension or the single-peaked distribution. For delay, there is a fine array of delaying tactics in legislatures, such as filibustering or the old device of disappearing quorums.

Beyond delay, although often in conjunction with it, prospective losers can attempt to add a dimension to the space. This restructuring – from a model where an equilibrium is likely to exist to one where it is not – allows a clever heresthetician to define a hyperplane separating the voters into a new majority-minority division that is advantageous to him or her. Such attempts at restructuring are one of the main activities of politics. Political leaders constantly seek to raise new dimensions (as did Magnuson), to reinterpret old ones (as did the Whigs of the 1830s who made slavery a national rather than a local issue in prelude to the Civil War), and to dismiss issues on which they feel uncomfortable (as in the cry "That's not a political issue" of centrist politicians in response to the abortion issue in the 1970s). Political scientists in general have not understood that these activities follow a pattern rooted in the nature of the decision process: Any set of voters can be divided into majority and minority in myriad ways, and such redivision can occur as soon as a one-dimensional equilibrium is upset. Hence, they have not generalized about this feature of politics. One of the great virtues of the spatial model is that, by using it, the importance and pervasiveness of changing dimensions is readily recognized.

An institutional feature of decision that allows considerable heresthetical manipulation, regardless of whether an equilibrium of tastes exists, is sequential decision, usually by successive balloting as in the amendment or successive procedure in parliamentary bodies. Because these institutions involve decisions at one balloting that influence choice at a subsequent balloting, it is possible that voters use their votes at the initial ballot, not to choose what they immediately prefer, but to set the scene for and influence the outcome of the subsequent ballot. In this so-called strategic voting, people vote on the initial ballot for an alternative that, were there no subsequent ballot, they would otherwise oppose.

In parliamentary bodies this maneuver often involves a "killer amendment," wherein at stage one the heresthetical voter helps to attach an amendment, perhaps even a disliked amendment, to a motion he or she opposes, an amendment that will render the revised motion unpalatable and unsupportable to some of its previous proponents, who then vote at the second stage with the heresthetical voter against the amended bill. (For some well-studied examples, see: on the Powell amendment, Denzau, Riker, and Shepsle 1985; Enelow 1981; Riker 1986; on the 17th amendment, Riker 1986; on the Panama treaty, Enelow and Koehler 1980. Shepsle and Weingast argue that strategic voting is an almost universal feature of procedure under open rules, in Shepsle and Weingast 1987, 1988.) Strategic voting in sequential decision is certainly heresthetical and has no rhetorical element because, entirely without persuasion, some voters are put into a position wherein they believe themselves compelled to vote against (for) something they had previously favored (opposed).

When a stable equilibrium (that is, a Condorcet winner) exists, it will be arrived at if everyone votes strategically, but often the decisive feature of this situation is that, in representative bodies, not everyone dares to vote strategically. When representatives choose among alternatives, considerations about representation – concern about constituents' approval of ideological utterances – may overwhelm considerations about outcomes – concern about constituents' appreciation for legislative consequences (Denzau, Riker, and Shepsle 1986). So one way to defeat an expected equilibrium outcome is to complicate the selection by strategic voting. In general, sequential strategic voting is a version of changing dimensions because a new dimension (such as a "killer" amendment) is added to consideration.

Strategic voting is not limited to the sequential case. In single-stage selection among candidates, voters often face institutional structures that allow, indeed encourage, voting for their second choice rather than their first in order to bring about a better outcome than would occur if they voted for their first. Thus, in plurality elections supporters of weak candidates may vote for their second-best choice to help him or her beat their third choice (Riker 1982). While this maneuver might seem to involve something other than movement between one and two dimensions, it does share this feature of heresthetic because the method of voting encourages the voter to think about two standards simultaneously: his or her taste in candidates, and the prospects of victory for the several candidates. The voters' choice is then some combination of judgments on these two scales.

Another kind of strategic voting, common in legislatures, is vote trading, which also requires a two-dimensional space (Riker 1982a). When two or more legislators take opposing views on a pair of issues, on both of which they provide the margins of victory on the winning sides, and on both of which, taken together, a majority would prefer an outcome different from what would occur under decision one at a time, then it is possible for them to reverse their votes. This results in greater individual satisfaction, for by reversing outcomes, each wins on his or her more-preferred issue. Measuring satisfaction on two issues requires at least two dimensions and, in general, vote trades on n issues require that the issues be measured in n-space.

Another large class of heresthetical devices consists of manipulation of agendas. Like the other devices here described, most such manipulation depends on exploiting either the other voters' lack of information or the difference between one- and two-dimensional distributions. In one dimension, if equilibria exist and if the voters are fully informed about each others' tastes, they can probably foil most attempts at agenda control. For example, in the Plott and Levine experiment on agenda control, when the subjects were inadvertently allowed to increase their knowledge of others' tastes, they immediately adjusted their behavior to choose the Condorcet winner. When, however, the experimenters restricted subjects' information to what was revealed in the balloting, they were driven to choose precisely what Plott and Levine intentionally forced them to choose (Plott and Levine 1978). For another example, in the story from the *Letters* of the younger Pliny, which Farquharson used as the running example in his path-breaking book on strategic voting, Pliny, as presiding officer, attempted to control the agenda in the Roman Senate to his own advantage by substituting a ternary method of voting for the usual binary one. His main opponent recognized what Pliny sought to do and responded by voting strategically to produce exactly the Condorcet equilibrium that the customary procedure would have produced. Pliny's effort failed for exactly the same reasons as the one failure in the Plott-Levine experiment, because a Condorcet winner existed and the voters knew enough to find it despite the chairman's obfuscation for agenda control (Farquharson 1969; Riker 1986).

Another kind of agenda control is based squarely on the number of dimensions. By McKelvey's agenda theorem, if there are two or more dimensions, then, under majority rule, all the points in the space are in a cycle. Hence, a fully informed agenda-setter with complete control may, by successive votes, force the final decision on any point in the space he chooses (Schofield 1978; McKelvey 1979). He may, however, be constrained by the shape of the distribution of tastes to relatively small movements within the smallest figure in the space bisected by or tangent to all the hyperplanes dividing the voters into simple majorities (Ferejohn, McKelvey, and Packel 1984). Since, in the real world, agenda-setters ordinarily do not have control over all amendments, there are probably no direct real-world analogues of this theoretical possibility of manipulation (but see Romer and Rosenthal 1978). Furthermore, there is always the chance of jumping from a one-dimensional space (with an equilibrium point) to a two-dimensional one (without equilibrium) by means, for example, of appropriate amendments. Most legislative bodies have rules, enforced with varying degrees of vigor, that permit only germane amendments. Of course, the pressure for nongermane amendments comes from people who are trying to introduce a second dimension, without an equilibrium, so that all the alternatives will be in a cycle. One important kind of agenda control is, then, the ability to admit or prohibit nongermane amendments, either to escape from or stay in one dimension.

One of the advantages of the spatial model for viewing political life is that it allows for just this expansion and contraction of dimensions, which, in the model, are surrogates for the ebb and flow of issues in the real world. Since manipulation of the number and relevance of issues is just about the center of politics, the spatial model allows us to utter generalizations about the most important kinds of political strategies. The secret is that the model concerns equilibria in the distribution of tastes relative to some given parameters, while the real manipulation of issues is itself a manipulation of real parameters.

RHETORIC

As we turn to rhetoric, the model is less obviously helpful, although I believe it will probably turn out to be extremely useful as we learn more about persuasion. Rhetoric is intended to relocate people's ideal points on parameters. Like heresthetic, this is a social process, but it also involves working a significant change inside individual psyches. Heresthetic merely involves displaying the relevance of a dimension, recalling it from latent storage to the center of psychic attention. This process is probably not threatening to most people because it does not require that they acknowledge that they previously erred. Persuasion, on the other hand, involves changing opinion and, implicitly at least, requires recognition of error. In this sense, rhetoric involves more vigorous manipulation of other people's psyches than does heresthetic.

The difference in emphasis alters the problem of interpretation from the social to the psychic. For understanding heresthetic, which involves individual psyches only with respect to the recall of the latent, we want to know chiefly about the effect of the changed dimensions on equilibria, a truly and exclusively social phenomena. But for understanding rhetoric, which, while social with respect to the interaction of rhetor and auditor, is psychic with respect to changed ideal points, we want to know chiefly about the way the rhetor's oratory affects private judgments. Thus, heresthetic is studied mainly by techniques of social science, while rhetoric is studied mainly by techniques of psychological science. Since the spatial model is entirely social, with tastes taken as given, one should expect it to be less useful in studying rhetoric than in studying heresthetic.

It is not surprising, therefore, that most makers of spatial models have not thought it worthwhile to examine changes in voters' tastes, at least changes in the short run. Insofar as they bother to justify this simplification, they say that, since persuasion is difficult and expensive, politicians are unlikely to expend energy on a probably fruitless task. In other contexts for studying tastes, such as price theory, scientists have similarly assumed, without serious distortion of their models, that tastes are constant in the time period of equilibration. Of course, ever since Veblen, a minority of economists, as well as many psychologists, have speculated about the origin of tastes. But no one has put forward a theory any more precise than Veblen's notion of conspicuous consumption or Maslow's notion of a hierarchy of goals. Neither of these ideas are much help for investigating the kind of changes in taste that might be important in price theory or spatial models of politics.

In the study of advertising, where, if anywhere, persuasion and changes of taste might be expected to be important, there are two quite different approaches by critics of society, on the one hand, and by economists, on the other. Social critics emphasize the immediate malleability of tastes and believe that advertisers persuade unsuspecting consumers to waste money on unnecessary or shoddy goods. The difficulty with this position is that, while innocents of course exist and are mulcted, the bulk of advertising is directed at normally intelligent and skeptical consumers, whose tastes are probably not so easily manipulated. Consequently, economists usually interpret advertising as information about products that satisfy some preexisting (though possibly latent) taste. The argument for this interpretation is based on the assumption that to persuade, that is, to change tastes, is more difficult and expensive than to inform or to cater to existing tastes. It follows that rational producers prefer the less costly informing to the more costly persuading. That is, they prefer to develop products that satisfy existing (possibly latent) tastes than to persuade people to desire already developed but unwanted products. Furthermore, producers get more-or-less immediate feedback from advertising, so they know what information works and what does not. With a speedy and systematic method of monitoring the effect of advertising on sales, it makes sense to search for products that fit tastes. Thus, it is so cheap to discover tastes that it is not worthwhile to change them. In this view, therefore, tastes are assumed to be constant, although perhaps varying in salience.

Political advertisers are in a different position from commercial advertisers. Businesses can change their products with relative ease, but political parties, one of the main products of which is ideology, cannot. Nor can parties get speedy feedback: The political feedback cycle is every four years in the United States, as compared to several weeks for commercial advertisers. Furthermore, because of their commitment to an ideology, parties and even individual politicians are confined to a restricted range on a dimension, at least in the short run. Too sharp or great a shift along a dimension exposes them to a loss of credibility. A politician's move from an extreme right to an extreme left, for example, seems so opportunistic that voters infer that he believes nothing. They reciprocate by believing nothing he says.

Because political advertisers must thus remain in inherited-issue neighborhoods and have therefore an incentive to persuade voters to join them there, the case for constant tastes for voters is not as clear-cut as the case for constant tastes for buyers. Persuasion is politically necessary for fixed politicians to attract voters to their neighborhoods. So political advertisers, unlike business advertisers, have a compelling motive to persuade. If they succeed, then voters' tastes cannot be constant.

Since psychological theory about persuasion is not well developed (Petty, Ostrom, and Brock 1981), we do not know much theoretically about rhetoricians' effectiveness, although we do have available a vast number of case studies of particular speeches and works of art. From the case study analysis we know that rhetoricians are constantly engaged in myth making, reshaping ideologies, and recasting causality, as well as in devising all sorts of emotional appeals, fortifying loyalties, invoking patriotism, intensifying devotion to cults, and so on. This is why politicians employ and honor propagandists and even political philosophers. Still, even granting that persuasion is necessary for political success and that politicians are persuaders by vocation, we do not know how well politicians persuade, or how much persuasion occurs, or whether it has marginal effects on social outcomes.*

A MODEL FOR CHANGING TASTES

In order to understand rhetoric and persuasion in terms of the spatial model, it is necessary to have a spatial model in which acts of persuasion make sense. It is unfortunate that the spatial model as usually presented does not allow for voters' positions to change and thus precludes persuasion (Austen-Smith and Riker 1987; Fink 1987; Enelow and Hinich 1984). The typical spatial model provides one space that contains both alternatives and outcomes, which are, therefore, treated as identical. Dimensions of this space measure characteristics of alternatives (such as candidates or motions) and it is assumed, usually without explicit mention, that the same characteristics define the

---

*It is regrettable that rhetoric has not been studied in a systematic way. Instruction, probably ever since the pre-Socratics, seems to have proceeded by analysis of examples, so students have learned mainly by analogy, not by generalization. This means that rhetorical theory consists mainly of categorization of occasions for and types of speeches, of figures of speech, and of principles of wisdom – as distinct from knowledge – about procedures of writing. In the last decade, psychologists and information theorists have studied the conditions under which audiences are receptive to appeals (Petty, Ostrom, and Brock 1981; Calvert 1985). But very few scholars have ever generalized about the content of appeals or attempted to test their persuasiveness. Thus, political and commercial advertisers alike are so devoid of theory that they must devise appeals by brainstorming and test their success by market experiments and survey research.

outcomes consequent to the choice of an alternative. Thus, a winning candidate's policy stances and characteristics in alternative space become, after the election, policy directions in the more-or-less identical outcome space.

But suppose the alternative space, which contains motions or platforms, and the outcome space, which contains judgments on motions adopted or candidates elected, are different, even with different dimensions. Suppose further that the alternative space contains a motion with an outcome which, when translated to outcome space, occasions various interpretations by participants so that the function that carries the outcome from alternative space to outcome space differs among persons. Consider, for example, a minimum wage bill as an alternative. Everyone knows it will raise the income of some poorly paid wage-earners, but everyone also knows it will cause some unemployment. Thus, the judgment on the bill in the outcome space varies, from those who approve because of its wage effect, to those who disapprove because of its employment effect.

Therein lies the opportunity for persuasion, which is observable by us because the uncertainty of individual interpretation is revealed by the separation of the alternative space from the outcome space. In this two-space model, the content of persuasion is the offering of reasons for auditors and readers to believe that some outcome ought to be differently judged from the way participants have previously judged it.

RHETORICAL THEORY

In order to understand and generalize about persuasion, one should be able to describe how rhetorical appeals actually work on individual psyches to move them from one ideal point to another on dimensions in the outcome space. Unfortunately we know almost nothing about this psychological process, so we are initially stymied in the construction of a rhetorical theory.

Fortunately, however, there is an indirect approach that depends, not on understanding the psychological process, but rather on interpreting the behavior of rhetors. For this analysis, we assume that experienced rhetors know something about how persuasion works on their own issues. If they then use a particular technique frequently, we can infer that this technique is believed to be persuasive. Furthermore, if many rhetors use the technique, it is then widely believed to be persuasive. Given such wide belief, we can ask why the particular technique might be persuasive, and the answer will, I believe, yield a theory of rhetoric that does not necessarily require a well-verified psychological theory as its base.

To illustrate this procedure, I offer an observation about the content of appeals in political campaigns. Campaigns are joint efforts in the sense that many rhetors participate. Their choices of appeal vary, but often they tend to emphasize particular appeals so that they often appear to be coordinated, even when they are not. To me this implicit consensus on tactics indicates an implicit consensus on the effectiveness of persuasion. This socially identifiable agreement thus provides a quasi-objective feature of persuasion. While it might also seem to be impossible to generalize about campaigns because each one is unique, rhetoricians have always classified and generalized about the properties and effectiveness of forms of argument and figures of speech. What I propose is no different, except that a campaign is a lengthier text than rhetoricians usually explicate. The difference is that traditional rhetoric has never had a basis for examining effectiveness, while the implicit consensus on appeals, with its implicit evidence of rhetors' belief in persuasiveness, provides a basis for judging the classes of argument.

My main observation about the content of campaign rhetoric is this: When the alternatives concerned are motions (rather than candidates), campaigners on each side emphasize the dreadful consequences of the failure (or success) of the motion they advocate (or oppose). Usually these predicted disasters are extremely unlikely but, presumably, plausible to their auditors. The auditors' judgments on the disasters are certainly in the outcome space, not in the alternative space.

Two examples of campaigns will illustrate such behavior by more or less uncoordinated rhetors: the successful campaign over the ratification of the Constitution and the unsuccessful campaign over the ratification of the Equal Rights Amendment.

In the campaign over the Constitution (Fink and Riker 1988), the main issue in the alternative space was the degree of consolidation of the states into a federation with a strong central government. (Some revisionists of the progressive era – J. Allen Smith, Charles Beard, Carl Becker, and others – have argued that the issue was a type of class struggle. This was indeed how one side in 1787 wanted the voters to interpret the alternative in the outcome space. But the actual decision in ratification, as both sides in 1787 recognized, was the degree of governmental consolidation.) The difference of opinion concerned the interpretation, in the outcome space, of the consolidation the Constitution provided for. Those who successfully called themselves Federalists argued that the then-existent federation was disintegrating and that, unless the proposed consolidation occurred, disastrous civil and foreign war, economic decline, and confiscation of property would follow. The people who reluctantly accepted the name Anti-Federalists argued that the consolidation would destroy traditional liberties, shield officials from popular control, and result ultimately in oligarchy or tyranny. It seems clear now that both arguments were extremely exaggerated predictions of extremely unlikely events. We know that consolidation produced none of the dire effects predicted by the Anti-Federalists. Concurrently we can also safely assume that, had ratification failed and a second convention been called (as Anti-Federalists wished), it would have proposed a less centralized and more easily acceptable government but one sufficient to coordinate commerce and pay off the war debt. In short, both sides exaggeratedly predicted a preposterous disaster from the success of the other.

The same kind of false exaggeration characterized the campaign over the Equal Rights Amendment (Mansbridge 1986). The main argument of its supporters was that women were, in the absence of the amendment, doomed to an inferior economic status. This was embodied in the ubiquitous slogan "59 cents," which meant that women earned only 59 cents for every dollar earned by men. The opponents, on the other hand, argued that the amendment would completely change the role of women in society by, for example, such innovations as unisex toilets and conscripted combat duty. The main chronicler of this campaign (Mansbridge) pointed out that feminists erred in emphasizing "59 cents" because even by the time the amendment failed, the relative economic position of women had improved considerably and would, presumably, continue to do so. On the other hand, the exaggerated claims about unisex toilets and combat duty were equally unrealistic – the former an absurd joke, the latter opposed by all but a few extreme feminists. It is undoubtedly true that the role of women in this society is changing for mainly economic reasons – the need to utilize women's labor outside the home – but there is nothing to suggest that the amendment would have speeded up the process in the ways the proponents and opponents predicted. So in this case also, uncoordinated rhetors on both sides emphasized unlikely, dreadful consequences.

Many other examples of this type of rhetorical appeal could be cited, for it seems to be almost universal in disputes about policy. If so, it must reflect campaigners' conviction that it is a successful tactic. And it does seem that in these two ratification campaigns, one can observe a degree of success.

The proto-Federalists of the early 1780s had attempted to centralize for some time (for example, with the proposals in 1781 and 1783 for a national tariff and with the Annapolis convention of 1786 on trade policy). Their arguments about impending disaster were well known everywhere by 1787 and doubtless contributed greatly to the agreement to hold the Constitutional Convention in May 1787, especially after the appearance of a trivial but frightening civil war in the fall of 1786. The initial reception of the Constitution in September 1787 seemed favorable, and ratification was not seriously opposed, except in Pennsylvania. So the proto-Federalists' rhetorical stance carried them through the initial stages of the proposal and probably seemed to them, as it seems to me, highly successful.

On the other hand, the Anti-Federalists' rhetorical stance was effective, during the almost year-long campaign, in mobilizing opposition to the Constitution, so that as early as February 1788, it appeared that ratification might well fail. This too represents rhetorical success. Much the same kind of success was achieved by both sides in the campaign over the ERA. Feminists' economic arguments about discrimination carried the proposal forward in the 1960s and through Congress in 1972 with relative ease. The initial momentum may thus be credited to all that went into the slogan "59 cents." The opposition stalled the ratification process with its vivid pictures of the defeminization of women and the reordering of the family. So, in this case also, the rhetorical prediction of unlikely disasters worked well for both sides.

Incidentally, the difference in outcomes between the two events is also relevant. In the ERA case the proponents lost, mainly, according to Mansbridge, because they refused to counter the opponents' rhetorical stance with a meaningless but apparently accommodating concession, the exclusion of combat duty for women. The Federalists, on the other hand, won because they agreed to adopt, after ratification, amendments recommended by the Anti-Federalists before ratification. The amendments they in fact accepted, however constitutionally valuable, were politically trivial in the sense that both Federalists and Anti-Federalists approved of them. (The Federalists ignored the amendments that the Anti-Federalists most urgently wanted.) I infer from this comparison that when a rhetorical stance emphasizing unlikely disasters seems about to stop the momentum of a campaign, it is heresthetically appropriate to offer more or less trivial amendments – trivial in the sense that they do nothing but forestall the predicted disasters that wouldn't have occurred anyway. The tactic of concession worked for the Federalists and, according to Mansbridge, would probably have worked for the ERA supporters. I take this as evidence in both cases that the rhetorical predictions were unrealistic. If the defect be curable by trivial concessions, then the prediction itself must be exaggerated and improbable.

How can one explain the rhetorical similarities in these two events? According to the method I suggested earlier, the best way is to examine the rationale of the rhetor. As a rational politician seeking to win by persuasion, his or her immediate goal is to utter persuasive arguments. The fact that predictions of unlikely disasters is so commonplace a stance implies that rhetors believe it works. So the question is: Why do they believe so? It may be that they speak without any theory or belief at all, and arrive at their preferred stance entirely by trials and errors with arguments. Their repeated discovery, then, that frightening predictions mobilize support implies an even deeper psychological question: Why is the number of auditors who appear to respond as rhetors desire sufficiently large to change outcomes?

I cannot give an assured answer to these questions, both of which require a nonexistent psychological theory of persuasion. But I can offer some possibilities. In the discussion of a new public policy, the voter is necessarily in the dark about the meaning or consequences of the proposed alternative. For example, there was no doubt in the fall of 1787 that the new Constitution centralized politics, but just how that centralization was to be judged was unclear. If the rhetor could show that, without ratification, the probability of foreign and civil war would be greater or, alternatively, that with ratification, the probability of subjugation to a new monarchical tyranny would be greater, he might hope for a popular judgment similar to his own. Quite possibly also, the greater the disaster, the greater the popular concern, entirely without any reference to the likelihood of the disaster. This, as Norman Schofield has suggested to me, is exactly the Rawlsian veil of ignorance (Rawls 1971). The voter knows disaster looms, has no idea of how likely it is, but does know that it must avoided at all costs. So, using the Rawlsian minimax strategy, he votes to minimize the chance of reaching the maximally bad outcome. It is not known to what degree real people choose in a Rawlsian fashion. Some experimenters suggest that most people prefer expected value calculations (Froelich, Oppenheimer, and Eavey 1987). But laboratory experiments are not likely to be decisive for judgments on truly important human concerns, which is precisely the point at which Rawlsian kinds of judgments might be expected to take place. And if a significant number of people do choose by the minimax standard, the greater the threat the rhetor can predict, then, entirely apart from its likelihood, the greater the rhetor's expectation of persuading voters to act cautiously by siding with the rhetor.

Some more-or-less-systematic evidence does suggest that voters behave in this way. Students of risk have frequently observed that the loss of utility from a unit of a negatively valued outcome is greater than the gain in utility from an equal unit of a positively valued outcome (Tversky and Kahneman 1979). A utility curve ranging over a wide distance of an axis measuring the quantity of a good is, as Peter Aranson has suggested, simply a rather unconventional way of asserting the law of diminishing marginal returns. Leaving aside Tversky and Kahneman's rather dubious claim that there is an inflection point at the origin in Figure 3.1a (which is derived from their analysis), it is clear that Figure 3.1b reflects diminishing marginal returns and is, of course, simply a transformation of their curve to a new origin. This identification of the two theories strengthens Tversky's and Kahneman's experimental evidence by linking it with the theoretical convictions of six generations of price theorists. While this evidence does not confirm an "avoid the worst" strategy by voters, it does confirm that voters, like experimental subjects, may be expected to take losses very seriously.

While this theory and evidence support the judgment of rhetors in predicting disasters, it does not suggest why they might prefer to emphasize extremely unlikely ones. Of course, there is some objective, negative association between the degree of disaster and its likelihood (that is, the greater the disaster, the less likely it is), so even the selection of a significant disaster implies that it is unlikely. But the association seems deeper than this artifactual one. In response to the rather mechanistic psychology of expected utility theory, many economists, psychologists, and social choice theorists have examined and even experimented with individual judgments of probabilities

William H. Riker

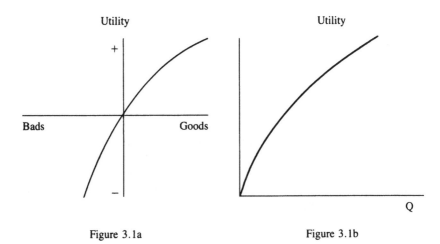

Figure 3.1a   Figure 3.1b

(Riker and Ordeshook 1973; Allais and Hagen 1979; Grether and Plott 1979). One repeated discovery in this research is that many people overestimate the probability of very unlikely events. (See Figure 3.2, where the diagonal depicts a one-to-one relation between subjective and objective probability and curve k reflects the subjective exaggeration of objectively unlikely events.)

It is unclear whether this subjective exaggeration is an innate feature of the human psyche or simply a reflection of the novelty of probability theory, which most people, even in our well-educated society, never internalize. Regardless of whether this is a universal human characteristic or merely an evanescent behavior likely to disappear in the next few hundred years, the effect of misestimates is a feature of all previous and present rhetoric and of the rhetoric of the foreseeable future.

It does not matter, either, whether the misunderstanding of probabilities is characteristic of all humans or simply of the gullible and credulous among us. The important fact is that, as long as the chance is considerable that a marginally significant number of people misestimate probabilities, then it will be entirely reasonable for rhetors to exploit the error to turn minorities into majorities. The way to do so is, of course, to predict unlikely horrors that will frighten the gullible into cautious voting.

Putting these two observations together allows me to state and explain the rationale of the rhetorical stance of induced dread. The stance is: *Attack an alternative by emphasizing its probability of causing unlikely but extremely negatively valued events.* Emphasizing an unlikely event encourages auditors and readers to overestimate its likelihood. When the unlikely event is negatively valued, the expected value of the outcome for auditors and readers is thus decreased by its value times the subjective probability that the event will

62

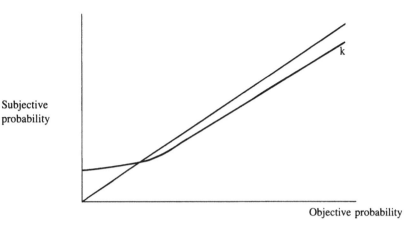

Figure 3.2

occur. By the strategy of induced dread, a rare and terrible outcome may thus dominate in the judgment on the outcome space. The rhetor expects, of course, that a revision of judgment on the outcome may lead voters to reject, in the alternative space, a decision for the alternative thus attacked.

We have thus an explanation of one extremely common rhetorical stance. It is not based on a theory about persuasion itself, but rather on an observation of the behavior and motivation of rhetors. In the absence of a satisfactory psychological theory, we can substitute a theory about the rational rhetor in the spatial model. The proportion of rhetorical action that has been or can be explained in this way is doubtless much smaller than the proportion of heresthetical action that can be similarly explained. Nevertheless, it says much for the prospect for successful analysis by means of the spatial model that even some rhetorical action, presumably mainly psychic in operation, can thus be interpreted.

REFERENCES

Allais, Maurice, and Ole Hagen, eds. 1979. *Expected Utility Hypotheses and the Allais Paradox*. Dordrecht: D. Reidel.

Austen-Smith, David, and William H. Riker. 1987. "Asymmetric Information and the Coherence of Legislation." *American Political Science Review* 81:897–918.

Black, Duncan. 1948. "On the Rationale of Group Decision Making." *Journal of Political Economy* 56:23–24.

———. 1958. *The Theory of Committees and Elections*. Cambridge: Cambridge University Press.

Calvert, Randall. 1985. "The Value of Biased Information: A Rational Choice Model of Political Advice." *Journal of Politics* 47:530–55.

Denzau, Arthur, William H. Riker, and Kenneth Shepsle. 1985. "Farquharson and Fenno: Sophisticated Voting and Home Style." *American Political Science Review* 79:1117–34.

Downs, Anthony. 1957. *An Economic Theory of Democracy.* New York: Harper & Bros.

Enelow, James M. 1981. "Saving Amendments, Killer Amendments and an Expected Utility Theory of Sophisticated Voting." *Journal of Politics* 43:1062–89.

Enelow, James M., and Melvin J. Hinich. 1984. *The Spatial Theory of Voting.* Cambridge: Cambridge University Press.

Enelow, James M., and David H. Koehler. 1980. "The Amendment in Legislative Strategy: Sophisticated Voting in the U.S. Congress." *Journal of Politics* 42:396–413.

Farquharson, Robin. 1969. *Theory of Voting.* New Haven: Yale University Press.

Feld, Scott L., and Bernard Grofman. 1988. "Necessary and Sufficient Conditions for a Majority Winner of n-Dimensional Spatial Voting Games: An Intuitive Geometric Approach." *American Journal of Political Science* (forthcoming).

Ferejohn, John A., Richard D. McKelvey, and E. W. Packel. 1984. "Limiting Distributions for Continuous State Markov Voting Models." *Social Choice and Welfare* 1:45–67.

Fink, Evelyn. 1987. *Political Rhetoric and Strategic Choice in the Ratification Conventions on the U.S. Constitution.* Rochester, N.Y.: University of Rochester Library.

Fink, Evelyn, and William H. Riker. 1988. "The Strategy of Ratification." In Bernard Grofman and Donald Wittman, eds., *The Federalist Papers and the New Institutionalism.* New York: Agathon, 220–57.

Froelich, Norman, Joseph Oppenheimer, and Cheryl Eavey. 1987. "Choices of Principles of Distributive Justice in Experimental Groups." *American Journal of Political Science* 31:606–36.

Grether, David, and Charles Plott. 1979. "Economic Theory of Choice and the Preference Reversal Phenomenon." *American Economic Review* 69:623–38.

Hammond, Thomas H., and Gary J. Miller. 1987. "The Core of the Constitution." *American Political Science Review* 81:1155–75.

Kramer, Gerald. 1977. "A Dynamical Model of Political Equilibrium." *Journal of Economic Theory* 16:310–34.

Mansbridge, Jane J. 1986. *Why We Lost the ERA.* Chicago: University of Chicago Press.

McKelvey, Richard D. 1976. "Intransitivities in Multidimensional Voting Models and Some Implications for Agenda Control." *Journal of Economic Theory* 12:472–82.

———. 1979. "General Conditions for Voting Intransitivities in Formal Voting Models." *Econometrica* 47:1085–1111.

———. 1986. "Covering, Dominance, and Institution-Free Properties of Social Choice." *American Journal of Political Science* 30:282–314.

Niemi, Richard. 1969. "Majority Decision-Making with Partial Undimensionality." *American Political Science Review* 62:488–97.

Niemi, Richard, and Jack Wright. 1987. "Voting Cycles and the Structure of Individual Preferences." *Social Choice and Welfare* 4:173–83.

Petty, Richard E., Thomas M. Ostrom, and Timothy C. Brock. 1981. *Cognitive Responses in Persuasion.* Hillsdale, N.J.: Lawrence Erlbaum Associates.

Plott, Charles, and Michael Levine. 1978. "A Model of Agenda Influence on Committee Decisions." *American Economic Review,* 68:146–60.

Plott, Charles. 1967. "A Notion of Equilibrium and Its Possibility under Majority Rule." *American Economic Review* 57:787–806.

Poole, Keith, and Howard Rosenthal. 1985. "A Spatial Model for Legislative Roll Call Analysis." *American Journal of Political Science* 29:357–84.

Rawls, John. 1971. *A Theory of Justice*. Cambridge: Harvard University Press.

Riker, William H. 1982a. *Liberalism against Populism: A Confrontation between the Theory of Social Choice and the Theory of Democracy*. San Francisco: W. H. Freeman and Company.

———. 1982b. "The Two-Party System and Duverger's Law: An Essay on the History of Political Science." *American Political Science Review* 76:753–66.

———. 1986. *The Art of Political Manipulation*. New Haven: Yale University Press.

Riker, William H., and Peter C. Ordeshook. 1973. *An Introduction to Positive Political Theory*. Englewood Cliff, N.J.: Prentice-Hall.

Romer, Thomas, and Howard Rosenthal. 1978. "Political Resource Allocation, Controlled Agendas, and The Status Quo," *Public Choice* 33:27–45.

Schofield, Norman. 1985. *Social Choice and Democracy*. New York: Springer Verlag.

———. 1978. "Instability in Simple Dynamic Games," *Review of Economic Studies* 45:575–594.

Shepsle, Kenneth A. 1972. "The Strategy of Ambiguity: Uncertainty and Electoral Competition." *American Political Science Review* 66:555–68.

———. 1979. "Institutional Arrangements and Equilibrium in Multi-Dimensional Voting Models." *American Journal of Political Science* 23:27–59.

Shepsle, Kenneth A., and Barry R. Weingast. 1984. "Uncovered Sets and Sophisticated Voting Outcomes with Implications for Agenda Institutions." *American Journal of Political Science* 28:49–74.

———. 1987. "The Institutional Foundations of Committee Power." *American Political Science Review* 81:86–104.

Smith, Richard. 1984. "Advocacy Interpretation, and Influence in the U.S. Congress." *American Political Science Review* 78:44–63.

Tversky, Amos, and Daniel Kahneman. 1979. "Prospect Theory: An Analysis of Decision under Risk." *Econometrica* 47:263–91.

4

Spatial Strategies When Candidates
Have Policy Preferences

DONALD WITTMAN
University of California,
Santa Cruz

I. INTRODUCTION

In *An Economic Theory of Democracy,* Anthony Downs characterized a political party as a team whose goal is to win the election. Although such an assumption concerning political parties is a reasonable first step, it is open to two important criticisms. The party may not be a team, and the goal of the party leaders may not be to win the election. Consider the latter criticism. It would be strange if the voters were interested in policy and not the members of the political party, especially so because government policy is a public good shared by all. Even if candidates were interested only in winning, the need to win election primaries would force the candidates to adopt positions more in line with the concerns of the median voter of the political party (or, more generally, of their constituencies). Since the party's median voter wants to maximize his/her expected utility from the election outcome, the political party's candidate would then adopt a position that maximized the party's median voter's expected utility from policy outcome.[1] Treating the political party as a team also ignores the principal/agent problems that arise when monitoring is imperfect or when agreements are not completely enforceable. The winning candidate might enact policies that are more consistent with his/her own desires than those of the voters. In a nutshell, winning may be a means to enact policy, rather than policy being a means toward winning.[2]

Here, we will assume that candidates maximize expected policy implementation. This approach not only has more realistic assumptions but, as will be shown in the following pages, also has a much richer set of empirical predictions. All of this comes at a cost, however. Modeling candidates with policy preferences involves more complicated mathematical expressions, as can be seen in the following expression:

$$W^{x^*}(x, y) = P(x, y)U^x(x) + [1 - P(x, y)]U^x(y) \qquad (1.1)$$

Strategies When Candidates Have Policy Preferences

That is, candidate X's expected utility equals the probability that X wins times the utility that X receives from the vector of policy positions, x, that are implemented when X wins, plus the probability that Y wins times the utility that X receives when policy vector y is implemented.

Even if P and U are concave in x, it is not generally true that W^{x^*} is concave or quasiconcave in x. Indeed, once one has discovered the conditions that ensure concavity or quasiconcavity of W^{x^*}, it is relatively easy to add on a term that allows X to maximize a weighted sum of expected utility and probability of winning. Hence, since Wittman (1983), researchers employing expected utility models have typically used the following synthesized form:

(a) $W^x(x, y) = P(x, y)U^x(x) + [1 - P(x, y)]U^x(y) + EP(x, y)$ (1.2)

(b) $W^y(x, y) = P(x, y)U^y(x) + [1 - P(x, y)]U^y(y) + E[1 - P(x, y)]$

where E is a weighting of winning per se – the larger E is, the more the candidate values winning.

In this chapter, we survey the main results of the policy implementation model. In Section 2, we show the existence of a divergent policy equilibrium when there is imperfect information and candidates maximize expected policy outcome. In Section 3, comparative static results are derived; Section 4 considers credible policy commitments. Section 5 investigates outcomes when policies are dependent upon previous policy choices. In Section 6 we consider the multiple candidate election, and Section 7 is devoted to the perfect information case.[3]

We try to use one basic model throughout, for the following reasons: (a) It is pedagogically easier when one uses a consistent framework; (b) the presentation here is more general than much of the literature; and (c) the variations in approach are often not interesting mathematically, and they arrive at similar conclusions.[4]

2. EXISTENCE OF A DIVERGENT EQUILIBRIUM WHEN THERE IS IMPERFECT INFORMATION

A. Assumptions

The various models in this genre have made similar assumptions regarding the utility functions. Letting M^x, M^y be the vector (in R^k) of most preferred positions for candidates X and Y, respectively, it is assumed that $M_j^x \leq M_j^y$. It is further assumed that

$U^i(z)$ is a concave twice differentiable function of z with a
maximum at M^i, $i = x, y$.   (2.1)

To ensure that the strategy space is continuous and compact and to prevent bizarre outcomes, such as candidate X wanting candidate Y to win (because X prefers Y's platform over X's platform), certain restrictions are placed on the set of choices available to the candidates.

i. $|x_j - M_j^x| \leq |y_j - M_j^x|; |y_j - M_j^y| \leq |x_j - M_j^y|$.
ii. $U^x(M^x + v) = U^x(M^x - v)$ and $U^y(M^y + v) = U^y(M^y - v)$,
   where v is a vector.
iii. $x_j \leq M_j^y; M_j^x \leq y_j$ (2.2)

Equation (2.2i) ensures that x is closer than y is to X's most preferred position, and y is closer than x is to Y's most preferred position.

Equation (2.2ii) makes U^i symmetric around M^i. In combination with (i), this assumption prevents the candidates from preferring the other candidate's platform. One could relax the symmetry assumption (as long as the strategy space remains convex). Equation (2.2iii) ensures continuity. The strategy space (2.2) is drawn in Figure 4.1.

We next turn our attention toward the probability function.

$$P(x, y) = \sum_{i=1}^{n} \frac{P^i(x, y)}{n}, \qquad (2.3)$$

where P^i is the probability that voter i votes for candidate X. P^i (and therefore P) is greater than zero and less than one and a twice differentiable concave function of x and convex function of y.[5]

B. Existence of an Equilibrium

In this subsection we demonstrate the existence of a divergent policy equilibrium. Because the theorems deal with a unidimensional issue space, x and y will be treated as unidimensional vectors, and the partials of P^i with respect to x and y will be denoted by P_x^i, P_y^i, respectively. We shall also use the notation U_z^i to refer to $U^{i\prime}(z)$. $(|P_{xx}^i P_{yy}^i| \geq P_{xy}^{i2})$.

Theorem 1. A. If the issue space is unidimensional, the candidates maximize weighted expected utility (1.2), $U_{zz}^i(z) < 0$ for $i = X, Y$ (2.1), the (2.2) restrictions on the strategy space holds, and the (2.3) restrictions on the probability function hold, then an equilibrium exists.
B. If $E = 0$ or $P_x = -P_y$ when $x = y$, and $M^x < M^y$, then the candidates' policies diverge.[6]

Proof: Our first task is to show that W^x and W^y are quasiconcave in x and y, respectively.

Quasiconcavity is demonstrated by showing that when the first order conditions hold with equality, the second derivatives are negative (that is, there is at most one peak). Taking the first derivative of (1.2a) with respect to x and

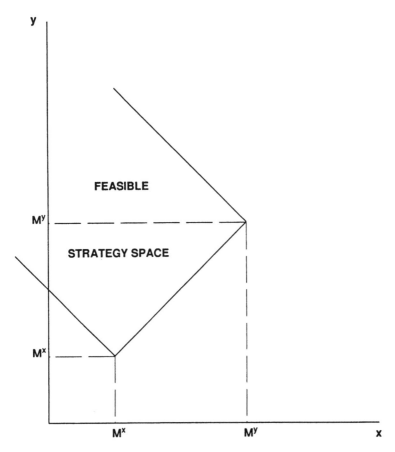

Figure 4.1. X must be less than or equal to M^y. y must be greater than or equal to M^x. x must be at least as close to M^x as y is to M^x. y must be at least as close to M^y as x is to M^y.

(1.2b) with respect to y, and letting $Z^x \equiv U^x(x) - U^x(y) + E$ and $Z^y \equiv U^y(y) - U^y(x) + E$, we have the following relationships:

(a) $W_x^x = P_x[U^x(x) - U^x(y) + E] + U_x^x(x)P = P_xZ^x + U_x^x(x)P$
(b) $W_y^y = -P_y[U^y(y) - U^y(x) + E] + U_y^y(y)[1 - P]$
$\qquad = -P_yZ^y + U_y^y(y)[1 - P]$ (2.4)

The second derivatives are then

(a) $W_{xx}^x = P_{xx}Z^x + U_{xx}^x(x)P + 2U_x^xP_x$.
(b) $W_{yy}^y = -P_{yy}Z^y + U_{yy}^y(y)[1 - P] - 2U_y^yP_y$.   (2.5)

69

$P_{xx} \leq 0$, $U^x_{xx} < 0$, $Z^x \geq 0$, and $P > 0$ by assumption. Hence, the first term in (2.5a) is nonpositive, and the second term is negative. The third term is nonpositive if U^x_x and P_x are of opposite signs. It is readily seen that equation (2.4a) cannot equal zero if U^x_x and P_x are either both (strictly) negative or both (strictly) positive. Therefore, the third term in (2.5a) is nonpositive, and the whole expression is negative. Hence the function is quasiconcave.[7]

A similar proof demonstrates that W^y is quasiconcave in y.

By assumption, the strategy space is continuous and compact. Hence, we can immediately apply the following existence by Debreu:

Theorem (Debreu): A noncooperative equilibrium exists if W^x is quasiconcave in x, continuous in y, and defined on a continuous and compact set, and W^y is quasiconcave in y, continuous in x, and defined on a continuous and compact set.

Hence an equilibrium exists.

We next demonstrate divergence. Assume to the contrary: that $x^* = y^*$. An equilibrium exists at $x^* = y^*$ only if

$$W^x_x = P_x E + U^x_x(x)P \geq 0$$
$$\text{and } W^y_y = -P_y E + U^y_y(y)[1 - P] \leq 0. \tag{2.6}$$

Otherwise, X could increase his expected utility by decreasing x (he can't increase x beyond y^*), and/or Y could increase her expected utility by increasing y.

Since $M^x < M^y$, the following inequalities hold: $M^x \leq x^* = y^* \leq M^y$, with at least one of the inequalities being strict. Assume that $y^* < M^y$. W^y_y must be nonpositive. Yet $U^y_y(y)[1 - P] > 0$. Therefore, both P_y and E must be greater than zero (if $E = 0$, then we have already arrived at a contradiction). But $P_x = -P_y$ at $x = y$. Therefore, $W^x_x < 0$ since $P_x < 0$, $E > 0$ (if $W^y_y \leq 0$), and $U^x_x(x) \leq 0$. Therefore, an equilibrium does not exist at $x = y$.[8]   Q.E.D.

It is easy to see that the divergence result carries over to higher dimensions. That is, if an equilibrium exists in a multidimensional space, it must diverge. Yet, proving the existence of an equilibrium is an extremely tedious and unrewarding job. The method of attack is much the same as in the unidimensional case, but one must demonstrate that n by n Hessians of second derivatives are negative definite to prove quasiconcavity.[9] Additional restrictions on the probability and utility functions are needed. (We will not bother with the proof here. The interested reader may consult Wittman 1983 for the proof of the two-dimensional case.) If candidates maximize plurality, one can exploit the fact that in equilibrium the positions will be identical. No such quick fix is available when candidates maximize policy implementation. So far, no one has had the audacity to start with the assumption that W^x is quasiconcave in x (a multidimensional vector) instead of deriving it from primitives.

Strategies When Candidates Have Policy Preferences

Candidates with policy preferences can be recast as a model where the goal of the candidates is to win their party nomination, but the members of the party want to maximize expected policy outcome. Once again, it is necessary to restrict choices to prevent perverse (and mathematically complicated) situations from arising. In this case, we do not want any member of the party to prefer that the candidate from the other party wins; furthermore, we want singlepeakedness within the party. This is accomplished by the following definitions and assumptions.

Let M^{xj} be the most preferred point (in R) of the jth member of party X, and let M^{yj} be the most preferred point of the jth member of party Y. The party members do not value winning per se. (2.7)

(a) Let $\hat{x}(M^x, y)$ be the x that maximizes the utility of party X when M^x is its most preferred position and Y has chosen y.[10] $\hat{x}$ is a continuous positive monotonic function of M^x (that is, the larger M^x, the larger $\hat{x}$). There exists some $M^{x'}$, $M^{x''}$ such that $\hat{x}(M^{x'}, y) = M^x - |M^x - y|$ (the lower bound on feasible x) and $\hat{x}(M^{x''}, y) = M^y - |M^y - y|$ (the upper bound on feasible x).

(b) Let $\hat{y}(x, M^y)$ be the y that maximizes the utility of party Y when M^y is its most preferred position and X has chosen x. $\hat{y}$ is a continuous positive monotonic function of M^y. There exists some $M^{y'}$, $M^{y''}$ such that $\hat{y}(x, M^{y'}) = M^x + |M^x - x|$ and $\hat{y}(x, M^{y''}) = M^y + |M^y - x|$ (the upper bound on feasible y). (2.8)

The continuity and boundary requirements on $\hat{x}$ and $\hat{y}$ mean that the set of possible $\hat{x}$ ($\hat{y}$) spans the set of possible x (y).

(a) The expected utility of member j in party X from positions $\hat{x}(M^x, y)$, y is a quasiconcave function of M^x with the peak at M^{xj}. That is, each member j of party X is assumed to have greater expected utility the closer M^x is to M^{xj}.[11]

(b) The expected utility of member j in party Y from positions x, $\hat{y}(x, M^y)$ is a quasiconcave function of M^y with the peak at M^{yj}. (2.9)

Theorem 2: Assume that there are two political parties and two candidates running for each party's nomination. Assume that each candidate maximizes the probability that he will win the party's nomination, and that each member-voter in the party wants to maximize expected policy implementation in the general election, and that (2.7)–(2.9) hold. If the median position of party X is M^{xm} and the median position of party Y is M^{ym}, then the equilibrium electoral positions will be

$$x^* = \hat{x}(M^{xm}, y^*), \quad y^* = \hat{y}(x^*, M^{ym}).$$

Donald Wittman

That is, the candidates will act as if they have the party's median member's utility function.[12]

Proof: We start with the equilibrium outcome (x^*, y^*) established in Theorem 1. If $M^{ym} = M^y$ and $M^{xm} = M^x$, then $x^* = \hat{x}(M^{xm}, y^*)$ and $y^* = \hat{y}(x^*, M^{ym})$. Given y^*, a majority of voters in the X primary prefer M^{xm} as a preferred position and its associated choice $\hat{x}(M^{xm}, y^*) = x^*$ to any other position. x^* is the choice most preferred by M^{xm}, the median voter. Since there is a positive monotonic relationship between M^x and $\hat{x}$, a majority of voters will prefer x^* to any other choice, $\hat{x}'$. Since $\hat{x}$ spans the set of possible x, there exists no other choice that a majority of X prefer to M^{xm}. The candidates can win the primary election only by satisfying a majority of members in the party. Therefore, they will choose that x^* associated with maximizing the expected utility of the median member. Hence, the candidates in party X will maximize the expected utility of the median voter. A similar logic holds for the members of Y. Thus, if x^*, y^* are the equilibrium positions when candidates have utility for policy, x^*, y^* are also the equilibrium positions when candidates are interested only in winning the primary and the median voters of the parties have the utility functions postulated previously for the candidates. Q.E.D.

Note that if all candidates had a similar desire to win the general election and this desire were greater than zero, then we would have the more general model with $E > 0$. One could also consider the case where primaries had uncertainty and where the candidates had policy preferences that were tempered by competition for the nomination. Undertaking such an analysis would be much more complex. Recent work by Enelow (1988) has made important strides in our understanding.

The next intellectual step is to make the membership of the party endogenous. Aldrich (1983) assumes that party membership is based on propinquity of interests. Thus, a person would be a member of a party if and only if he or she were within a certain distance from the median party member (or possibly, the nearest candidate). This is a clever and possibly realistic alternative to the assumption that members join the party to influence policy positions. While Aldrich has made steps in developing a theory of endogenous parties, no one has developed a rigorous theorem that makes party membership and candidate position jointly dependent.

Theorems 1 and 2 are theories of party and candidate cleavage (when $M^x \neq M^y$). They contrast strongly with the basic result of the Downsian-type models (plurally maximizing and maximizing the probability of winning) where parties tend to produce identical policies.[13] Considerable evidence suggests that there are persistent ideological differences between the political parties and that the candidates do not represent the median voter. For example, Poole and Rosenthal (1984), looking at the U.S. Senate from 1959 to 1980, show that senators in the same state but in different parties are highly dissimilar while senators from the same state and party are very similar. In a more ambitious study covering all congressional voting from 1789 to 1985, Poole and Rosenthal (1988) show that party cleavages and ideology were important factors in determining the voting patterns. Ginsburg (1976) also shows persistent differences between the major political parties in the United States from 1844 to 1968. Page's (1978) analysis of campaign texts and transcripts from 1932 onward demonstrated clearly detectable differences between the policy stands of the Republican and Democratic candidates. These differences are parallel to those of their party identifiers and activists. Similarly, Tufte (1978) measured party platforms and statements by the president and his economic advisors as well as preferences by the rank and file, and shows that Republican party ideology places higher priority on low inflation and Democratic ideology on low unemployment.

In addition, a large body of work provides evidence that "party" has important economic effects. Works by Hibbs (1977), Beck (1982), and Chappel and Keech (1986b) show that "party in office" has an effect on the unemployment rate. Frey and Schneider (1978) found that conservative (Republican) presidents tend to restrict expenditures, ceteris paribus. Tabellini and La Via (1986), Chappell and Keech (1988), and Alesina and Sachs (1988) show that Republican administrations have been associated with tighter monetary policy.

One of the most important results of the Downsian model is that both candidates will have a 50 percent chance of winning if the voters treat them symmetrically (that is, when they have identical platforms, they each have a 50 percent chance of winning). In the following theorem, we demonstrate that when candidates have policy preferences, both candidates may have a 50 percent chance of winning even when there is no symmetry and they choose different platforms.

Theorem 3: Assume that $M^x < x^* < y^* < M^y$, $E = 0$, the candidates have linear utility functions (that is, $U^x(z) = C^x - A^x z$ and $U^y(z) = C^y + A^y z$, and that either $P_y = P_x$ for all $x < y$ or $P_x \leq P_y$ when $P > .5$, $P_x \geq P_y$ when $P < .5$, and $P_x = P_y$ when $P = .5$.[14] Then the probability of either candidate winning is $.5$.[15]

Proof: With an interior equilibrium $W^x_x = 0 = W^y_y$. (2.4) can then be rewritten as follows:

$$\frac{P_x}{P} = \frac{1}{y^* - x^*} = \frac{P_y}{1 - P} \tag{2.10}$$

If $P_y = P_x$, then $P = 1 - P$ and $P = .5$. If $P_y = P_x$ for all $x < y$, then our work is done. If $P_x \leq P_y$ when $P > .5$, $P_x \geq P_y$ when $P < .5$, and $P_x = P_y$ when $P = .5$, then it immediately follows that (2.10) can hold only at $P = .5$.

Q.E.D.

Donald Wittman

3. COMPARATIVE STATICS: THE EFFECT OF BIAS AND LEVEL OF INFORMATION

Comparative statics is a very powerful method for generating emprical hypotheses. In this section I will show how the expected policy maximization equilibrium changes when the level of information and degree of bias change. I will compare these results to the comparative statics results when candidates maximize only the probability of winning.

It is necessary to create variables that capture the notion of bias and level of information. Therefore, we redefine P^i as follows:

$$P^i(x, y) = \tfrac{1}{2} + B + sp^i(x, y). \tag{3.1}$$

Where x and y are unidimensional vectors, $s > 0$, and $p^i(z, z) = 0$.[16]

B is bias, the preference for or against the candidate regardless of the candidate's present policy position. Thus, if most of the voters were registered as Democrats, we would expect the Democratic candidate to have a greater than 50 percent chance of winning the election even if both candidates took identical positions. If X stands for the Democratic party, then $B > 0$. Incumbency may also affect B.

s is voter sensitivity. The larger s is, the more probability changes when policy position changes. Increased sensitivity can result from the voters being more informed about the candidates' positions (either because the election is dealing with issues important to the voters or because the office is more important) or because the electoral district is more competitive.[17]

Letting $P = \sum_{i=1}^{n} P^i/n$, we have the following characterization of P:

$$P = 1/2 + B + sp(x, y). \tag{3.2}$$

In this section we make use of the following assumption regarding the elasticity of p_i:

$$\frac{|p_{xx}|}{|p_x|}, \frac{|p_{yy}|}{|p_y|} \geq \frac{|p_{xy}|}{|p_x|}, \frac{|p_{xy}|}{|p_y|} \tag{3.3}$$

The first order conditions (2.4) for an interior maximum can be rewritten as follows:

(a) $W^x_x = sp_x[U^x(x) - U^x(y) + E] + U^x_x[1/2 + B + sp(x, y)]$
$= sp_x Z^x + U^x_x(x)P = 0$
(b) $W^y_y = -sp_y[U^y(y) - U^y(x) + E] + U^y_y[1 - 1/2 - B - sp(x, y)]$
$= -sp_y Z^y + U^y_y(y)[1 - P] = 0$ $\tag{3.4}$

74

The hessian, $|H|$, of second derivatives is then:

$$\begin{bmatrix} W^x_{xx} & W^x_{xy} \\ W^y_{yx} & W^y_{yy} \end{bmatrix} = \tag{3.5}$$

$$\begin{bmatrix} sp_{xx}Z^x + U^x_{xx}(x)P + 2U^x_x(x)sp_x & sp_{xy}Z^x - sp_xU^x_y(y) + sp_yU^x_x(x) \\ -sp_{xy}Z^y + U^x_x(x)sp_y - U^y_y(y)sp_x & -sp_{yy}Z^y + U^y_{yy}(y)[1 - P] - 2sp_yU^y_y(y) \end{bmatrix}$$

Theorem 4: If $M^x < x^* < y^* < M^y$, $E = 0$, the elasticity assumption holds, the utility functions are linear, $p_x = p_y$, and $|H| > 0$, then an increase in B will result in a decrease in both x^* and y^*.[18]

Proof: In order to find the effect of an increase in B, we first take the total differential:

$$dW^x_x = W^x_{xx}dx + W^x_{xy}dy + W^x_{xB}dB = 0 \tag{3.6}$$

$$dW^y_y = W^y_{yx}dx + W^y_{yy}dy + W^y_{yB}dB = 0$$

We already have all the parts except W^x_{xB} and W^y_{yB}.

$$W^x_{xb} = U^x_x = -sp_xZ^xP^{-1}$$

$$W^y_{yB} = -U^y_y = -sp_yZ^y[1 - P]^{-1} \tag{3.7}$$

The last equalities in each line are obtained from the first order conditions (3.4). We find the effect of an increase in B on x via Cramer's rule:

$$dx = \frac{\begin{bmatrix} -W^x_{xB} & W^x_{xy} \\ -W^y_{yb} & W^y_{yy} \end{bmatrix}}{|H|}$$

$$= \frac{\begin{bmatrix} sp_xZ^xP^{-1} & sp_{xy}Z^x - sp_xU^x_y(y) + sp_yU^x_x(x) \\ sp_yZ^y[1 - P]^{-1} & -sp_{yy}Z^y + U^y_{yy}(y)[1 - P] - 2sp_yU^y_y(y) \end{bmatrix}}{|H|} \tag{3.8}$$

By Theorem 3, when the utility functions are linear (and the other conditions are satisfied), $P = .5$, $U^x_z = -A^x$, and $U^y_z = A^y$.[19] Multiplying through by $|H|P/s^2 > 0$, we get the following relationship:

$$dx\frac{|H|\,P}{s^2} = -p_xp_{yy}Z^xZ^y - 2p_xp_yZ^xA^y - p_yp_{xy}Z^xZ^y - p_yp_xZ^yA^x + p_yp_yZ^yA^x$$

$$= p_xp_{yy}Z^xZ^y - 2p_xp_yA^xA^y[y - x] - p_yp_{xy}Z^xZ^y$$

$$- p_yp_xA^yA^x[y - x] + p_yp_yA^yA^x[y - x] \tag{3.9}$$

The first term is nonpositive (by assumption p_{yy}, Z^x, $Z^y \geq 0$; by the first order conditions $p_x > 0$ when $U^x_x < 0$). We will next show that it swamps the

Donald Wittman

third term (that is, their sum is nonpositive). Dividing the first by the third term, we get the following:

$$\frac{p_x p_{yy}}{p_y p_{xy}} \tag{3.10}$$

The absolute value of this term is greater than or equal to one by the elasticity assumption. The second and fourth terms are negative, and their sum is three times as large as the fifth term if $p_x = p_y$, as we have assumed. Therefore, x^* decreases. A similar exercise shows that y^* also decreases. One does not have to go through the math to understand the logic, however. An increase in bias for X is the same as a decrease in bias for Y. Therefore, y^* will decrease. Q.E.D.

This theorem has demonstrated that an increase in bias in favor of X will result in both equilibrium positions moving toward X's most preferred position. The intuition behind the result is as follows: In equilibrium, X equates marginals. When there is an exogenous increase in the probability of X winning, X trades off some of this added probability for increased utility from winning so that the marginals are again equated. At the same time, Y will have to make up for its exogenous loss of probability by trading off utility from winning for increased probability of winning.

If candidates were only interested in maximizing expected vote share, then bias would have no effect on the positions taken by the parties. Since the comparative static results for the Downsian and the policy maximization model differ, we can subject them to empirical tests.

There are many reasons for bias, including incumbency advantages (due to seniority on committees and name recognition) and larger party registration. Achen (1977), in his study of 1958 congressional elections, found that winning Republican incumbents were further away from the median vote as a group than the Democrats they defeated, and that Democratic incumbents were further away (on nonsocial welfare issues) from the median voter than their Republican challengers, and that incumbents were always further away from the median than challengers in the same party in other districts.

Another form of bias is party registration. Candidates in the party with the greater registration figures would take advantage of this bias in their favor, while candidates in the minority party would have to give the voters a better deal in order to make up for the bias. In turn, this would lead to the majority party getting a lower percentage of the vote than its percentage of party registration. Wittman (1983), looking at all forty-three California congressional districts, found that the percentage of the vote share of the party with a majority registration was less than the percentage of registration of the majority party, as predicted by Theorem 4.

We next look at the effect on the equilibrium positions when s increases.

76

Strategies When Candidates Have Policy Preferences

Theorem 5: If $M^x < x^* < y^* < M^y$, $E = 0$, $B = 0$, the elasticity assumption holds, the utility functions are linear, $p_x = p_y$, and $|H| > 0$, then an increase in s will result in an increase in x^* and a decrease in y^*.[20]

Proof: Once again we take total differentials of the first order conditions:

$$dW_x^x = Y_{xx}^x dx + W_{xy}^x dy + W_{xs}^x ds = 0$$
$$dW_y^y = Y_{yx}^y dx + W_{yy}^y dy + W_{ys}^y d = 0 \qquad (3.11)$$

All we need to find are W_{xs}^x and W_{ys}^y. From the first order conditions (3.4), we obtain the following relationships:

$$U_x^x(x) = -\frac{sp_x Z^x}{P}; \; U_y^y(y) = \frac{sp_y Z^y}{1-P} \qquad (3.12)$$

$$W_{xs}^x = p_x Z^x + pU_x^x(x) = p_x Z^x - \frac{psp_x Z^x}{P}$$

$$W_{ys}^y = -p_y Z^y - pU_y^y(y) = -p_y Z^y - \frac{psp_y Z^y}{1-P} \qquad (3.13)$$

By Theorem 3, linear utility functions imply that $P = 1/2 + B + sp = .5$. Since $B = 0$ by assumption, $p = 0$. Hence, $W_{xs}^x = p_x Z^x$ and $W_{ys}^y = -p_y Z^y$. Once again we solve for the change in x via Cramer's rule.

$$|H|d_x = \begin{bmatrix} -W_{xs}^x & W_{xy}^x \\ -W_{ys}^y & W_{yy}^y \end{bmatrix} = \begin{bmatrix} -p_x Z^x & sp_{xy} Z^x + sp_x A^x - sp_y A^x \\ p_y Z^y & -sp_{yy} Z^y - 2sp_y A^y \end{bmatrix} \qquad (3.14)$$

$$sp_x Z^x p_{yy} Z^y + sp_x Z^x 2p_y A^y - sp_y Z^y p_{xy} Z^x - sp_y Z^y p_x A^x + sp_y p_y Z^y A^x \qquad (3.15)$$

The first term in (3.15) is positive and is greater than or equal to the absolute value of the third term (by the elasticity assumption). Therefore, their sum is nonnegative, even if $p_{xy} < 0$. The second term is positive, while the fourth and fifth terms cancel out when $p_x = p_y$.

Therefore, x will increase when s increases. A similar proof shows that y will decrease when s increases. Q.E.D.

The intuition for these results is straightforward. If the voters were totally insensitive to the candidates' policy positions (that is, probability of winning was not affected by the candidates' positions), then each candidate would always choose his or her most preferred position. When voters respond to policy position, each candidate must compromise position by trading off preferred policy for an increased probability of winning. The more sensitive the voters are to a policy change, the more costly is any move away from the maximal winning position toward the candidate's preferred position.

Once again, the pure Downsian model predicts no change when the exogenous variable, this time s, changes. Hence, once again, we can test the different implications of the two models.

Donald Wittman

Theorem 5 predicts that the more salient the issue and the greater the competitiveness of the district, the greater the congruence between voter preferences and candidate choices. Looking at voting referenda in California, roll call voters on related issues by state legislators, the saliency of the issue, and the competitiveness of the district (measured by the legislator's percent victory in the previous election), Kuklinski and Elling (1977) discovered that increased saliency and competitiveness resulted in greater congruence between legislative behavior and district voting. Hansen's (1975) cross-section study showed that concurrence between citizens and leaders was significantly higher in communities with higher levels of participation and contested elections. Both these variables are good proxies for s. Hence, these studies confirm the policy maximization model.

Thus a variety of tests have produced results consistent with the model presented here but contrary to the pure Downsian model.

Other comparative static results are possible. For example, Wittman (1986) shows that increased risk aversion by the candidates will result in x^*, y^* converging toward the median. The logic (and the math) is very similar to the case of increased sensitivity by the voters. As the candidates become more risk averse, they are more willing to trade off policy for a greater probability of winning.

4. CREDIBLE COMMITMENTS

Heretofore we have implicitly assumed that candidates keep their promises. Nevertheless, there is no third party enforcer to ensure that election promises are met. In this section we consider the issue of credible commitments and time-consistent behavior.

We first consider the situation when there is only one election. We assume that the voters know the candidates' most preferred positions and that they have rational expectations regarding the actual choice by the winning candidate. In addition, we make the following two assumptions:

> The winning candidate chooses the platform that maximizes his
> or her discounted expected utility. (4.1)
> Voters have rational expectations. They know that the winning
> candidate will maximize his or her discounted expected utility. (4.2)

Theorem 6: In a one period election, each candidate will choose his own most preferred position. X will win the election with probability, $P(M^x, M^y)$.[21]

Proof: We proceed by backward induction. If there is only one election, then the winning candidate will implement his most preferred position. The voters have rational expectations. Therefore, they will vote for X with probability, $P(M^x, M^y)$. Q.E.D.

Strategies When Candidates Have Policy Preferences

We next turn our attention to the infinitely repeated election game. We make the following assumptions:

$$\bar{U}^x(z) = \sum_{t=0}^{\infty} \left(\frac{1}{1+r}\right) U^x(z_t); \quad \bar{U}^y(z) = \sum_{t=0}^{\infty} \left(\frac{1}{1+r}\right)^t U^y(z_t) \qquad (4.3)$$

The discount factor, $0 < 1/[1 + r] < 1$, is identical for both parties. z_t is the unidimensional policy implemented in time t.

$$\text{The party chooses the same policy every time period.} \qquad (4.4)$$

This assumption makes sense because the present value of the expected payoff is the same every time period.

Theorem 7: (a) Given assumptions (4.3) and (4.4), an equilibrium, $\bar{x}^*$, $\bar{y}^*$,
exists for the credible commitment game.
(b) This equilibrium will not be at M^x, M^y or at x^*, y^* ($M^x < x^*$
$< y^* < M^y$), the equilibrium of the promises always kept game.[22]

Proof: Assume that X has won the election in period 0. Then his discounted payoff is

$$\bar{W}^x = U^x(x) + \frac{1}{r}[P(x, y)U^x(x) + [1 - P]U^x(y) + PE]$$

$$= U^x(x) + \frac{1}{r} W^x. \qquad (4.5)$$

By assumption, X will choose the same x every time he wins the election if he chooses x in the present time period. Thus the present value for the next and future elections is a multiple of $1/r$. The only credible choice is the one that maximizes his expected discounted utility. Thus for the present period, the probability of winning the present period's election does not enter into X's calculations.

Taking the first derivative of (4.5) with respect to x we get:

$$\bar{W}^x_x = \frac{1}{r} W^x_x + U^x_x. \qquad (4.6)$$

The second derivative is then:

$$\bar{W}^x_{xx} = \frac{1}{r} W^x_{xx} + U^x_{xx}. \qquad (4.7)$$

The proof of quasiconcavity follows the one used earlier. The assumptions concerning the convexity of the strategy space and continuity of the payoff function also hold. Therefore, an equilibrium exists.

We next turn our attention to the location of this equilibrium. It is readily established that if $M^x < x^*$, $y^* < M^y$, then $\bar{x}^*$, $\bar{y}^* \neq M^x$, M^y. $U^x_x(M^x)$, $U^y_y(M^y)$

$= 0$. Therefore $\bar{W}^x_{\tilde{x}} = \frac{1}{r} W^x_{\tilde{x}}$ and $\bar{W}^y_{\tilde{y}} = \frac{1}{r} W^y_{\tilde{y}}$ at $x, y = M^x, M^y$. Hence, if M^x, M^y is not an equilibrium (that is, the first order conditions do not hold) in the promises-always-kept game, it is not an equilibrium in the credible commitment game.

$W^x_{\tilde{x}}(x^*, y^*) = 0 = W^y_{\tilde{y}}(x^*, y^*)$ when $M^x < x^* < y^* < M^y$. Therefore, $\bar{W}^x_{\tilde{x}}(x^*, y^*) = U^x_{\tilde{x}}(x^*) < 0$ and $\bar{W}^y_{\tilde{y}}(x^*, y^*) = U^y_{\tilde{y}}(y^*) > 0$ at x^*, y^*. Thus, x^*, y^* is not an equilibrium for the credible commitment game. Q.E.D.

We can see at the margin that the candidates want to move toward their most preferred positions. With a few additional assumptions, one can establish that $M^x < \bar{x} < x^* < y^* < \bar{y} < M^y$, where $\bar{x}, \bar{y}$ are the equilibrium choices in the credible commitment game.

Wittman (1973) argued that concave utility functions would create incentives for the parties to present identical positions to avoid risk – thus the rise of bipartisanship and the tendency for issues to become nonissues. The problem of credible commitment arises again, however. The parties may not be able to enforce a contract on the winning office holder. Alesina (1988b) has extended the previous model to include the possibility of credible commitments by the parties to a uniform policy. The threat points in the bargaining game are the outcome of the game presented in Theorem 7. Again the credible commitment does not lead to the same outcome (identical positions) as would exist if promises were binding.

Having infinitely lived parties allows for credible promises and overcomes the problem of backward unraveling that exists when there is only a finite number of elections. Yet parties are staffed by finite-lived politicians. Alesina and Spear (1987) show how credible commitments between future candidates and incumbents allow the basic model presented in Theorem 7 to still hold. The intuition is as follows: The party's future candidates reward the present incumbent for implementing policy consistent with the party's long-run interests. Since there are gains from trade and the commitment is credible, the arrangement will be undertaken.[23]

In this section, we have considered the issue of credible commitments and time consistency. In comparison to the promises-always-kept model, the results are magnified. Divergence is likely to be greater. The comparative statics analysis in the infinitely repeated credible commitment game will provide similar qualitative results to those found in the promises-always-kept election.

5. TIME-DEPENDENT EFFECTS

Policies pursued in the present can affect policy outcomes in the future, and present elections can influence future elections. Both of these possibilities interacting with macroeconomic variables create interesting macrodynamics. In this section we consider several rational-expectations macrocycle models.

The first model integrates congressional and presidential elections. Policy is a weighted function of congressional membership (by party) and party affiliation of the president. The median voter is most likely to be between the most preferred positions of the parties.[24] In presidential election years, there is a tendency to split the ticket so that government policy is near the median voter. The outcome is never fully anticipated, however; and for reasons that will be more fully explained later, the ex post weight will be away from the median voter toward the winning presidential candidate. Therefore, in the mid-term election, the voters will tend to vote for the party in opposition to the president thereby moving policy closer to the median. Because the outcome of the presidential election is not fully anticipated, macroeconomic effects will be associated with the outcome. These effects will tend to disappear by the second half of the presidential term. We will now present these ideas more formally.

Let the ex post policy implementation in time t (t = 1, 2) be:
$$v_t = x^* + C[P^{ct}x^* + [1 - P^{ct}]y^*]$$
if X has won the presidential election
$$v_t = y^* + C[P^{ct}x^* + [1 - P^{ct}]y^*]$$
if Y has won the presidential election $\hspace{2cm}$ (5.1)

where P is the probability that X will be elected president, P^{ct} is the percentage of Congress affiliated with party X in time period t, and C ($0 < C < 1$) is the weight that Congress has on policy. t = 1 signifies both a presidential and congressional election; t = 2 is the midterm election involving only Congress. We assume that $x^* = M^x$ and $y^* = M^y$ – these are credible commitments in the finite game (see Theorem 6).

$$E[v_i] = M^m \hspace{2cm} (5.2)$$

In all elections, the median voter tries to balance the positions of Congress and the presidency so that the ex ante outcome is close to the median voter's most preferred position.

It is assumed that P^{ct} is known even before the election. This assumption makes the proofs simpler, but ultimately all that is needed is that the variance of the congressional outcome is less than the variance of the presidential outcome. If the probability of presidential candidate X winning the election is P, then the variance is $P[1 - P]$ if $y^* = 1$ and $x^* = 0$. If the probability of a particular congressman winning is P, then the variance of P^c is $P[1 - P]/435$. Even taking into account the possibility that estimation of P is more difficult for the legislative district then for the nation, the variance of Congress (here the House of Representatives) is smaller because proportion is not all or

Donald Wittman

nothing (if we accept the assumption that legislative outcomes are a linear function of the proportion).

Theorem 8: Assume (5.1) and (5.2) hold. (a) The midterm election will reduce the number of seats in Congress held by the presidential party, and (b) if unanticipated policy has macroeconomic effects, then there will be macro effects arising from election 1 but not from election 2.[25]

Proof: For $0 < P < 1$, the ex post outcome of the presidential election is not the same as the ex ante expectation; that is, the outcome is not fully anticipated, even with rational expectations.[26] The outcome of the congressional election is equal to the ex ante expectation. Therefore, if Y (X) has won the presidential election, then $v_1 > (<) E[v_1] = M^m$. Hence, in the next election, P^c, the percentage of Congress belonging to party X will increase (decrease).

The presidential election (1) has some surprises. The outcome of the midterm election has no surprises since P^{c2} is fully anticipated once election 1 has taken place. Therefore, only election 1 will have macroeconomic effects.
Q.E.D.

Theorem 8 provides one explanation for macroeconomic and political cycles even when voters are fully rational.

A number of empirical regularities are consistent with this model. Since World War II, the party holding the White House has lost vote share in midterm elections both in the House and in the Senate. Alesina and Sachs (1988), Alesina (1988a), and Chappel and Keech (1988) have shown that real GNP tends to increase at above-average rates in the first two years of Democratic administrations and to increase at below-average rates in the first two years of Republican administrations, while the second halves of the two administrations show very little difference.

Alesina and Rosenthal (1989b) provide a number of tests of this model versus competing models (such as retrospective voting and irrational expectations) and find that these other models add little, if any, explanatory power.[27]

This model is an important first step in integrating the various branches of government into a general theory of policy outcome. Future models might encompass a more detailed analysis of (1) the party system in Congress and its interaction with the presidency and semiautonomous bodies such as the Federal Reserve, (2) rational voting behavior when preferences vary across and within legislative districts, and (3) the infinite horizon case.

We next consider the possibility that policy during one term of office can affect policy payoff's in later terms. Because the party in power is not assured that it will be in power in later terms, it undertakes different policies than it would if the party had permanent tenure. Thus, this analysis seeks to determine how Democrats should behave if they know that they may be succeeded in office by Republicans, and how their behavior (regarding the tradeoff between inflation and recession, for example) changes when the probability of a Republican victory changes. The analysis is much more complicated when policy in one term affects choices in later terms. One has to make special assumptions in order to make the model work, and a greater number of special cases are possible. This area is just starting to be mined, and there will be significant intellectual payoffs from those models that yield the most insightful results. Here we discuss two important steps in this process.

Before delving into the particular models, it is useful to consider why the previous analysis is unlikely to carry over at the same level of generality. In the previous sections there was a one period model or a multiperiod model with each party choosing the same policy from one period to the next. Here, the policies of one period interact on policies in the ensuing period(s), and except in special cases, the party will enact different policies depending on which party won the previous election(s).[28] Even if we can establish that the expected payoff within any election period is quasiconcave, we may not be able to show that the present discounted expected payoff is quasiconcave (since the sum of quasiconcave functions need not be quasiconcave).[29]

Our next theorem considers an economy in which the first term can leave debt or surplus to the succeeding administration but the net deficit over the two time periods must equal zero. Because the candidates have different preferences over policy, the incumbent in the first time period will leave his successor (possibly himself) with debt. The intuition for this result is that the opposition's expenditures do not bring as much utility to the incumbent as do the incumbent's expenditures. The incumbent will therefore spend more now and leave less for the second period. We will now proceed to the formal analysis.

$$U_i^x = G_i^\alpha B_i^\omega; \ U_i^y = G_i^\omega B_i^\alpha \tag{5.3}$$

where G_i is expenditures on guns and B_i is expenditures on butter in time period i ($i = 1, 2$), $0 < \alpha \neq \omega > 0$ and $\alpha + \omega < 1$.

$$T_1 + T_2 = G_1 + G_2 + B_1 + B_2. \tag{5.4}$$

That is, taxes equal expenditures. We will assume that $T_1 = T_2$.[30]

$P\left(\dfrac{G_2^x}{B_2^x}, \dfrac{G_2^y}{B_2^y}\right)$ is the probability that X wins the second election, $\tag{5.5}$

where the superscripts stand for party. Putting the terms in ratios is a quick way of assuming that the indifference curves of the voters (from whence the probability functions are derived) have the same slope along a ray and that the probability that X wins the election is independent of the level of expenditures (but not of the composition).

We assume that the incumbent in time period 1 can commit expenditures only for time period 1 and that the two period budget deficit is zero. We once again assume that candidates' promises cannot be enforced (that is, once in office they will maximize their expected utility) and that the voters are rational.

Theorem 9: Given the above assumptions, if the probability of reelection is less than 1, then the incumbent in time period 1 will leave a deficit to the succeeding administration even though the incumbent would not leave a deficit if he were assured of victory. The lower the chance of reelection and the more opposed the candidates' preferences are (that is, the larger $|\alpha - \omega|$), the greater the deficit. [31]

Proof: If X wins the second period election, then X will find the saddle point of the following Lagrangian:

$$G_2^{\alpha} B_2^{\omega} + \lambda[T_1 + T_2 - G_1 - G_2 - B_1 - B_2] \tag{5.6}$$

The first order conditions are then: [32]

$$\text{(a) } \alpha G_2^{\alpha-1} B_2^{\omega} - \lambda = 0; \text{ (b) } \omega G_2^{\alpha} B_2^{\omega-1} - \lambda = 0 \tag{5.7}$$

Setting (a) = (b), we get the following equivalent relationships:

$$\frac{\alpha B_2}{\omega G_2} = 1 \text{ or } B_2 = \frac{G_2 \omega}{\alpha} \tag{5.8}$$

Equation (5.8) gives us the relationship between G_2 and B_2. We next interpret this in terms of the allowable expenditure in the second period, Z_2.

$$Z_2 = G_2 + B_2 = G_2 + G_2 \frac{\omega}{\alpha} = G_2 \left[1 + \frac{\omega}{\alpha} \right] = G_2 \frac{\alpha + \omega}{\alpha}. \tag{5.9}$$

Equivalently,

$$G_2 = Z_2 \frac{\alpha}{\alpha + \omega} \text{ and } B_2 = Z_2 \frac{\omega}{\alpha + \omega}. \tag{5.10}$$

Hence, if X wins the second election, X's utility is:

$$\alpha^{\alpha} \omega^{\omega} \left(\frac{Z_2}{\alpha + \omega} \right)^{\alpha+\omega} \tag{5.11}$$

If Y wins the second period election, then Y will find the saddle point of the following Lagrangian:

$$G_2^{\omega} B_2^{\alpha} + \lambda[T_1 + T_2 - G_1 - G_2 - B_1 - B_2] \tag{5.12}$$

The first order conditions are then:

$$\text{(a) } \omega G_2^{\omega-1} B_2^{\alpha} - \lambda = 0; \text{ } \alpha G_2^{\omega} B_2^{\alpha-1} - \lambda = 0 \tag{5.13}$$

Setting (a) = (b), we get the following equivalent relationships:

$$\frac{\omega B_2}{\alpha G_2} = 1 \text{ or } B_2 = \frac{G_2 \alpha}{\omega} \tag{5.14}$$

Again, these are ratios. We solve in terms of Z_2. If Y wins,

$$Z_2 = G_2 + B_2 = G_2 + G_2 \frac{\alpha}{\omega} = G_2 \frac{\alpha + \omega}{\omega}. \text{ Hence,} \tag{5.15}$$

$$G_2 = Z_2 \frac{\omega}{\alpha + \omega}, \text{ and } B_2 = Z_2 \frac{\alpha}{\alpha + \omega}. \tag{5.16}$$

Therefore if Y wins the second election, X's utility is

$$\alpha^\omega \omega^\alpha \left(\frac{Z_2}{\alpha + \omega} \right)^{\alpha + \omega}. \tag{5.17}$$

Putting all the pieces together (X's utility in the first period plus 5.11 and 5.17), if X is the incumbent in period 1, then X's constrained expected utility is

$$\alpha^\alpha \omega^\omega \left(\frac{Z_1}{\alpha + \omega} \right)^{\alpha + \omega} + P\alpha^\alpha \omega^\omega \left(\frac{Z_2}{\alpha + \omega} \right)^{\alpha + \omega}$$

$$+ [1 - P]\alpha^\omega \omega^\alpha \left(\frac{Z_2}{\alpha + \omega} \right)^{\alpha + \omega} + \lambda[T_1 + T_2 + Z_1 + Z_2]. \tag{5.18}$$

Note that the optimal relationship between B_1 and G_1 is independent of level and therefore we can write the utility in the first period in a similar form to the utility that X derives if X wins the second period.

The first order conditions with respect to Z_1 and Z_2 are then:

(a) $(\alpha + \omega)\alpha^\alpha \omega^\omega \left(\dfrac{Z_1}{\alpha + \omega} \right)^{\alpha + \omega - 1} - \lambda = 0$ \hfill (5.19)

(b) $P(\alpha + \omega)\alpha^\alpha \omega^\omega \left(\dfrac{Z_2}{\alpha + \omega} \right)^{\alpha + \omega - 1}$

$\quad + [1 - P](\alpha + \omega)\alpha^\omega \omega^\alpha \left(\dfrac{Z_2}{\alpha + \omega} \right)^{\alpha + \omega - 1} - \lambda = 0.^{33}$ \hfill (5.19)

Equivalently,

$$[\alpha^\alpha \omega^\omega] \left(\frac{Z_1}{\alpha + \omega} \right)^{\alpha + \omega - 1}$$

$$= [P\alpha^\alpha \omega^\omega + [1 - P]\alpha^\omega \omega^\alpha] \left(\frac{Z_2}{\alpha + \omega} \right)^{\alpha + \omega - 1} = 0. \tag{5.20}$$

If $P = 1$, then $Z_2 = Z_1$, since both sides of (5.20) are otherwise identical. Since $T_1 = T_2$ and their sum is constrained to be equal to the sum of Z_1 and Z_2, the budget is balanced in both time periods.

We will now show that for $P < 1$, the expression in square brackets on the left hand side of the equality is greater than the expression in square brackets on the right hand side of the equality. In turn, this implies that $Z_1 > Z_2$, since each is raised to the same negative power $(\alpha + \omega - 1)$.

We first show that

$$\alpha^\alpha \omega^\omega > \alpha^\omega \omega^\alpha. \text{ Equivalently,} \tag{5.21}$$

$$\left(\frac{\alpha}{\omega}\right)^{\alpha-\omega} > 1. \tag{5.22}$$

In equation (5.22), if $\alpha > \omega$, then the expression in parentheses is greater than 1, and it is raised to a power greater than zero. Therefore the whole expression is greater than 1. If $\alpha < \omega$, then the expression in parentheses is less than one, but it is raised to a negative power, making the whole expression again greater than one.

Thus the expression in the square brackets on the left hand side of equation (5.20) is greater than the weighted average in the square brackets on the right hand side. As already argued, this implies that $Z_2 < Z_1$. In turn, this implies a deficit in the first period.

The bigger the expression in brackets on the left hand side relative to the expression on the right hand side, the bigger Z_1 relative to Z_2. Thus as $1 - P$ increases, so does Z_1. From (5.22) it can be seen that as α and ω become more dissimilar (by adding δ to α and subtracting δ from ω when $\alpha > \omega$), the brackets on the left hand side of equation (5.20) once again become relatively larger than the brackets on the right hand side, and thus Z_1 increases. Q.E.D.

The following theorem attempts to generalize the approach used in Theorem 9. We will drop the special assumptions used in Theorem 9 and instead make use of the following assumption (in addition to the relevant assumptions presented in sections 1 and 2):

Let $U_t^i(z^1, z^2, \cdots, z^t)$ be i's utility ($i = X, Y$) in time period t, (5.23)

where U^{i_t} is a concave function of the z^j, the multidimensional policy implemented in period j.

Note that utility in period t is only indirectly a function of policies in previous time periods, since the previous time period policies affect outcomes and utilities in the present.[34]

Because discounted expected payoffs involve combinatorics, their characterization is awkward. We will therefore restrict our analysis to the three-election-period case.

If X is the incumbent in the first time period, X maximizes:

$$W^x = U^x_0(x^0) + P\left[U^x_1(x^0,x^1)\frac{1}{(1+r)} + PU^x_2(x^0,x^1,x^2)\frac{1}{(1+r)^2}\right.$$

$$\left. + [1 - P]U^x_2(x^0,x^1,y^2)\frac{1}{(1+r)^2}\right]$$

$$+ [1 - P] \left[U^{x_1}(x^0, y^1) \frac{1}{(1 + r)} + P U^{x_2}(x^0, y^1, x^2) \frac{1}{(1 + r)^2} \right.$$

$$\left. + [1 - P] U^{x_2}(x^0, y^1, y^2) \frac{1}{(1 + r)^2} \right] \tag{5.24}$$

where x^0, x^1, and x^2 are the choice variables.

Theorem 10: If P is fixed and the candidates maximize expected discounted utility, then an equilibrium exists.[35]

Proof: With P fixed, expected discounted utility is concave, since it is a sum of concave functions. Therefore, all the conditions for an equilibrium are again satisfied. Q.E.D.

Since policy has no effect on election probabilities, we have credible commitment (to the candidate's own interests). McKibben, Roubini, and Sachs show how an exogenous change in P affects the macroeconomy. Putting some restrictions on P and performing a comparative statics analysis would allow us to derive similar results. But for spatial, as opposed to macroeconomic, theory, the case where policy has no effect on P is uninteresting, and therefore we will not derive its results here.[36]

Additional effects take place over time (for example, candidate reputations in retrospective voting). Alesina and Cukierman (1987) consider the possibility that voters learn about the incumbent's preferences only through policy. If the policy is ambiguous, the incumbent makes s (the sensitivity parameter) smaller, and, as in our earlier result, this allows the incumbent to choose policies that are, on average, closer to his most preferred position.

In this and the previous section, we have considered policy interactions and credible commitments. These topics are foreign to the Downsian model, where both parties choose identical policies and always keep their promises.

6. MULTICANDIDATE ELECTIONS

Multicandidate elections create special analytic problems when candidates have policy preferences. In a plurality election, increasing one's own chance of winning is likely to reduce the nearest competitor's chance of winning and possibly increase the farthest away competitor's chance of winning. This possibility may make the functional relationship nonconcave. In parliamentary systems, we need to predict the winning coalition and its choice (when there is no median). Here we present one very simple model. This area has room for much more research, especially regarding parliamentary systems.

Consider a plurality model where there are m pairs of political parties (X^i, Y^i, $i = 1, \cdots, m$).

Donald Wittman

The probability that X^i wins is $P^{x^i}(x^i, y^i)$.

The probability that Y^i wins is $P^{y^i}(x^i, y^i)$.

(6.1)

That is, the probability of X^i winning is just a function of x^i, y^i.

$$\sum_{i=1}^{m} (P^{x^i} + P^{y^i}) = 1.$$

The objective functions of x^i and y^i are:

$$W^{x^j} = \sum_{i=1}^{m} [P^{x^i}(x^i, y^i) U^{x^j}(x^i) + P^{y^i}(x^i, y^i) U^{x^j}(y^i)]$$

$$W^{y^j} = \sum_{i=1}^{m} [P^{x^i}(x^i, y^i) U^{y^j}(x^i) + P^{y^i}(x^i, y^i) U^{y^j}(y^i)]$$

(6.2)

Theorem 11: An equilibrium exists in this multicandidate election. It has the same comparative statics results as the two candidate election.[37]

Proof: The first and second derivatives are identical to those of the two candidate election (since x^j has no effect on P^{x^i} or P^{y^i} for $i \neq j$). Therefore, all the earlier results hold for the multicandidate contest.   Q.E.D.

7. ELECTIONS WITH PERFECT INFORMATION

Heretofore we have assumed that the voters vote with probability greater than zero and less than one. By contrast, in this section, there is only probabilistic voting when both candidates offer the same utility to the voter. We demonstrate the existence of an equilibrium under the assumption that the voters' preferred points are symmetrically distributed. However, without this extreme restriction on the distribution of voter preferences, an equilibrium is unlikely to occur. We therefore turn the analysis toward disequilibrium models.

We make the following assumptions regarding the voters' and candidates' utility functions:

The indifference curves of voters and candidates are spheres with the center at the voter's or candidate's most preferred point. That is, $U^i(\|x - M^i\|)$, $i = 1, \cdots, n, x, y$. $U_{|z|}(\|z\|) < 0$. (7.1)

This assumption is standard but somewhat more restrictive than necessary. We assume that n is odd. Without loss of generality, we will assume that $M^m = 0$, a vector of zeroes. We also assume that the utility functions of the candidates are continuous.

We will make use of the following definition:

Strategies When Candidates Have Policy Preferences

The distribution of voters is radially symmetric if all $M^i \neq M^m$ can be divided into cognate pairs M^i, M^{n+1-i} such that $M^i = -|k_i|M^{n+1-i}$. (7.2)

We will no longer require that a candidate obtain at least as great utility from his own position as he does from the other candidate's position (thus we drop assumption (1.2)).

Theorem 12: Assume that voters vote for X if they prefer x to y, vote for Y if they prefer y to x, and vote for X with probability .5 if they are indifferent between x and y. Assume that the voters are distributed radially symmetric and that campaign promises are always kept.[38] If $E > 0$, then a unique equilibrium exists at M^m.[39]

Proof: Existence:

If $x^* = y^* = M^m$, then X's expected utility is $U^x(M^m) + .5E$. If X chooses any other point, X will lose the election, M^m will again be implemented, and his expected utility will be reduced to $U^x(M^m)$. The explanation for X losing the election follows: The median voter(s) prefer M^m to any other point, x. At most $\frac{n-1}{2}$ prefer x to M^m. By radial symmetry, this implies that at least $\frac{n-1}{2}$ voters, not including the median, strictly prefer M^m to x. Hence, X's expected utility decreases if he moves from M^m. A similar argument holds for Y. Therefore, M^m is an equilibrium.

Uniqueness:

We prove in turn that each of the following cases cannot be equilibria. If $x^* \neq y^*$ and one candidate, say Y, always wins, then X could improve his utility by choosing x^* to equal y^*. In this way, implemented policy is not changed, but X gains $.5E$. Therefore, the conditional statement could not be an equilibrium.

If $x^* = y^* \neq M^m$, then either candidate could move marginally closer to M^m, thereby increasing his welfare (since the increase in utility from an additional $.5E$ outweighs the marginal decrease (if any) in utility from the inferior implemented policy.

If $x^* \neq y^*$ and each candidate has a 50 percent chance of winning, then X can improve his utility by marginally moving closer to the median voter, thereby increasing his probability of winning to 100 percent. Again, by continuity of the utility function, this increase due to E will outweigh the loss (if any) from a marginally different policy implementation.   Q.E.D.

This existence and uniqueness theorem reinforces the result in the earlier section, which showed that as s (sensitivity) increases, the candidates move closer together. Here, in the limit, they are identical.[40]

Unfortunately, with even the slightest deviation from perfect radial symme-

89

try, an equilibrium does not exist for vote-maximizing candidates, and there is every reason to believe that this nonexistence result will usually be the case when candidates have preferences.[41] A large number of papers have explored alternative solution concepts for the plurality-maximizing model (for example, the Copeland winner, the uncovered set, the yolk) when voters are not distributed radially symmetric. Very little has been done to apply the analogous concepts to the case where candidates have policy as a goal (if the opposition always wins, or if a set of policies are equally effective in terms of winning, why not choose the most preferred policy from this set?). Here we provide one example. We show that when candidates have policy preferences election outcomes occur within particular subsets of the set of potential policy choices. There is considerable room for research in this area.

Wittman (1977) considered the following model.

> If X (Y) is the winning candidate in election t,
> then $x^{t+1} = x^t (y^{t+1} = y^t)$. (7.3)
> Voter i votes for the incumbent if the incumbent is strictly closer
> to M^i than the opposition is to M^i. (7.4)

Otherwise the voter always votes for the opposition.

> The opposition candidate is assumed to choose a position that
> maximizes his expected utility in time period t. If no position
> both increases his expected utility and wins, then the opposition
> will choose a position identical to that of the incumbent and
> win (that is, the value of winning per se is second in the
> lexicographical ordering).[42] (7.5)

We will use the following three definitions.

> Let S^j be a set of (N + 1)/2 most preferred positions.
> (7.6)
> There are $\binom{N}{(N+1)/2}$ distinct S^j.

> S^x is a minimax set for X, if for every set S^i, $i \neq x$ there exists
> an $M^j \in S^i$ such that $\|M^j - M^x\| \geq \|M^k - M^x\|$ *for all* $k \in S^x$.
> S^y, a minimax set for Y, is defined in the same way. (7.7)

> B^x (B^y) is the minimax ball if it is the smallest ball with center
> M^x (M^y) containing the most preferred points of S^x (S^y). See
> Figure 4.2. (7.8)

Theorem 13: Every x^t (y^t) for $t > 1$ is in the minimax ball B^x (B^y).

Proof: Assume that Y is the incumbent for election $t + 1$. If $y^t = y^{t+1}$ is not an element of the Pareto optimal set defined by S^x and M^x, then there exists an

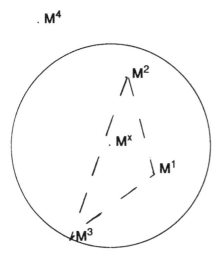

Figure 4.2. B^x is the minimax ball. The dotted line is the Pareto Optimal set defined by S^x and M^x.

x^{t+1} in the Pareto optimal set strictly preferred by all of the members of the set, including X, to y^{t+1}. Since this set has at least a majority of voters, x^{t+1} is a winning position. If X does not choose a point in this set, by assumption he must choose a winning position $x^{t+1'}$ that is not farther away from M^x than x^{t+1}; therefore, $x^{t+1'} \in B^x$. If y^{t+1} is an element of the Pareto optimal set defined by S^x and M^x and there exists a point $x^{t+1''}$ that is an element of a sphere with center M^x and radius $\|M^x - y^{t+1}\|$, which is, itself, contained in B^x and which is preferred by a majority of voters, then X will choose $x^{t+1''}$. If no such point exists, then X will choose $x^{t+1'''} = y^{t+1}$ and satisfy his lexicographic desire for winning.   Q.E.D.

Wittman (1977) also considers an income distribution game and shows that, over time, the equilibrium converges to a situation where almost all the income goes to the candidates.

Chappel and Keech (1986a) have forsaken any hope for analytic solutions. Instead, they have tried to simulate the election. Using the same basic model as described above but with three voters, their results corroborate the results reported here. With perfect information, cycling occurs, but it is limited and repetitive. With imperfect information, more uncertainty results in the candidates diverging more; while bias in favor of one candidate results in both candidates moving toward the most preferred position of the favored candidate.

8. CONCLUDING REMARKS

Having outlined the major theoretical and empirical developments of the policy implementation model, I would like to speculate on where we are likely to see new results in the next two or three years.

I have already suggested that parliamentary models, disequilibrium perfect information models, and political macro-models are likely to produce interesting results in the near future. More complex institutional models, involving different policy makers, possibly in different economies, are also likely to be a growth area. Finally, the role of asymmetric information in elections should bring new insight into the candidates with policy preferences literature.

APPENDIX

Proposition: If $M^x < x^* < y^* < M^y$, $U^i(x)$ is linear in z, and either the elasticity assumption holds, or $P_{xy} = 0$, or $p_x = p_y$, then $|H| > 0$.[43]

Proof:

Let $U^x(z) = A - A^x z$ and $U^y(z) = A + A^y z$, where $A^x, A^y > 0$. (A.1)

Then $|H|$ reduces to the following expression:

$$\begin{bmatrix} sp_{xx}Z^x - 2A^x sp_x & sp_{xy}Z^x + sp_x A^x - sp_y A^x \\ -sp_{xy}Z^y + A^y sp_y & -sp_{yy}Z^y - 2sp_y A^y \end{bmatrix} \quad \text{(A.2)}$$

$$= s^2 Z^x Z^y [-p_{xx}p_{yy} + p_{xy}p_{xy}] + 4s^2 A^x A^y p_x p_y - 2s^2 p_{xx} Z^x A^y p_y$$

$$+ 2s^2 p_{yy} Z^y A^x p_x - 2s^2 p_x p_y A^x A^y + s^2 p_y^2 A^x A^y + s^2 p_x^2 A^y A^x$$

$$+ s^2 p_{xy} Z^y A^x [p_x - p_y] + s^2 p_{xy} Z^x A^y [p_x - p_y] \quad \text{(A.3)}$$

The first term is positive since Z^x, Z^y and the terms in the brackets are positive by assumption. p_x, $p_y > 0$ by the first order conditions (since U_z^x, $- U_z^y < 0$ by assumption). Therefore, the second term is positive. The second term is twice as large as the fifth term. The third and fourth terms are positive since $-p_{xx}$, $p_{yy} > 0$ by assumption. The sixth and seventh terms are also positive.

If either $p_{xy} = 0$ or $p_y = p_x$, then the eighth and ninth terms equal zero.

If $\dfrac{|p_{yy}|}{|p_y|}, \dfrac{|p_{xx}|}{|p_x|} > \dfrac{|p_{xy}|}{|p_y|}, \dfrac{|p_{xy}|}{|p_y|}$, then the second and third terms swamp the eighth and ninth terms.

Terms eight and nine can be rewritten as follows:

$$2s^2 p_{xy} A^x A^y [y - x] p_x - 2s^2 p_{xy} A^x A^y [y - x] p_y. \tag{A.4}$$

Dividing the left hand term in (A.4) into the third term in (A.3) and the right hand term in (A.4) into the fourth term in (A.3), we get the following relationship:

$$\frac{p_{xx}}{p_{xy}} \frac{p_y}{p_x} \text{ and } \frac{p_{yy}}{p_{xy}} \frac{p_x}{p_y} \tag{A.5}$$

Both expressions are greater than zero by the elasticity assumption. Thus $|H|$ is positive. Q.E.D.

NOTES

1 This will be made more precise later in the chapter.
2 In economic markets, opportunism is reduced but not eliminated by competition. Because elections involve relatively few candidates, there are greater rents to be gained by the participants. As will be shown, when there is imperfect information, political duopoly does not exhaust all profits even when one candidate's goal is only to win the election.
3 Sections 3, 4–5, 6, and 7 are independent of each other and need only sections 1 and 2 for understanding.
4 We try to phrase the theorems in such a way that they can be proven in a few steps. With one or two exceptions, we are successful in this endeavor.
5 Making P the sum of the individual probability of voting functions changes P from a probability of winning function to an expected vote function. W^x is then a weighted mandate – the greater x's plurality and the more extreme x is, the smaller the x that is actually implemented. This weighted mandate view seems to accord with reality. Landslide elections allow the candidate to implement more extreme policies. In a parliamentary system, the relationship between the size of the plurality and government behavior is even closer. Without much bother one can start with utility functions and/or allow abstentions. For a more extensive discussion of probability of voting functions, see the chapter by Coughlin in this volume. Enelow (1988) use PF2 density functions which are not in general concave.
6 Theorem 1 is a unidimensional version of a theorem presented in Wittman (1983). Hansson and Stuart (1984) provide an existence theorem that is a special case of Theorem 1. They have a more restricted strategy space, have a "one voter" model, and use a more specific probability function.
7 It should be clear that $U_{zz}^i < 0$ is not critical. Any of the following would have produced similar results: $E > 0$ and $P_{xx}, -P_{yy} < 0$; or there exists no point z such that $P_i = U_z^i(z) = 0$ for $i = x, y$.
8 Mitchell (1987) assumed that candidates X and Y maximize $EP + U^x(x)$, and $E[1 - P] + U^y(y)$, respectively. In this case, the candidate is not interested in policy implementation; instead, he achieves higher utility from having a "good" platform. However, the first derivatives are similar when $x = y$, and consequently, the conditions for divergence are nearly identical,
9 Actually, it is more complicated than that. Letting H stand for the hessian of second-order partials, W^x is quasiconcave in x if for every vector V such that $V^tV = 1$, $\sum_{j=1}^{k} V_j W_{x_j}^x = 0$ *implies* $V^tHV < 0$, where V^t is the transpose of V.

10 We know that there is only one $\hat{x}$ since $W_{xx}^x < 0$ (see equation 2.5). However, having a unique $\hat{x}$ is not critical.

11 (2.8) and (2.9) allow the theorem to hold, but they do not start with first principles. The following is the type of assumption that would be needed for such a venture: Each member j of political party i has utility function, $f(\|M^{ij} - z\|)$; that is, all members of the party have concave utility functions that are identical except for the bliss point.

12 This theorem is loosely based on Coleman (1971, 1972). See also Aranson and Ordeshook (1972).

13 Of course, in its most general formulation (such as Hinich, Ledyard, and Ordeshook 1972), plurality maximization need not lead to convergence (especially so, if the candidates are not treated symmetrically).

14 The latter assumption is appropriate when candidates with inferior positions have greater marginal productivity.

15 This proposition is based on Wittman (1970).

16 The assumption of unidimensionality is for heuristic purposes. Relaxing this assumption makes the proofs considerably longer with little additional enlightenment. Making B and s vary across individuals (that is, having B^i and s^i) would also make the analysis more complicated without much additional insight. See Wittman (1983) for the more general case.

17 This latter characterization makes sense if we view P as probability of winning rather than expected vote.

18 The theorem holds under more general conditions, but the proof is arduous and unrewarding. In the Appendix we demonstrate that $|H| > 0$. For related proofs, see Wittman (1983, 1986).

19 When $M^x < x^*$, $U_z^x < 0$.

20 This theorem is related to a theorem by Wittman (1983).

21 This theorem is due to Alesina (1988b). P should be interpreted as probability of winning.

22 This theorem is based on Alesina (1988b). I use a different probability assumption and a more general utility function. The proof proceeds somewhat differently.

23 The future candidates may provide ex-presidents with a role in the party if they have "behaved." It is not entirely clear why such promises are credible.

24 This assumption is most natural, but not required.

25 This theorem is (loosely) based on the work of Alesina and Rosenthal (1989a). Note that policy can have effects in a rational expectations framework only if contracts are written before the election and they are not contingent.

26 Alesina (1987) has a theoretical paper investigating the macroeconomic effects of presidential elections. Alesina and Rosenthal (1989a) can be seen as a generalization of this earlier paper.

27 Another test of the model would be to see whether close presidential elections (with the least anticipated outcome) have the strongest macroeconomic effects.

28 Alesina's "inflation game" (1986) extended the work of Barro and Gordon (1983) to include two political parties. However, the optimal policy in any time period is independent of the previous policies (the state variables) and therefore belongs under our previous analysis where policy of one period does not affect policy in future periods.

29 In this footnote I consider two possible resolutions to this problem. (1) Start with the equilibrium outcome under the no policy affect across time period model and marginally add future period policy effects in a comparative statics analysis. (2)

Consider some simple quadratic formulae for the effect of policy on future policy and see whether the present discounted payoff is quasiconcave.

30 We have neither interest nor discounted value in this simple model.

31 This theorem is based on Alesina and Tabellini (1987) and related work on deficits by Tabellini and Alesina (1988). My utility function is different from theirs (they use additive utility functions), and the proofs are dissimilar. Their work also has more details about the economy.

32 Cobb-Douglas utility functions will yield interior solutions.

33 Note that Z_1 and Z_2 have no effect on P. By assumption, P is affected by expenditures only in period 2. The level will be the same whoever wins, and the probability depends only on the ratio of guns to butter in the second period.

34 This formulation is quite general and may even allow for history or memory of past policy positions as long as it ultimately enters into utility in a concave fashion.

35 This theorem is based on McKibben, Roubini, and Sachs (1987). Their paper uses a dynamic programming framework, but the complexity of the problem prevents them from fully exploiting the Bellman equations. They also make specific assumptions regarding payoffs (quadratic) and transition probabilities (linear). This enables them to develop a particular macromodel, which we do not discuss here.

36 In Theorem 9, policy in the first period does not affect probability of winning in the second period, but (anticipated) policies in the first period affect probabilities of winning in the first period and (anticipated) policies in the second period affect probability of winning in the second period.

37 These assumptions are more restrictive than the assumptions required to demonstrate the existence of an equilibrium when candidates are only interested in winning (see Wittman 1987).

38 If M^x, M^y were the only credible policies by X and Y, respectively, then that candidate with the preferred position closest to M^m would win.

39 The existence (but not uniqueness) result is based on Wittman (1977) and Calvert (1985). $E > 0$ is not required for existence and is not always necessary for uniqueness.

40 Calvert (1985) used this result to argue that any differential between the parties is slight. But we have shown that this convergence is a limiting case. He also considers the imperfect information case. Starting with a situation in which candidates only value winning and hence having a convergent equilibrium, adding a little bit of interest in policy will only make the candidates slightly diverge. But of course this too is a limiting case. We have shown that divergence increases as E or s (sensitivity) decreases, and, in the limit, the positions chosen coincide with the candidates' most preferred positions.

41 An equilibrium can be shown to exist under special circumstances. Consider the case where the most preferred positions of three voters form an isoscoles triangle and M^x bisects the base and M^y is below the base on a line segment through the top of the triangle and M^x. Then M^x is an equilibrium point if $E = 0$. There is no point that Y and a majority of voters prefer to M^x.

42 The players are very myopic in this game. The present opposition does not consider how his choice in the present election may influence his opponent's choices in future elections. It is unlikely that a non-myopic analysis can be accomplished for this game since it is so discontinuous. The probabilistic approach in the previous section is more amenable to such an analysis. Except for the goal of the candidates, this model has assumptions that are identical to those used by Kramer (1977) in his analysis of plurality maximizing parties.

43 $p_{xy} = 0$ is a special case of the elasticity assumption.

Donald Wittman

REFERENCES

Abramowitz, A. 1980. "A Comparison of Voting for U.S. Senator and Representatives in 1978." *American Political Science Review* 74:633–40.

Achen, C. 1977. "Measuring Representation." *American Journal of Political Science* 21:805–15 (Nov.).

Aldrich, J. 1983. A Downsian Spatial Model with Party Activism. *American Political Science Review* 77:974–90.

Alesina, A. 1985. "Does the Median Voter Like Budget Deficits?"

———. 1986. "Macroeconomic Policy in a Two-Party System" (Ph.D. Thesis, Harvard University).

———. 1987. "Macroeconomic Policy in a Two-Party System as a Repeated Game." *Quarterly Journal of Economics* 102:651–78 (August).

———. 1988a. "Macroeconomics and Politics." *NBER Macroeconomic Annual 1988*. Cambridge: MIT Press, 3:13–52.

———. 1988b. "Credibility and Policy Convergence in a Two-Party System with Rational Voters." *American Economic Review,* 78:796–805.

Alesina, A., and Alex Cukierman. 1987. "The Politics of Ambiguity." NBER Working Paper No. 2468 (December).

Alesina, A., and Howard Rosenthal. 1989a. Moderating Elections, Carnegie-Mellon, GSIA Working Paper No. 88-89-54.

———. 1989b. "Partisan Cycles in Congressional Elections and the Macroeconomy." American Political Science Review 83:373–98 (June).

Alesina, A., and Jeffrey Sachs. 1988. "Political Parties and the Business Cycle in the United States, 1948–1984." *Journal of Money, Credit and Banking* (February):63–84.

Alesina, A., and Stephen Spear. 1987. "An Overlapping Generations Model of Electoral Competition." NBER Working Paper No. 2354 (July).

Alesina, A., and Guido Tabellini. 1987. "A Political Theory of Fiscal Deficits and Government Debt." NBER Working Paper No. 2308 (July).

Alt, James. 1985. "Political Parties, World Demand and Unemployment: Domestic and International Sources of Economic Activity." *American Political Science Review* 49 (December):1016–140.

Aranson, P., and P. Ordeshook. 1972. "Spatial Strategies for Sequential Election." In *Probability Models of Collective Decision Making,* eds. R. Niemi and H. Weisberg. Columbus, Ohio: Merrill.

Barro, R., and D. Gordon. 1983. "Rules, Discretion and Reputation in a Model of Monetary Policy." *Journal of Monetary Economics* (July): 101–22.

Beck, N. 1982. "Parties, Administrations, and American Macroeconomic Outcomes." *American Political Science Review* 76 (March):83–94.

———. 1984. "Domestic Political Sources of American Monetary Policy: 1955–82." *Journal of Politics* (August):786–817.

Bental, B., and U. Ben Zion. 1975. "Political Contributions and Policy – Some Extensions." *Public Choice* 30:1–13.

Bernhardt, D., and D. Ingberman. 1985. "Candidate Reputation and Incumbency Effect." *Journal of Public Economics* 27 (June):47–67.

Brams, S. 1978. *The Presidential Elections Game.* New Haven: Yale University Press.

Calvert, R. 1985. "Robustness of the Multidimensional Voting Model: Candidates' Motivations, Uncertainty and Convergence." *American Journal of Political Science* (February):1056–70.

Chappell, H., and W. Keech. 1985. "A New View of Political Accountability for Economic Performance." *American Political Science Review* 79 (March):10–27.

96

Strategies When Candidates Have Policy Preferences

──────. 1986a. "Policy Motivation and Party Differences in a Dynamic Spatial Model of Party Competition." *American Political Science Review* 80 (September):881–899.

──────. 1986b. "Party Differences in Macroeconomic Policies and Outcomes." *American Economic Review* (May):71–74.

──────. 1988. "The Unemployment Consequences of Partisan Monetary Policy"

Coleman, J. S. 1971. "Internal Processes Governing Party Positions in Elections." *Public Choice* 11:35–60.

──────. 1972. "The Positions of Political Parties in Elections." In *Probability Models of Collective Decision Making,* eds. R. Niemi and H. Weisberg. Columbus, Ohio: Merrill.

Cox, G. 1984. "An Expected-Utility Model of Electoral Competition." *Quality and Quantity* 18:337–49.

Debreu, G. 1952. Existence of a social equilibrium. *Proceedings of the National Academy of Sciences.*

Downs, A. 1957. *An Economic Theory of Democracy.* New York: Harper.

Enelow, J. 1988. "A New Approach to the Spatial Theory of Electoral Competition with Expected-Utility Maximizing Candidates." Stony Brook: SUNY, Department of Political Science.

Frey, B. S., and F. Schneider. 1978. "An Empirical Study of Politico-economic Interaction in the U.S." *Review of Economics and Statistics* 60:174–83.

Ginsburg, B. 1976. "Elections and Public Policy." *American Political Science Review* 70:41–49.

Hansen, S. 1975. "Participation, Political Structure and Consequence." *American Political Science Review* 69:1181–99.

Hansson, Ingemar, and Charles Stuart. 1984. "Voting Competitions with Interested Politicians: Platforms Do Not Converge to the Preferences of the Median Voter." *Public Choice* 44:431–41.

Havrilesky, Thomas. 1987. "A Partisan Theory of Fiscal and Monetary Regimes." *Journal of Money, Credit and Banking.* 19 (August):308–25.

Hibbs, D. 1977. "Political Parties and Macroeconomic Policy." *The American Political Science Review* (December):1467–87.

──────. 1979. "Inflation, Unemployment and Left-Wing Political Parties: A Reanalysis." *American Political Science Review* 73:185–90.

──────. 1988. *The American Political Economy: Electoral Policy and Macroeconomics in Contemporary America.* Cambridge: Harvard University Press.

Hinich, M. J., J. D. Ledyard, and P. Ordeshook. 1972. "Nonvoting and the Existence of Equilibrium under Majority Rule." *Journal of Economic Theory* 4:144–53.

Kramer, G. 1977. "A Dynamical Model of Political Equilibrium." *Journal of Economic Theory* 16:310–34.

Kuklinski, J. 1977. "District Competitiveness and Legislative Roll-call Behavior: A Reassessment of the Marginality Hypothesis." *American Journal of Political Science* 21:627–738.

──────. 1978. "Representativeness and Elections: A Policy Analysis." *American Political Science Review* 72:165–77.

──────. 1979. "Representative–Constituency Linkage: A Review Article." *Legislative Studies Quarterly* 4:121–41.

Kuklinski, J., and R. C. Elling. 1977. "Representational Role Constituency Opinion and Legislative Roll-Call Behavior." *American Journal of Political Science* 21:135–47.

Lau, L., and B. Frey. 1971. "Ideology, Public Approval and Government Behavior." *Public Choice* 10:20–40.

Donald Wittman

Lindbeck, A., and J. Weibull. 1989. "Political Equilibrium in Representative Democracy." Institute of International Studies Seminar Paper No. 426, University of Stockholm.

Mann, T., and R. Wolfinger. 1980. "Candidates and Parties in Congressional Elections." *American Political Science Review* 74:617–32.

McKibbin, Warwick, Nuriel Roubini, and Jeffrey Sachs. 1987. "Dynamic Optimization in Two-Party Models." NBER Working Paper (April).

Mitchell, D. W. 1987. "Candidate Behavior under Mixed Motives." *Social Choice and Welfare* 4:153–60.

Page, B. 1978. *Choice and Echoes in Presidential Elections: Rational Man in Electoral Democracy.* Chicago: University of Chicago Press.

Payne, J. 1979. "Inflation, Unemployment, and Left-wing Political Parties: A Reanalysis." *American Political Science Review* 73:181–85.

Persson, T., and L. E. O. Svensson. 1987. "Why a Stubborn Conservative Would Run a Deficit: Policy with Time-Inconsistent Preferences" (mimeo).

Petry, F. 1982. "Vote-Maximizing versus Utility-Maximizing Candidates: Comparing Dynamic Models of Bi-Party Competition." *Quality and Quantity* 16:507–26.

Poole, K. T. and H. Rosenthal. 1984. "The Polarization of American Politics." *The Journal of Politics* 46:1061–79.

———. 1988. "The Spatial Stability of Congressional Voting: 1789–1985." Speech at the Legislative Institutions, Practices, and Behavior Conference, Hoover Institution (February).

Robertson, D. 1976. *A Theory of Party Competition.* London: John Wiley & Sons.

Rothenberg, J. 1965. "A Model of Economic and Political Decision Making." In *The Public Economy of Urban Communities*, ed. J. Margolis. New York: AMS Press.

Schlesinger, J. 1975. "The Primary Goals of Political Parties: A Clarification of Positive Theory." *American Political Science Review* 69:840–49.

Schumpeter, J. A. 1950. *Capitalism, socialism, and democracy.* New York: Harper & Brothers.

Tabellini, G. 1987. "Domestic Politics and the International Coordination of Fiscal Policies."

Tabellini, G., and A. Alesina. 1988. "Voting on the Budget Deficit."

Tabellini, G., and Vincenzo La Via. "Money, Debt and Deficits in the U.S." forthcoming *Review of Economics and Statistics.*

Tufte, E. 1978. *Political Control of the Economy.* Princeton: Princeton University Press.

Wittman, D. A. 1970. "Theories of Optimal Party Decision-Making." (Ph.D. thesis, University of California, Berkeley).

———. 1973. "Parties as utility maximizers." *American Political Science Review* 67:490–98.

———. 1975. *"Political Decision-Making."* In *Economics of Public Choice.* eds. R. Leiter and G. Sirkin. Cyrco Press.

———. 1977. "Candidates with Policy Preferences: A Dynamic Model." *Journal of Economic Theory* 14:180–89.

———. 1983. "Candidate Motivation: A Synthesis of Alternative Theories." *American Political Science Review* 77:142–57.

———. 1986. "Final Offer Arbitration." *Management Science.*

———. 1987. "Elections with N Voters, M Candidates and K Issues." In *The Logic of Multiparty Systems,* ed. M. J. Holler. Dordrecht: Kluwer Academic Publishers. Pp. 129–34.

5

A Decade of Experimental Research on Spatial
Models of Elections and Committees

RICHARD D. MCKELVEY

California Institute of Technology

PETER C. ORDESHOOK

California Institute of Technology

ABSTRACT

The Euclidean representation of political issues and alternative outcomes, and
the associated representation of preferences as quasiconcave utility functions,
is by now a staple of formal models of committees and elections. This theoretical development, moreover, is accompanied by a considerable body of
experimental research. We can view that research in two ways: as a test of the
basic propositions about equilibria in specific institutional settings, and as an
attempt to gain insights into those aspects of political processes that are poorly
understood or imperfectly modeled, such as the robustness of theoretical
results with respect to procedural details and bargaining environments. This
essay reviews that research so that we can gain some sense of its overall
import.

*   *   *

A considerable body of political theory represents alternative outcomes or
policies by a subset of n-dimensional Euclidean space, and assumes that we
can represent individual preferences over these outcomes by quasiconcave
utility functions with internal satiation points. By imposing this particular
structure on alternatives and preferences, we can deduce a variety of substantively informative results, such as the Median Voter Theorem in elections, and
the generic emptiness of cores in cooperative political games (cf. Plott 1967,
Schofield 1983). Correspondingly, the special case of Euclidean preferences,
introduced by Davis and Hinich (1966, 1968), form the basis for the most
extensively developed models of two general classes of political institutions –
elections and committees. Although Euclidean preferences do not necessarily

99

Richard D. McKelvey and Peter C. Ordeshook

yield the most general models, they allow us to formulate estimatable statistical models of preference parameters (see Enelow and Hinich 1985 for a general survey). Furthermore, with them we secure a benchmark against which to compare other theoretical results, especially those that concern the relative importance and impact of alternative institutions in the determination of outcomes (cf. Kramer 1972; Shepsle and Weingast 1981; Riker 1984).

This latter issue about the effects of alternative institutional structures is the take-off point for the literature this essay reviews – experimental research on spatial models. Briefly, we can view that research, commencing with Fiorina and Plott's (1978) experiments on committee decision making, in two ways. On the one hand, we can interpret it as testing the basic propositions that such models offer about equilibrium outcomes in two specific institutions – two-candidate, majority rule elections and n-person, majority-rule committees. Since an important part of this theoretical research consists of ascertaining the impact of procedures such as the requirement of unusual majorities, issue-by-issue voting, and agendas, experimental research seeks to test the related theoretical propositions. On the other hand, we can view experimentation as providing insight into those aspects of political processes that are poorly understood or imperfectly modeled, such as the robustness of theoretical results with respect to particular procedural details and nuances in bargaining environments. This essay reviews that literature so that we can gain a clearer sense of the role of specific experiments with respect to these two views.

I. THE BASIC THEORETICAL STRUCTURE AND RESULTS

We begin by introducing some notation that allows us to formulate the central theoretical results of spatial models about Condorcet winners. These results are the focus of nearly all experimental research that we review. Briefly, if we let $X \subseteq R^m$ denote the set of feasible alternative outcomes (usually a closed and convex set, such as the set that corresponds to a budget constraint), and $N = \{1, 2, \ldots, n\}$ the set of voters or committee members, then the associated utility function for person $i \in N$, $u_i:X \rightarrow R$, is written as a function of $x = (x_1, x_2, \ldots, x_m)$, with the understanding that $u_i(x)$ is characterized in particular by the ideal point of person i, $x^*_i = (x^*_{i1}, x^*_{i2}, \ldots, x^*_{im}) \in X$.

Although theoretical results that seek generality impose the weakest assumptions possible on u_i, experimental research is facilitated if intuitively simple forms are used. Hence, the majority of experimental research proceeds by using the Euclidean metric. Briefly, if A is a symmetric, positive-definite matrix, then $u_i(x) = -(x^*_i - x)A(x^*_i - x)'$. In this instance, i's indifference contours in X are concentric ellipses, where A determines the specific form and orientation of those ellipses. If A is a diagonal matrix ($a_{ij} = 0$ for all $i \neq j$), then a transformation of the axes renders A equal to the identity matrix I,

$u_i(x)$ becomes the simple distance metric, and indifference contours are circles. In anticipation of some experimental results that we review, we note that one alternative to this formulation is the city block metric, defined by $u_i(x) = -\Sigma|x^*_{ij} - x_j|$. In this case, indifference contours over X are concentric squares, with diagonals parallel to the coordinates of X.

From the perspective of experimental research, the most-relevant theoretical results concern the conditions for the existence of Condorcet winners – outcomes that defeat all other alternatives in X in a majority vote. (We cannot review that research in detail here.) But we should cite Plott's (1967) result for general quasiconcave and continuous preferences. If the number of voters is odd and if at most one person's ideal is at the presumed Condorcet point, Plott gives necessary and sufficient conditions for the existence of that point in terms of the pairwise symmetry of voter utility gradients. This result shows that the existence of a Condorcet point is rare in multidimensional issue spaces. Indeed, if utility functions are everywhere differentiable, then generically Condorcet winners do not generically exist (Schofield 1983).

Despite these results, we can construct preference configurations that yield a Condorcet winner, and this theoretical research is an especially useful starting point for experimental research. In one dimension, Plott's symmetry condition reduces to Black's (1962) theorem, which is that if utility functions are single-peaked (strictly quasiconcave) and if the number of voters is odd, then the Condorcet winner exists and corresponds to the electorate's median ideal point. If the number of voters is even or if utility functions have "flat peaks," then a Condorcet winner may not exist, but there will exist a set of alternatives that cannot be defeated in a majority rule vote, called the majority rule core. In multiple dimensions when all voters have preferences based on Euclidean distance, the symmetry conditions for a Condorcet point are equivalent to the results of Davis, Hinich, and Degroot (1972), who show that a necessary and sufficient condition for the existence of a Condorcet point is that there exist a median in all directions. Given this requirement's fragility, this also shows that Condorcet winners are rare. With respect to city-block preferences, the existence of a Condorcet winner is assured, but only if the dimensionality of X is one or two (Rae and Taylor 1971).

To interpret experimental results correctly, it is important to understand that establishing an alternative as a Condorcet winner is not equivalent to predicting that alternative as the eventual outcome. The definition of the Condorcet winner refers only to a property of the social preference relation under pairwise voting and simple majority rule, and the social scientist's interest in it stems from the implicit judgment that if such a winner exists, then collective decision-making institutions ought to select it, whereas if an institution does not select it, then we ought to have good reasons for regarding the selected outcomes as legitimate social choices. Thus, our research typically begins with the question "Does institution_____yield the Condorcet winner as the eventual outcome if such a winner exists, and what kind of outcomes does this institution yield if there is no Condorcet winner?"

Most theoretical and experimental research about voting, committees, and legislatures seeks answers to this question. Hence, an important part of that research is the specification that the situation be modeled in such a way that we link individual decisions and collective outcomes to the concept of the Condorcet winner. This means that before making any prediction we must look at the game-form implied by the specific institutions that society uses to choose outcomes – the strategies available to decision makers and the preferences over these strategies implied by preferences over outcomes in X.

This approach yields the principal, descriptive reason for interest in the concept of a Condorcet winner – namely, the apparent variety of game-forms that render such winners' predicted outcomes. Two important game-forms are two-candidate elections and n-person cooperative committees. With respect to elections, if X denotes the strategy spaces of each of two candidates who are competing for electoral victory under simple majority rule, if N is the set of voters, if all voters have perfect information about the candidates' strategies, if candidates have perfect information about voter preferences, and if all persons vote for the candidate whose strategy they most prefer, then a Condorcet winner, if it exists, is the unique Nash equilibrium strategy for both candidates in the corresponding two-candidate, zero sum game. With respect to cooperative committees, if N denotes the members of a committee that must choose an alternative in X, if the committee uses simple majority rule, and if the strategic character of procedures is described by a characteristic-function representation in which majority coalitions can secure anything in X and all other coalitions can secure nothing, then the Condorcet winner corresponds to the game's core – to an outcome that no coalition has the means or the desire to upset.

Similar analysis also establishes the Condorcet winner as the predicted outcome for other institutional arrangements. For example, if a committee or legislature proceeds by an agenda in which alternatives or amendments to the status quo can be considered only issue-by-issue, and if preferences correspond to unweighted Euclidean distance $(A = I)$, then, regardless of whether voters act strategically or nonstrategically (in the sense of always choosing sincerely), the unique, stable outcome is the one that corresponds to the median preference on every issue – the issue-by-issue median (if we look only at committees in which all members always vote sincerely, we can drop the requirement that A equal I to establish that a stable outcome exists; cf. Kramer 1972, but see Enelow and Hinich 1983 for an analysis with uncertainty). Since Condorcet winners, if they exist, must correspond to a median in all directions, issue-by-issue voting yields Condorcet winners as eventual outcomes.

A Decade of Experimental Research on Spatial Models

Not all game-forms, however, imply the selection of Condorcet winners. If all voters are sincere, if one voter is exogenously selected as an agenda setter, and if this agenda setter can form an agenda of any type over a part of the feasible set (in this instance, a finite subset of R^m), then even if the Condorcet winner appears on the agenda, nearly any alternative can be made to prevail. On the other hand, if all voters are sophisticated in the sense that they look ahead to final consequences and vote accordingly, and if a Condorcet winner is on the agenda, then that winner will be selected (see Ordeshook and Schwartz 1987 for a review of these results, and Levine and Plott 1977 for some experimental verification). With respect to elections, if three or more candidates compete under plurality rule, then even if the election concerns a single issue, the Condorcet winner generally is not an equilibrium strategy for any candidate – equilibrium strategies, if they exist, are lotteries (mixed strategies) over a subset of the issue space (Cox 1987).

These results leave us with five questions – three theoretical and two experimental. The first experimental question is straightforward: If a Condorcet winner exists and if a game-form predicts that winner as the outcome, will it be selected? The theoretical questions engendered by these results are, first, if a Condorcet winner does not exist, what outcomes should we predict; second, what role does the concept of a Condorcet winner play in alternative institutional arrangements (under alternative game-forms); and what solution hypotheses are appropriate for games with empty cores or for game-forms that fail to yield a plausible noncooperative equilibrium? The subsidiary experimental question is: What support can we find for theoretical extensions, and how might experimental research suggest viable theoretical approaches?

These questions organize the experimental research that we review. First, with respect to committees, that research includes:

1. testing the core (Condorcet winner) as a predictor in cooperative committee processes;

2. testing the robustness of the core with respect to variations in procedures.

Second, with respect to two-candidate elections and the relevance of Condorcet winners to final outcomes,

3. ascertaining whether candidates converge to Condorcet winners in two-candidate elections;

4. ascertaining whether candidates converge to Conforcet winners when the information of candidates and of voters is incomplete.

Third, with respect to situations in which preferences are configured so that no Condorcet winner describes the social preference order under simple majority rule,

Richard D. McKelvey and Peter C. Ordeshook

5. identifying possible bounds on the strategies of election candidates, such as those hypothesized by concepts like the uncovered set;

6. developing and testing alternative cooperative solution hypotheses, such as the Competitive Solution;

7. ascertaining the circumstance under which alternative procedural restrictions, such as issue-by-issue voting or the requirement of unusual majorities, induce equlibria.

2. CONDORCET WINNERS IN SIMPLE COMMITTEES

The seminal experimental essay dealing with spatial preferences is Fiorina and Plott's (1978) study of cooperative committees. Using the configuration of ideal points $(x_1, \ldots, x_5)$ shown in Figure 5.1a and a payoff structure that induces circular indifference contours so that the ideal point of voter 5 is a Condorcet point, the broad outline of their procedure is as follows: Beginning with a status quo point (the extreme upper-right corner of the grid), any subject can be recognized by the chair (experimenter) to offer a feasible alternative as a proposed change in the status quo. If this motion is seconded, the alternative is put to a majority vote against the status quo, with the winner becoming the new status quo. This process is repeated until some subject makes a motion to adjourn that is seconded and approved by a majority. Fiorina and Plott consider four experimental contexts, distinguished by two variables: high versus low payoffs, and experiments in which subjects could discuss alternatives after motions are seconded versus experiments in which all discussion is precluded. (In all of the experiments that we review, to ensure that the spatial dimensions, and not mere monetary rewards, are the "issues" under consideration, subjects are prohibited from revealing anything about the cardinal nature of their payoffs or from devising schemes for dividing their winnings at the termination of an experiment.) Figure 5.1a summarizes the final outcomes of the "high payoff" experiments; Figure 5.1b reports the "low payoff" outcomes (no general pattern of significant differences between the "with communication" and "without communication" is apparent in their data).

One reaction to these data is that, because only a minority of outcomes correspond to the Condorcet point, we ought to reject the simple hypothesis that "Cooperative majority rule committees choose Condorcet winners if such a winner exists." On the other hand, we can see that most outcomes – at least for the high payoff experiments – are "close" to the Condorcet point in terms of Euclidean distance, and that this point appears to serve as a important focus for most committees. Indeed, Figure 5.2b summarizes the outcomes of a procedurally equivalent series of experiments using committees with from twenty-three to forty-five subjects (Plott 1977). Figure 5.2a shows the dis-

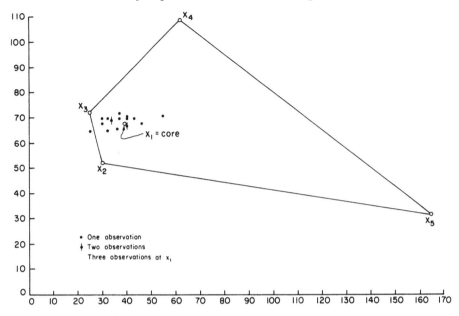

Figure 5.1a. High Payoff Observations (from Fiorina and Plott 1978)

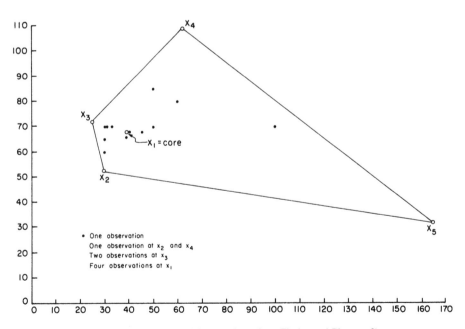

Figure 5.1b. Low Payoff Observations (from Fiorina and Plott 1978)

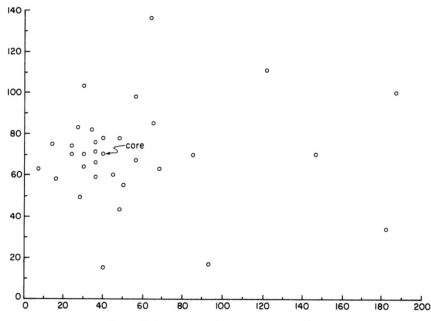

Figure 5.2a. Distribution of Individual Optima (from Plott 1977)

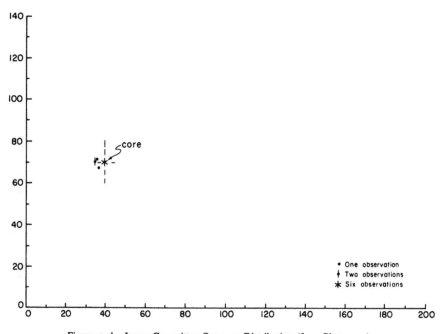

Figure 5.2b. Large Committee Outcome Distribution (from Plott 1977)

tribution of ideal points for the largest committee. Six of nine outcomes now correspond identically to the core. Hence, the deviations that Figures 5.1a and 5.1b report may be merely the artifact of a small experimental committee (which are magnified by decreasing the subjects' monetary incentives).

Yet, some aspects of the details of Fiorina and Plott's procedures warrant emphasis. First, the method whereby subjects are recognized to make motions appears to place the experimenter in too central a role. Do subjects perceive the recognition rule as random or as biased toward particular subjects, such as those who have not previously made a motion? Second, because subjects do not know each other's preferences (even ordinally), it is more appropriate to describe the corresponding game-form as a game of incomplete information. Our concern here is the fact that with incomplete information, other institutions occasion seemingly perverse predictions about Condorcet winners (Ordeshook and Palfrey 1988) and there is no guarantee, a priori, that Fiorina and Plott's procedure avoids such possibilities. Third, the game-form implied by a sequential parliamentary procedure should be modeled, since that form need not correspond to one in which we predict a Condorcet winner. Indeed, using the subjects' incomplete information, we can speculate that the predictions rendered by a carefully drawn (and probably intractable) model of the situation will include, but will not be limited to, the Condorcet point. In a series of finite-alternative experiments, however, Salant and Goodstein (1987) confront many of these issues directly with a revised parliamentary procedure. Salant and Goodstein's conclusion that "committees . . . are much more likely to select the Condorcet point when 'high intensity' preferences are used" (p. 17) nevertheless reaffirms Fiorina and Plott's conclusions, although they accept the necessity for introducing the notion of a threshold in order to explain deviations from predicted outcomes.

The objections to Fiorina and Plott's procedure are summarized by the concern that the implied noncooperative extensive-form game of incomplete information is not known to yield a Condorcet winner as an equilibrium outcome. Rather than revise this procedure incrementally so that we can deduce predicted outcomes directly from its game-form, however, Berl et al. (1976) report on a series of experiments using the preference configuration in Figure 5.3 in which a procedure is implemented that attempts to approximate the rules identifying a cooperative extensive form game as closely as possible (although this essay has an earlier publication date than that of Fiorina and Plott, the inspiration for this research came from earlier drafts of Fiorina and Plott's essay). In this instance, subjects are informed about each other's ordinal preferences, and in lieu of a specific parliamentary procedure, subjects can discuss alternatives freely, without interference from the experimenter. And any majority at any time is free to end the experiment after reaching an agreement. The data that Figure 5.3 portrays strengthen Fiorina and Plott's conclusions about the attractiveness of the core.

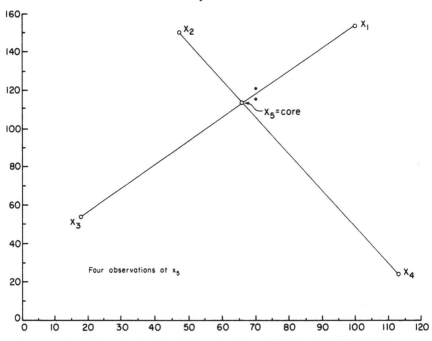

Figure 5.3. Outcomes with Discussion (from Berl et al. 1976)

One objection to both the Fiorina-Plott and Berl et al. experiments is that with circular indifference contours, the Condorcet winner is necessarily "central" – the distribution of ideal points must be radially symmetric so that the Condorcet winner corresponds to the ideal point that lies on the intersection of the straight lines connecting the ideals of diametrically opposite voters (assuming that at most one voter's ideal is at the presumed Condorcet point). Thus, such a point may be chosen because it is deemed equitable by subjects or because it is a "natural" focal point. Fiorina and Plott, however, also report on experiments using elliptical indifference contours, and the results (see Figure 5.4) corroborate their earlier conclusions.* For a more dramatic asymmetry in the location of the core with respect to ideal points, Berl et al. provide a series of three-person experiments in which city-block utility functions are induced, and in which, with an appropriate rotation of the axes, the core gives the appearance of benefiting one or two specific subjects and thus does not appear to be equitable. Figure 5.5a and 5.5b summarize their results. Finally, Figure 5.6 summarizes the outcomes of some experiments reported by

*This figure and Figure 5.7b are drawn according to the reported data. In each case one observation in the original figure is inconsistent with that data.

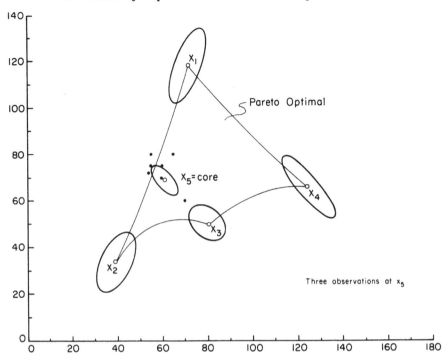

Figure 5.4. Elliptical Indifference Curves (from Fiorina and Plott 1977)

Plott (1978, 1979) using the Fiorina-Plott procedures applied to rhomboid indifference contours with the orientations shown in the figure. In general, all of these variations confirm the attractiveness of the core as a solution hypothesis.

Although we might quibble about the procedural dissimilarities in these experiments, a more serious issue concerns the special role of Euclidean preferences and spatial alternative sets. The experimental data that we have reviewed thus far supports the hypothesis that

if preferences and alternatives are spatial, if a Condorcet winner exists, and if procedures imply a game-form (or "approximate game-form") that links this winner to the core, then that winner is the final outcome, either identically or approximately.

McKelvey and Ordeshook (1981), however, offer a series of finite-alternative core experiments in which with one preference configuration the core is selected less than half the time, whereas with another configuration the core is selected every time (see also Eavey and Miller 1984b). A variety of straight-forward hypotheses (such as considerations of equity, indifference to payoff

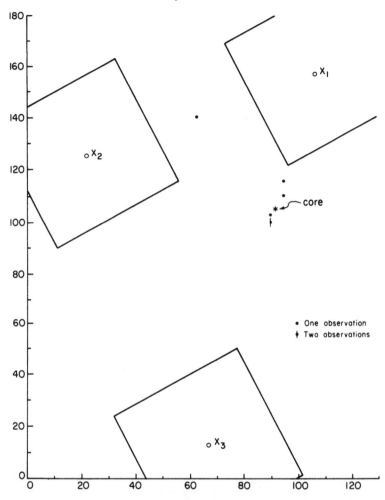

Figure 5.5a. City-Block Outcomes (from Berl et al. 1976)

magnitudes, the experience of subjects, and the completeness of information) fail to explain this discrepancy. These experiments, then, raise the question whether spatial configurations with Condorcet winners can be found that will yield equivalent discrepancies. Thus, we must ask: Is the support that the core receives in the Fiorina-Plott and Berl et al. experiments an artifact of the fortuitous selection of ideal point configurations, or is there something special about spatial representations? The first part of this question can only be "answered" by additional experimentation, although the evidence to date strongly suggests that the core's support in spatial experiments is not an

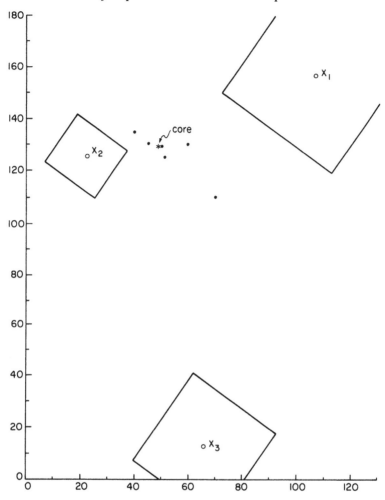

Figure 5.5b. City-Block Outcomes (from Berl et al. 1976)

artifact. The second part suggests that our explanations of experimental is missing an element outcomes – that a satisfactory explanation must also tell us why people react to a spatial structure differently than they react to other topological representations of alternatives and preferences.

Despite these caveats, experimental research supports the prediction that, at least in alternative sets with a spatial structure, the core (Condorcet winner) of a committee game emerges as the final outcome. Indeed, a comparison of the Fiorina-Plott with the Berl et al. experiments suggests (but does not establish) that, because they employ different procedures, this prediction is robust to

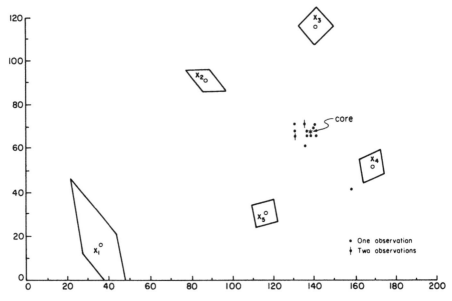

Figure 5.6. Rhomboid Indifference Curves (from Plott 1978)

slight variations in procedural details. As further evidence for this suggestion, McKelvey and Ordeshook (1984) offer a series of experiments that graft an important variation of the Fiorina-Plott parliamentary procedure onto their own design. Specifically, these experiments use an identical parliamentary procedure in which subjects must formally make motions to change the status quo, and so forth, with the exception that a motion can differ from the status quo on only one issue. That is, voting must proceed issue-by-issue, with the opportunity to reconsider issues in any sequence. And as before, two types of experiments are considered: those that allow discussion and those that preclude discussion among subjects. Thus, agreements to trade votes across issues implicitly (as is possible in the Fiorina-Plott experiments via the opportunity to make motions that differ from the status quo on both issues simultaneously) or explicitly are prohibited in the first case, but not in the second. Theoretically, however, we know that if preferences are characterized by simple Euclidean distance, then regardless of whether discussion is or is not permitted, the core and the Condorcet winner remain equivalent (Kramer 1972). Figure 5.7a and 5.7b plot the results of these experiments with discussion permitted and with it not permitted. In general, this data can be seen to support the theoretical prediction of the core and the insensitivity of this prediction to possibilities for communication.

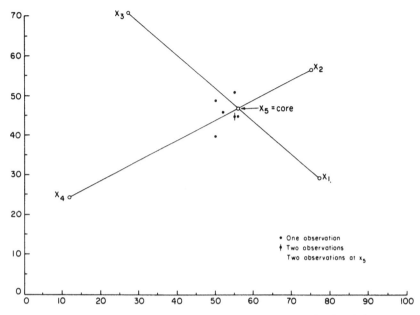

Figure 5.7a. Issue-by-issue Voting Outcomes with Discussion Precluded (from McKelvey and Ordeshook 1987)

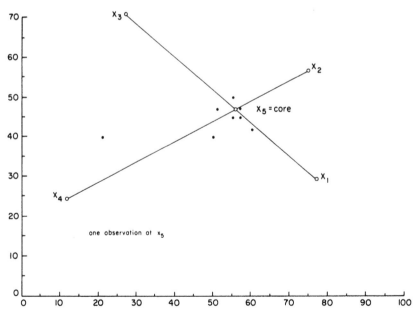

Figure 5.7b. Issue-by-issue Voting Outcomes with Discussion Permitted (from McKelvey and Ordeshook 1987)

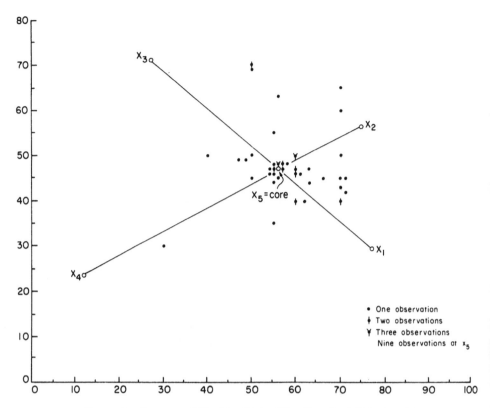

Figure 5.8a. Outcomes of First Five Trials of Five-Voter Spatial Election with an Equilibrium (from McKelvey and Ordeshook 1982)

3. CONDORCET WINNERS IN SIMPLE ELECTIONS

Turning now to elections, we are surprised how little experimental research there is to report, even though our prediction – that candidates will converge to a Condorcet point if it exists – is identical to the prediction that we make in the committee setting. McKelvey and Ordeshook (1982) provide a series of two-candidate, two-dimensional elections with a Condorcet winner – the same preference configuration as the one shown in Figures 5.7a and 5.7b – and, thus, with a unique Nash equilibrium for the corresponding two-candidate zero sum game. In these experiments, only the candidates are subjects: voters are artificial actors who simply vote for the candidate closest to their ideal. Each experiment consists of a sequence of trials in which the same two subjects choose strategies after observing each other's previous choice and the electoral outcome. Figures 5.8a and 5.8b summarize the candidates' choices

114

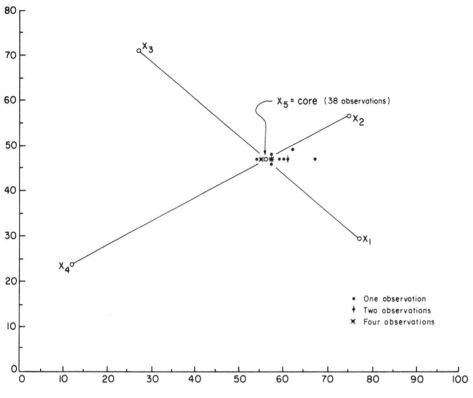

Figure 5.8b. Outcomes of Last Five Trials of Five-Voter Spatial Election with an Equilibrium (from McKelvey and Ordeshook 1982)

in the first five and last five trials, and they document the convergence of choices to the Condorcet point.

In the preceding experiments, the subjects (candidates) are perfectly informed about the preferences of each member of the electorate, and the simulated electorate is assumed to be informed about the candidates' issue positions – the voters choose on the basis of the candidates' actual strategies. In reality, of course, electorates typically are poorly informed about the policies that candidates will implement if elected, and candidates may have only noisy data about voter preferences. As a partial response to such considerations, Plott (1977) offers a series of ten experiments in which candidates are uninformed about the preferences of voters (the number of voters varies in these experiments between nineteen and forty-one). Voters know the positions of the candidates, and candidates are allowed to query the electorate about preferred directions of change (such as, "How many would like me to move

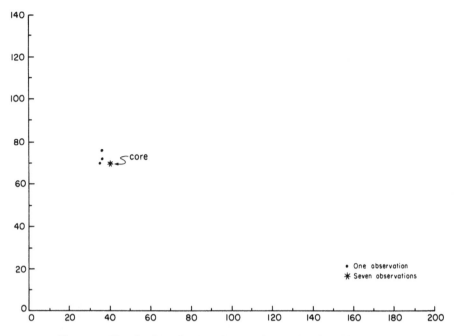

Figure 5.9. Two-Candidate Elections Outcome Distribution (from Plott 1977)

to the point _____?"). Also, a poll is conducted periodically in which the electorate is asked: "If the election were held now, how many would vote for _____?" Although Plott does not show that voting sincerely in the polls is a dominant strategy, if we assume that this is so, then each candidates' equilibrium strategy corresponds to the Condorcet point. Figure 5.2a shows the distribution of ideal points for the largest experiment, and Figure 5.9 shows the final experimental outcomes.

These experiments, nevertheless do not confront perhaps the most important feature of information in elections – the low levels of voters' information. McKelvey and Ordeshook undertook a series of theoretical results in conjunction with a series of experimental tests of those results, to ascertain the robustness of spatial election theory to such incomplete information. We cannot review the details of their theoretical analyses here (for a more comprehensive review, see McKelvey and Ordeshook 1985b, 1987), but, in brief, those analyses develop two general classes of models. The first model applies ideas taken from the rational expectations theory of markets to hypothesize that voters use a variety of readily available cues, such as public opinion polls and interest group endorsements, to estimate which candidate in a unidimensional or multidimensional spatial environment is closest to their ideal point.

The electorate is assumed to consist of both informed and uninformed voters, where informed voters know the candidates' issue positions (in the unidimensional case some portion of informed voters can correspond to a unitary actor that simply endorses the candidate closest to its ideal point), and where uninformed voters must rely on cues – endorsements and public opinion polls of the entire electorate – to make their decisions.

McKelvey and Ordeshook (1985b) report on two unidimensional experiments. In these experiments, each of which consists of a series of eight elections, candidates are completely uninformed about voter preferences. Each election begins with the selection of issue positions by the two candidates, followed by two polls of the electorate in which voters must identify the candidate they think they most prefer, followed by a vote to determine that election's winner. Half of the electorate (plus one) is told the candidates' strategies in each election, whereas each of the remaining voters is told (a) which candidate is to the left and which is to the right on the issue (via the interest group endorsement); (b) the outcome of each poll; and (c) the location of his or her ideal point relative to the entire electorate (such as whether it falls in the 30th percentile, counting from the left, the 35th percentile). In theory, this information is sufficient for the realization of a rational expectations equilibrium in which candidates converge to the electorate's median preference and all voters vote as if they had complete information about the candidates.

In the actual experimental data, uninformed voters vote "correctly," given their information, 84.9 percent of the time; Figures 5.10a and 5.10b, which graph the candidates' choices in each election, document their rapid convergence to the electorate's median preference. It appears, then, that the Median Voter Theorem, given an appropriate structure to incomplete information, is robust to such information. Yet, McKelvey and Ordeshook also report on a series of two-dimensional experiments, run an average of nine election periods, that are far less conclusive. From the perspective of uninformed voters, the details of these experiments differ from their unidimensional counterparts as follows: There is no interest group rendering an endorsement; the electorate is divided into three groups – each consisting of informed and uninformed subparts; a poll within each group is reported to the electorate; and each voter is told the position of his or her ideal point relative to the median preference within each group. Despite these changes, which are necessitated by the theoretical model, uninformed voters vote correctly 85.5 percent of the time. Only three of the six candidates, however, can be said to have converged to positions close to the overall median (see McKelvey and Ordeshook 1985a for a detailed analysis of the data).

We can hypothesize, of course, that multidimensional contests (as compared to unidimensional ones) present candidates with a sufficiently difficult decision environment so that even several election outcomes do not allow

Richard D. McKelvey and Peter C. Ordeshook

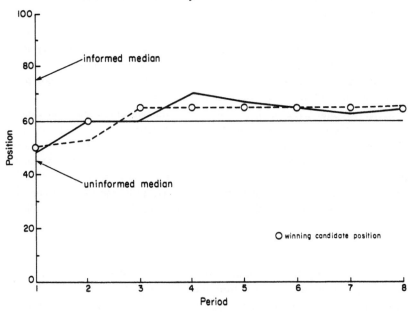

Figure 5.10a. Sequential Experiment (from McKelvey and Ordeshook 1985b)

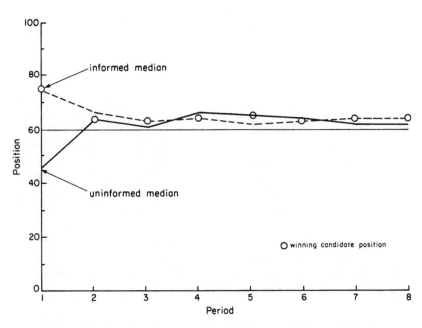

Figure 5.10b. Sequential Experiment (from McKelvey and Ordershook 1985b)

them to judge the directions in which they ought to move their issue positions (since sixty to ninety subjects are required to implement the experimental design, each experiment requires 3 to 4 hours to administer, which precludes additional trials). Thus, we can also conjecture that if the experiments were run longer, the candidates would converge – that additional data on victories and defeats would decrease the degrees of freedom that candidates have for choosing strategies. This conjecture, however, remains merely an unsubstantiated speculation.

Although subjects participate in a sequence of experiments so that they can learn to process the information made available to them, McKelvey and Ordeshook's first theoretical model in fact focuses on a single election and on the value to voters of cues that arise in a campaign. Yet, much of the empirical literature on voting suggests that voters vote retrospectively. In brief, the traditional retrospective voting hypothesis is that, in lieu of any knowledge about policies advocated by candidates and implemented by incumbents, voters know only their stream of income or welfare (compare Key 1966; Fiorina 1981). The empirical question, then, is whether retrospective voting in a spatial context generates signals that lead incumbents to implement Condorcet winners as policy. A second model and series of experiments is developed, then, which only permit voters to choose retrospectively (Collier et al. 1987; Grey, McKelvey, and Ordeshook 1986).

In this second set of experiments, each subject that plays the role of a voter is assigned a spatial utility function (simple Euclidean distance in either one or two dimensions) that is revealed to no one. Instead, the incumbent (initially selected at random) chooses a spatial position that is translated, via the assigned utility functions, into a payoff, and only this payoff is revealed to each voter. Voters must then choose between reelecting the current incumbent and electing the challenger. Notice that with this procedure, a challenger does not adopt a policy until he or she becomes an incumbent. Thus, election campaigns are nonexistent, voters must act on the basis of the past stream of payoffs associated with the two potential incumbents, and the sole source of information available to candidates is the history of spatial positions adopted by incumbents and the votes those spatial positions earned incumbents.

Evaluating voting behavior in this context is difficult. The absence of structure in each experiment means that voters could reasonably employ a great many alternative decision rules (for example, vote to reelect the incumbent if the incumbent's policy yields a payoff greater than the discounted average of the past, or greater than the discounted average of the challenger's past, or if the payoff is no worse than the payoff from the previous incumbent). But with respect to the more important question of what policies incumbents choose, these experiments suggest that, despite the limited information available to subjects, Condorcet winning spatial positions remain powerfully attractive to the candidates. Reporting both the unidimensional and the two-dimensional

Richard D. McKelvey and Peter C. Ordeshook

Table 5.1 *Estimates of regression*

	a	b	R^2
Unidimensional			
periods 1–5	39.3 (2.91)	.21 (.05)	.06 (15.5)
periods 11–15	22.0 (2.75)	.59 (.05)	.37 (14.6)
last 5 periods	17.0 (2.67)	.69 (.05)	.52 (12.5)
Two-dimensional			
periods 1–5	45.4 (4.14)	.06 (.07)	.00 (21.7)
periods 11–15	15.8 (2.46)	.64 (.04)	.56 (13.0)
periods 21–25	15.8 (2.58)	.67 (.04)	.56 (13.5)
periods 35–40	11.2 (2.38)	.77 (.04)	.66 (12.5)

experiments, Table 5.1 records the results of the simple regression $y = a + bx + e$, where x is the location of the electorate's median preference and y is the actual position adopted by the incumbent (in the case of two dimensions, each dimension is treated as a separate source of data for the regression). Notice that if incumbents converge identically to the median, then we would have a $= 0$ and $b = 1$. The data that this table reports show that such perfect convergence does not occur, but they confirm that, on average, the candidates do approach the median as the experiment proceeds.

At least for the limited information structure imposed by these experiments, then, the Condorcet winner remains attractive to candidates. This does not mean that the sole sufficient condition for the median's attraction is that it merely exist. The experiments reviewed in this section support the proposition that, experimentally, candidates will converge to equilibrium strategies – that the definition of rational choice offered by noncooperative game theory has empirical foundation. But we cannot conclude that Condorcet winners prevail if the situation's game-form is changed so that equilibrium strategies correspond to something other than that winner. Consider, for example, the fact noted earlier that even if an election is unidimensional or if the distribution of ideal points is radially symmetric, equilibrium strategies in general cannot correspond to the Condorcet winner if there are more than two candidates. The experimental evidence that Figure 5.11 summarizes supports this view. This figure shows the positions of victorious candidates in a series of three-candidate elections (Plott 1977). Although the data are near the Condorcet winner, a comparison of Figures 5.11 and 5.9 reveals that outcomes are more dispersed in three-candidate elections than in their two-candidate counterparts. Thus, the mere addition of a candidate changes equilibrium strategies, and this change is reflected in the experimental data.

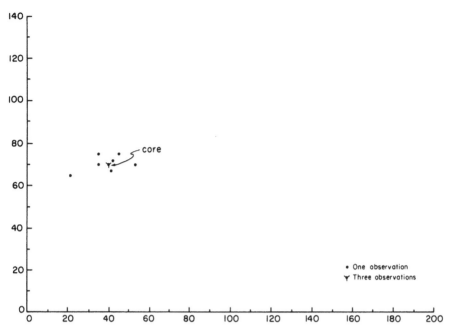

Figure 5.11. Three-Candidate Elections Outcome Distribution (from Plott
1977)

3. ELECTIONS WITHOUT PURE STRATEGY EQUILIBRIA

Much of the early research on spatial election models focused on sufficient
conditions for the existence of readily identifiable pure equilibrium strategies
for candidates. Indeed, owing to the obsession of this research with uncover-
ing such conditions, it is safe to infer that many scholars believed at the time
that little could be said about political outcomes if such strategies did not
exist. Even so, beginning with McKelvey and Ordeshook's (1979) development of the admissable set and Kramer's (1977) application of the minmax
set, and proceeding to the formulation and application of the uncovered set
(Miller 1980), we now have good theoretical reasons for supposing that candidates in two-candidate elections without a Condorcet winning platform will
not diverge "much" from the median voter preference on each spatial dimension (for specific bounds on the divergence, see McKelvey 1986). The uncovered set is especially important in this regards since all strategies outside
of it are necessarily dominated by strategies within it, in which case the
support set of mixed strategy equilibria must fall within the uncovered set.

As an initial test of these ideas, McKelvey and Ordeshook (1982) offer a

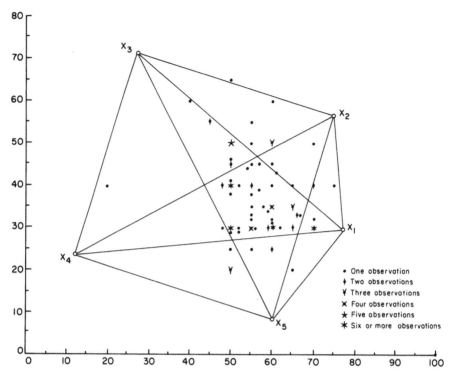

Figure 5.12a. Outcomes of First 5 Trials of Five-Voter Spatial Election without an Equilibrium (from McKelvey and Ordeshook 1982)

series of five- and nine-voter, two-candidate experiments. Figures 5.12a and 5.12b summarize the choices of candidates in the first and last five rounds of the five-voter experiments; Figures 5.12c and 5.12d summarize the nine-voter experiments (recall that the voters here are artificial and that only candidates are actual subjects). Three important conclusions are evident from these data. First, the candidates' strategies are not scattered randomly across the entire issue space; rather, they are constrained for the most part to Pareto-optimal positions. Second, the dispersion of positions decreases as the experiments proceed. Although the candidates do not appear to be converging to a specific point (compare these figures with Figure 5.8b), the candidates tend to select positions near the "middle" of the space – positions that fall generally in the support set of a mixed strategy solution to the game. Finally, the dispersion of positions is less with nine voters than with five voters. Hence, since the size of

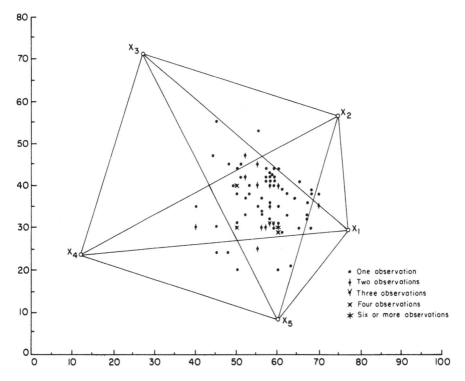

Figure 5.12b. Outcomes of Last 5 Trials of Five-Voter Spatial Election without an Equilibrium (from McKelvey and Ordeshook 1982)

the uncovered set decreases, in general, as the density of ideal points increases, these data are consistent with the hypothesis that candidates are attracted to positions within this set.

4. UNRESTRICTED MAJORITY RULE AND COMMITTEES WITHOUT CORES

Although sound reasons suggest that the description of mixed minmax strategies drawn from a static description of an election is of limited empirical relevance owing to the sequential nature of campaigns, the uncovered set itself is important because it places limits on undominated spatial positions. This fact, in turn, provides a theoretical basis for supposing that candidates

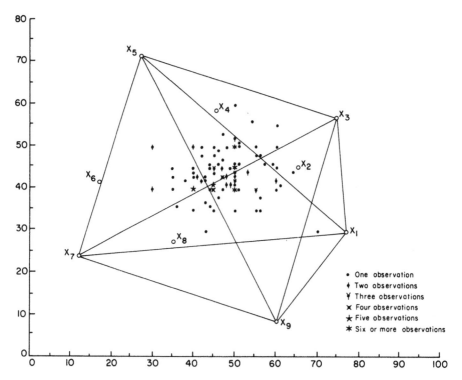

Figure 5.12c. Outcomes of First 5 Trials of Nine-Voter Spatial Election without an Equilbrium (from McKelvey and Ordeshook 1982)

will not "wander too far." But matters are far less clear for cooperative committees without cores. Although we can show that various cooperative solution concepts, such as the V-set, necessarily predict outcomes that are uncovered, our confidence in these concepts does not equal our confidence in the core or in the hypothesis that people will not choose dominated alternatives. Consequently, experimental research into cooperative spatial committees without cores serves more of an exploratory function – testing tentative ideas and suggesting alternative approaches. It is unfortunate that, owing to the specific concerns of individual researchers, this research comprises something less than a well-integrated experimental package. Indeed, procedures often are incomparable even though the experimental evidence suggests that variations in these procedures may be of profound significance.

One model of cooperative spatial committees without cores is McKelvey, Ordeshook, and Winer's (1978) competitive solution. In brief, the invention

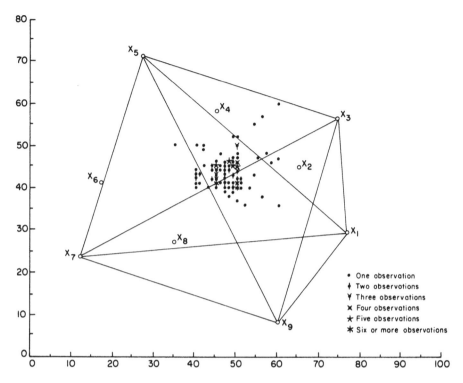

Figure 5.12d. Outcomes of Last 5 Trials of Nine-Voter Spatial Election without an Equilbrium (from McKelvey and Ordeshook 1982)

of competitive solution is a response, first, to the fact that concepts such as the main-simple V-set and the various bargaining sets are typically empty for spatial games without cores, and second, to the unreasonableness of the supposition that the absence of a core implies "chaos" in simple majority rule institutions. To test this solution hypothesis, McKelvey, Ordeshook, and Winer offer a series of spatial experiments in which (a) subjects are told the ideal points of other players, and everyone knows that all indifference contours are circles; (b) free and open discussion is permitted – no specific parliamentary voting mechanism is employed – with the sole prohibition that subjects cannot reveal their actual monetary payoffs; and (c) an experiment ends when some majority indicates that it has reached an agreement, and the members of that majority sign a document to that effect. Figure 5.13 reports the outcomes of six experimental sessions. Similarly, Figures 5.14a through 5.14d report on a series of sixty experiments reported by Ordeshook and

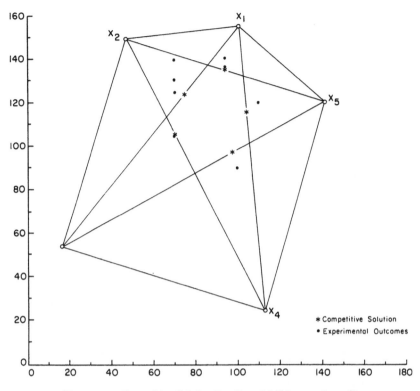

Figure 5.13. Competitive Solution Test (from McKelvey et al. 1978)

Winer (1980) that use weighted voting (the weights are the numbers beside each committee member's ideal point). In general, these data support the competitive solution and thereby disconfirm the supposition that the absence of the core implies chaos.

Laing and Olmstead (1978) report on a series of spatial experiments that use different configurations of ideal point but identical procedures, with one exception – subjects play a sequence of otherwise independent games. Their results are difficult to interpret because of the possibility of multiple-trial agreements among subjects. Indeed, Laing and Olmstead exclude two experimental sessions out of nineteen from their analysis, owing to explicit agreements to choose successively the ideal points of different players. With this qualification in mind, Figure 5.15 summarizes the outcomes from one of their preference configurations. This particular configuration is especially interesting because it does not appear to yield a competitive solution, and it thus serves as a counterexample to the conjecture that this solution exists in general for all simple games. To the extent that the outcomes in Figure 5.15 are close to an "approximate" solution, it suggests that although the competitive solution captures essential features of bargaining with spatial preferences, this concept either needs refinement or that a new hypothesis must be formulated that is consistent with the competitive solution's predictions.

Laing and Olmstead raise a theoretical problem for the competitive solution in particular, but with a series of finite alternative (nonspatial) experiments designed to discriminate among cooperative game-theoretic solution hypotheses, McKelvey and Ordeshook (1983) show that this solution needs not predict outcomes. In fact, the data they report suggest that the cardinality of utility plays an important role in the patterns of outcomes. Miller and Oppenheimer (1982) attempt a systematic study of the effects of the cardinality of preferences, and they also show that cardinality affects the performance of the competitive solution. It is evident, then, that much critical theorizing remains before any definitive conclusions can be reached concerning the specific outcomes that prevail in a cooperative environment.

The experimental evidence on cooperative games without cores, then, yields the following general conclusions. First, the absence of a core does not imply incoherence or chaos – patterns to the data warrant explanation. Second, "classical" solution hypotheses such as the V-set and the various bargaining sets are, as presently formulated, wholly inadequate. Third, the competitive solution captures an important feature of bargaining and coalition formation, but, for theoretical reasons, it cannot be regarded as a satisfactory general hypothesis. Finally, although the distribution of outcomes is somewhat sensitive to the cardinality of preferences when the core is not empty (see Salant and Goodstein 1987), cardinality appears to be more important when the core is empty.

5. COMMITTEES AND THE CONSEQUENCES OF INSTITUTIONS

The experiments that the previous section reviews concern a particular institution—unrestricted majority rule, but it represents only one institution drawn from a potentially infinite variety that might describe actual political systems. And alternative institutions can have significant theoretical consequences: They can change the nature of the core, they can induce a nonempty core for cases in which no such equilibrium exists under unrestricted majority rule, or they can render the core empty. An especially graphic illustration of the first possibility is offered by Kormendi and Plott (1982). Using a preference configuration and procedures that match the open-discussion experiments of Fiorina and Plott (1978), but which employ a nomonetary preference-inducement mechanism (student grades were dependent on their performance as

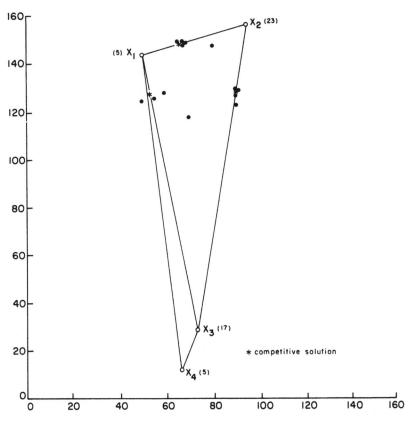

Figure 5.14a. Weighted Voting Test of Competitive Solution (from Ordeshook and Winer 1980)

subjects), Kormendi and Plott, in Figure 5.16a, report the results of seven experimental outcomes, all clustered tightly about the core. In Figure 5.16b, however, voter 4 is the only subject allowed to make motions. Hence, voter 4 must be a member of any coalition to upset the status quo, in which case the core corresponds to all outcomes that lie on the dashed line connecting 4's ideal point to the original core. Similarly, in Figure 5.16c, voter 4's role is given to voter 5 so that the core now corresponds to the dashed line shown there. Figure 5.16c especially shows how this simple procedural variation, by changing the core, changes the pattern of outcomes.

Laing and Slotznik (1987a) consider a different mechanism for inducing a nonempty core – four-fifths majority rule. In the five-person preference

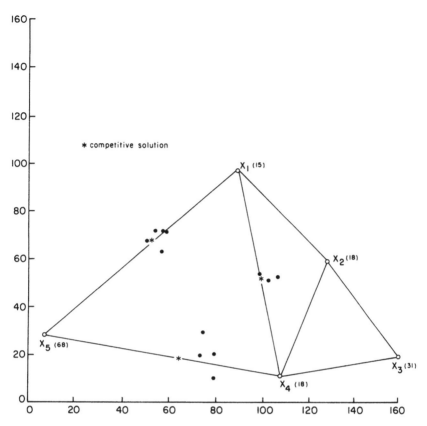

Figure 5.14b. Weighted Voting Test of Competitive Solution (from Ordeshook and Winer 1980)

configuration in Figure 5.17, the interior hatched quadrilateral (called the "heartland" by Laing and Slotznick) corresponds to those points that are Pareto-optimal for every winning coalition (every coalition with four or five members). Under simple majority rule, such points, if they exist, correspond to the core, whereas for the particular preference configuration in this figure, simple majority rule yields an empty core (indeed, this figure depicts Laing and Olmstead's example of a spatial game with no competitive solution). With unusual majorities, however, we cannot identify a core without referring to a status quo point, since we must also identify the outcomes that blocking coalitions can ensure. Suppose, then, that the point s' is the status quo. The two "lenses" attached to this point denote the alternatives that defeat s' under

129

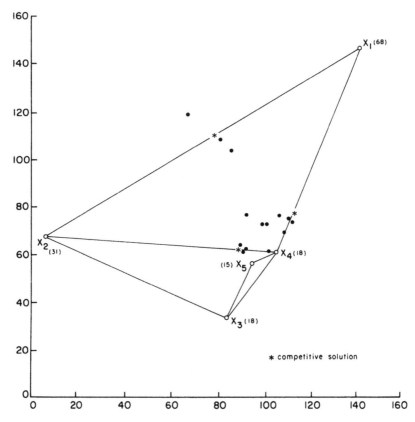

Figure 5.14c. Weighted Voting Test of Competitive Solution (from Ordeshook and Winer 1980)

four-fifths rule, and the intersection of these lenses with the heartland is the core of the corresponding game. If these lenses fail to intersect in the hatched region, as is the case with a status quo at s″, the core is empty. Hence, theoretically, we predict outcomes "near" or in the intersections of these lenses with the heartland when the status quo is s′, and although there is no specific prediction for this game when there is no core, we should anticipate a wider dispersion of outcomes when the status quo at s″.

Laing and Slotznick report on ten experiments using the preference configuration in Figure 5.17, as well as two other configurations, in conjunction with the open discussion procedures that McKelvey, Ordeshook, and Winer (1978) apply to their test of the competitive solution. Figure 5.17 reports their

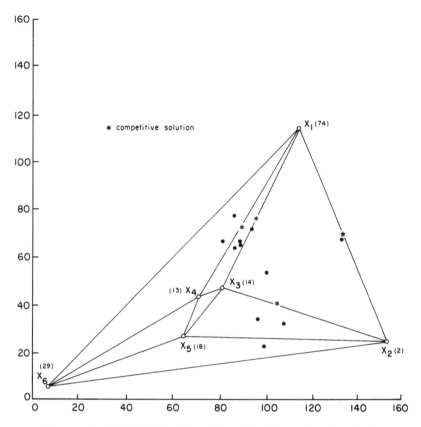

Figure 5.14d. Weighted Voting Test of Competitive Solution (from Ordeshook and Winer 1980)

data, where x's denote outcomes with the status quo at s', and o's denote outcomes with the status quo at s". In this instance, it is apparent that the evidence is merely suggestive and not conclusive. The x's do in fact tend to cluster more strongly than the o's, but only one x is in the core itself. The particular feature of Laing and Slotznick's procedure that may account for these discrepancies is the one we cite earlier: subjects play a series of experiments and are thereby allowed the opportunity to reach multitrial agreements. Indeed, two experimental series are deleted from the study owing to the explicit appearance of such an agreement. Grether, Isaak, and Plott (1981), for example, report on a series of single-trial experiments using unanimity rule that strongly support the theoretical prediction that unanimity renders

Richard D. McKelvey and Peter C. Ordeshook

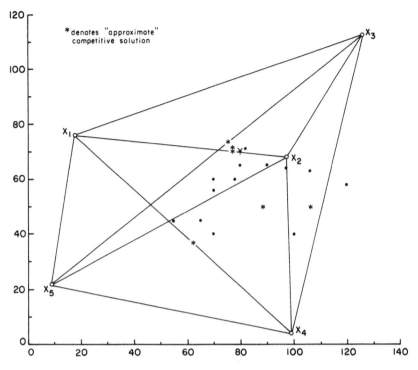

Figure 5.15. A Game Without a Competitive Solution (from Laing and Olmstead 1978)

the status quo as the unique core outcome. Laing and Sloztnick (1987b), on the other hand, describe a series of unanimity experiments in which, although the core performs better that all other hypotheses considered, sharp deviations from the core are evident. Again, though, they employ a procedure in which subjects play a sequence of games in which multitrial agreements are possible

The role played by a status quo depends, of course, on the procedural choice context. In Laing and Slotznick's experiments, that role is determined by the four-fifths voting requirement. An alternative possibility is that committees proceed by an endogenously determined agenda in which the status quo enters the agenda, as in the Fiorina-Plott experiments, as the first motion to be voted on (forward agendas), or as the alternative entered in the agenda's final stage (backward agendas). In a forward agenda, the status quo, theoretically at least, should play little role in the final outcome, whereas in the backward agenda, only outcomes that defeat the status quo should be selected. Wilson (1986) documents this fact in a series of experiments played by

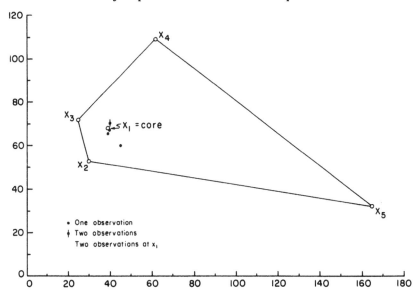

Figure 5.16a. No Agenda-Setter (from Kormendi and Plott 1982)

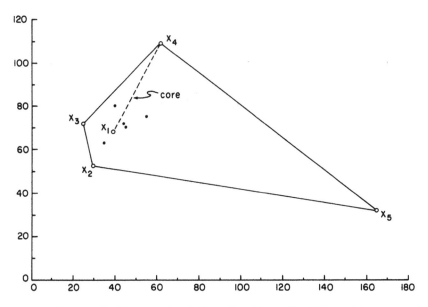

Figure 5.16b. Voter 4 as Agenda-Setter (from Kormendi and Plott 1982)

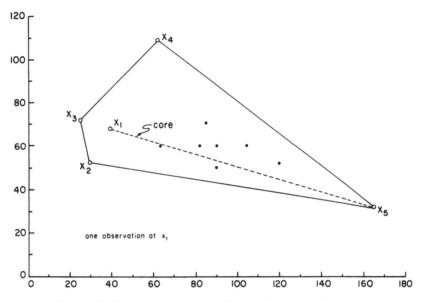

Figure 5.16c. Voter 5 as Agenda-Setter (from Kormendi and Plott 1982)

subjects, without discussion, over computer terminals. Figures 5.18a and b summarize his findings and show that with a backward agenda, outcomes always fall in the lenses that correspond to alternatives that defeat the status quo; with forward agendas, no such pattern is evident.

By precluding the possibility of direct communication and discussion, Wilson ensures that the agenda formed by a decentralized and computerized process is adhered to by committee members. Unfortunately, we have little theoretical knowledge about optimal strategies for endogenous agenda setting (for some results, see McKelvey 1986) and thus we cannot interpret further the dispersion of outcomes that Figure 5.18b reports. We can offer one speculation: If communication and coordination are allowed, other aspects of procedural structure should be less influential. Similarly, McKelvey and Ordeshook (1984) study a different procedural variant that induces a stable point for a preference configuration that does not yield a core under unrestricted majority rule.

In theory, if voting proceeds issue-by-issue without discussion, and if indifference contours are circles, then the unique stable point is the issue-by-issue median (Kramer 1972). Figures 5.19a and b summarize the outcomes of the experiments designed to test this hypothesis. The procedures adopted here

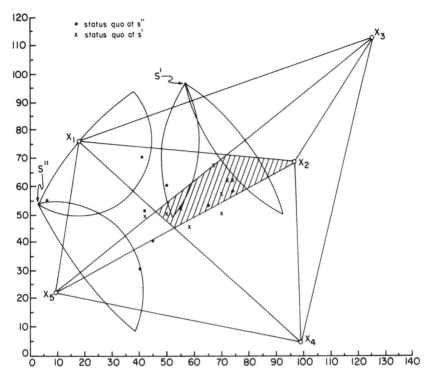

Figure 5.17. Four-Fifths Majority Rule (from Laing and Slotznick 1987a)

correspond identically to those that Fiorina and Plott use when subjects are not allowed to hold any discussion, with the exception that motions can differ from the status quo on only one dimension. The comparison of these figures with the data that Figure 5.13 reports when unrestricted majority rule is in force reveals the influence on outcomes of an issue-by-issue constraint. Notice, in particular, that unlike the experimental outcomes that prevail with unrestricted discussion (see Figure 5.13), nearly all outcomes here lie in the interior pentagon of the figures. Further, when preferences are rotated so as to move the location of the issue-by-issue median, the mean outcome tracks that point (compare Figures 5.19a and 5.19b).

The theoretical prediction that follows from Kramer's analysis supposes that committee members cannot communicate to form binding agreements. If such agreements are allowed, then the issue-by-issue procedural context as well as the specific orientation of ideal points in the space become the-

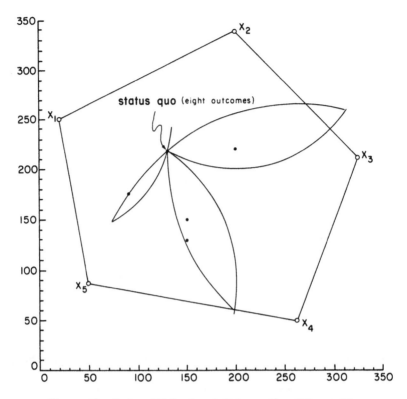

Figure 5.18a. Backward Voting Agenda Outcomes (from Wilson 1986)

oretically irrelevant, and the committee is effectively acting under unrestricted majority rule. With this argument in mind, McKelvey and Ordeshook also report on an experimental series that requires issue-by-issue voting, but which permits subjects to discuss matters freely prior to each vote. Figures 5.20a and 5.20b summarize their results, and the comparison of these data to the data in Figure 5.13, Figures 5.18a, and 5.18b is informative. Specifically, notice that the dispersion of outcomes in Figures 5.20a and 5.20b falls somewhere between the dispersion in Figure 5.13 and the dispersions in Figure 5.19a and 5.19b, and the mean outcome moves away from the issue-by-issue stable point. The inference drawn from these data is that as the constraints on the imposition of a procedure such as issue-by-issue voting are relaxed – as the costs of reverting to unrestricted majority rule are decreased – majority coalitions that find it in their interest to bypass restrictive procedures will in fact

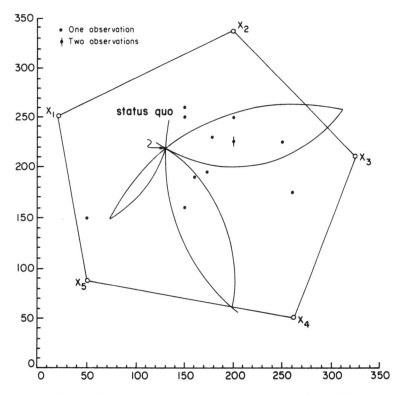

Figure 5.18b. Forward Voting Agenda Outcomes (from Wilson 1986)

bypass them. And if these costs are zero, outcomes should follow the pattern in Figure 5.13.

6. CONCLUSIONS

It has been slightly more than ten years since Fiorina and Plott and Berl et al. published their experimental results about cores and Condorcet winners. This research and the research proceeding from it tells us, first, that the concept of the core, at least in the context of spatial preferences and majority rule, is predictive for a wide range of institutions. Second, the Condorcet winner as an equilibrium strategy for candidates in two-candidate elections has impressive credentials as a predictive concept. There are disquieting notes, to be sure, such as those finite alternative experiments in which cores are not

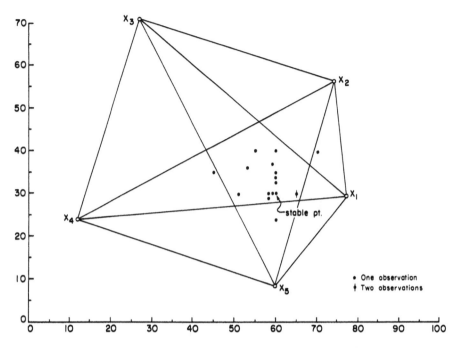

Figure 5.19a. Discussion Prohibited, Issue-by-issue Voting (from McKelvey and Ordeshook 1984)

chosen by subjects. But the experiments run to date leave no doubt that the development of political and economic theory must heed the definition of rational action encapsulated by these concepts.

Although experimental research gives us confidence in our theoretical research in situations in which a core exists, it can make a more impressive contribution. With the discovery that Condorcet winners are rare with spatial preferences and that cyclic social preferences can extend across the entire space of feasible alternatives (McKelvey 1976, 1979), some scholars were led to the belief that political processes are inherently unstable and unpredictable (Riker 1984). Others, believing that only the possibility of rendering unique predictions is removed if a game's core is empty, and the like, began the development of alternative equilibrium notions such as the uncovered set and the competitive solution. Experimental research supports this second view. In addition, it has guided the development of new equilibrium concepts, and has led us to reject outright ideas such as the V-set and the bargaining set, and to seriously question the generality of alternative cooperative solution hypotheses such as the competitive solution.

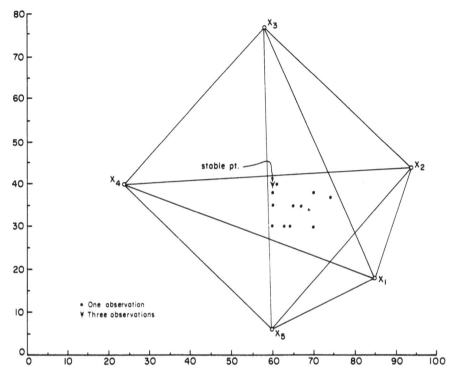

Figure 5.19b. Discussion Prohibited, Issue-by-issue Voting (from McKelvey and Ordeshook 1984)

Finally, experimental research contributes in a natural way to our understanding of the role of procedures and institutions in economic and political processes. Experimental research, by its very nature, is intimately involved with institutional design. Every set of instructions and every variable considered in the implementation of an experiment is an aspect of institutional design, which readers the experimentalist especially sensitive to institutions and their implications. Predictably, then, experimental research, taken as a whole, gives us a view of the sensitivity and insensitivity of outcomes to alternative formal and informal procedures. The data, for example, suggest that knowledge about the preferences of others plays little if any role in committees with unrestricted majority rule; procedures such as issue-by-issue voting can restrict outcomes and induce stability, but only to the extent that those procedures also limit the ability of committee members to communicate directly and negotiate agreements; the requirement that only unusual majorities can modify the status quo works in a theoretically proscribed way;

139

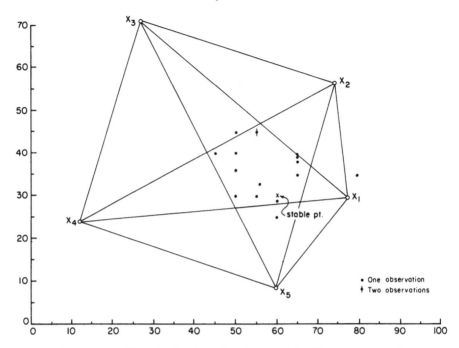

Figure 5.20a. Discussion Permitted, Issue-by-issue Voting (from McKelvey and Ordeshook 1984)

theoretical predictions work better in larger committees; and the theory of two-candidate elections is robust to important forms of incomplete information.

Experimentation also makes us sensitive to procedural effects about which we know little in theory. For example, Hoffman and Plott (1983) suggest that formal procedures can significantly effect the consequences of informal pre-meeting discussions. Quoting their conclusion at length, they surmise that

If the rule is simple majority, with no Robert's Rules provisions, the coalitions formed during the pre-meeting discussions simply vote in the agreed alternative with very little discussion or debate. Under the Robert's Rules provisions which can for discussions and the orderly submission of amendments, the proposal advanced by the pre-formed coalition is immediately challenged by amendment. During the ensuing discussion information is generated which reveals the potential advantages of other possibly successful motions . . . It seems that the institutional arrangements foster a search and informational gathering activity. [p. 34]

In summary, then, the experimental research that this essay reviews gives us considerable confidence that the large body of theoretical research into spatial models of committees and elections is not without sound empirical content.

140

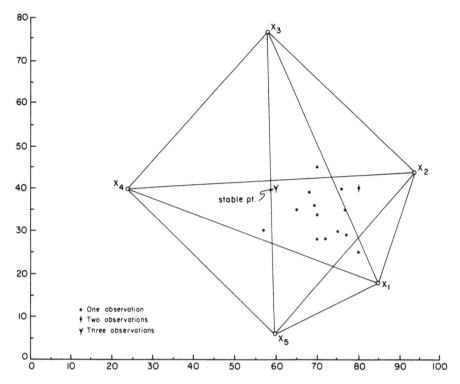

Figure 5.20b. Discussion Permitted, Issue-by-issue Voting (from McKelvey and Ordeshook 1984)

Certainly, those models may have to be elaborated before we can apply them directly to the study of, for example, the U.S. Congress, parliaments, and actual elections. But those same experiments, in addition to revealing fruitful avenues of opportunity for the theorist, also suggest how theoretical models can be adapted to environments outside the laboratory.

REFERENCES

Berl, Janet, Richard D. McKelvey, Peter C. Ordeshook, and Mark D. Winer, 1976. "An Experimental Test of the Core in a Simple N-Person Cooperative Nonsidepayment Game." *Journal of Conflict Resolution* 20, 3: 453–79.

Black, Duncan. 1958. *The Theory of Committees and Elections,* Cambridge: Cambridge Univ. Press.

Collier, Kenneth, Richard D. McKelvey, Peter C. Ordeshook, and Kenneth C. Williams. 1987. "Retrospective Voting: An Experimental Study," *Public Choice.*

Cox, Gary. 1987. "Electoral Equilibrium in Multicandidate Elections: Plurality vs. Approval Voting," Univ. of Texas (mimeo).

Davis, Otto A., and Melvin J. Hinich, 1966. "A Mathematical Model of Policy Formation in a Democratic Society." In J. L. Bernd, ed., *Mathematical Applications and Political Science* II, Dallas: SMU Press.

———. 1968. "On the Power and Importance of the Mean Preference in a Mathematical Model of Democratic Choice," *Public Choice* 5: 59–72.

Davis, Otto A., Melvin J. Hinich, and Morris DeGroot. 1972. "Social Preference Orderings and Majority Rule." *Econometrica* 40: 147–57.

Eavey, Cheryl, and Gary Miller. 1984a. "Bureaucratic Agenda Control: Imposition or Bargaining." *American Political Science Review* 78: 719–33.

———. 1984b. "Experimental Evidence on the Fallibility of the Core." *American Journal of Political Science* 28: 570–86.

Enelow, James, and Melvin J. Hinich. 1983. "Voting One Issue at a Time: The Question of Voter Forecasts." *American Political Science Review* 77: 435–45.

———. 1984. *The Spatial Theory of Voting*. Cambridge: Cambridge Univ. Press.

Fiorina, Morris P. 1981. *Retrospective Voting in American National Elections*, New Haven: Yale Univ. Press.

Fiorina, Morris P., and Charles R. Plott. 1978. "Committee Decisions Under Majority Rule: An Experimental Study." *American Political Science Review* 72: 575–98.

Grether, David. M., R. Mark Isaak, and Charles R. Plott. 1981. "The Allocation of Landing Rights by Unanimity Among Competitors." *American Economic Review* 71: 166–71.

Grey, Peter, Richard D. McKelvey, and Peter C. Ordeshook. 1986. "Some Experimental Results on Retrospective Voting in Multidimensional Elections." Paper presented at the 1986 Public Choice Society Meetings.

Hoffman, Elizabeth, and Charles R. Plott. 1983. "Pre-meeting Discussions and the Possibility of Coalition-Breaking Procedures in Majority Rule Committees." *Public Choice* 40: 21–39.

Key, V. O. 1966. *The Responsible Electorate*. New York: Vintage Press.

Kormendi, Roger C., and Charles R. Plott. 1982. "Committee Decisions Under Alternative Procedural Rules." *Journal of Economic Behavior and Organization* 3: 175–95.

Kramer, Gerald. 1972. "Sophisticated Voting Over Multidimensional Choice Spaces." *Journal of Mathematical Sociology* 2: 165–81.

———. 1977. "A Dynamical Model of Political Equilibrium." *Journal of Economic Theory* 16: 310–34.

Laing, James D., and Scott Olmstead. 1978. "An Experimental and Game Theoretic Study of Committees." In P. C. Ordeshook, ed., *Game Theory and Political Science*. New York: NYU Press.

Laing, James D., and Benjamin Slotznick. 1987a. "Viable Alternative to the Status Quo." *Journal of Conflict Resolution* 31: 63–85.

———. 1987b. "When Anyone Can Veto: A Laboratory Study of Committees Governed by Unanimous Rule." *Behavioral Science*.

Levine, Michael E., and Charles R. Plott. 1977. "Agenda Influence and Its Implications." *Virginia Law Review* (May): 561–604.

McKelvey, Richard D. 1976. "Intransitivities in Multidimensional Voting Models and Some Implications for Agenda Control." *Journal of Economic Theory* 16: 472–82.

———. 1979. "General Conditions for Global Intransitivities in Formal Voting Models." *Econometrica:* 1085–1112.

————. 1986. "Covering, Dominance, and the Institution-Free Properties of Social Choice." *American Journal of Political Science* 30, 2: 283–314.

McKelvey, Richard D., and Peter C. Ordeshook. 1979. "Symmetric Spatial Elections without Majority Rule Equilibria." *American Political Science Review*, 70: 1172–84.

————. 1981. "Experiments on the Core: Some Disconcerting Results for Majority Rule Voting Games." *Journal of Conflict Resolution* 25: 472–82.

————. 1982. "Two-Candidate Elections Without Majority Rule Equilibria: An Experimental Study." *Simulation and Games* 13: 311–35.

————. 1983. "Some Experimental Results That Fail to Support the Competitive Solution." *Public Choice* 40: 281–91.

————. 1984. "An Experimental Study of the Effects of Procedural Rules on Committee Behavior." *Journal of Politics* 46: 182–205.

————. 1985a. "Rational Expectations in Elections: Some Experimental Results Based on a Multidimensional Model." *Public Choice* 44: 61–102.

————. 1985b. "Elections with Limited Information: A Fulfilled Expectations Model Using Contemporaneous Poll and Endorsement Data as Information Sources." *Journal of Economic Theory* 36: 55–85.

————. 1987. "Elections with Limited Information: A Multidimensional Model." *Mathematical Social Science*, 14: 77–99.

McKelvey, Richard D., Peter C. Ordeshook, and Mark Winer. 1978. "The Competitive Solution for N-Person Games without Sidepayments: *American Political Science Review* 72: 599–615.

Miller, Gary, and Joe A. Oppenheimer. 1982. "Universalism in Experimental Committees." *American Political Science Review* 76: 561–74.

Miller, Nicholas. 1980. "A New Solution Set for Tournaments and Majority Voting." *American Journal of Political Science* 24: 68–96.

Ordeshook, Peter C., and Thomas Palfrey. 1988. "Agendas, Strategic Voting, and Signaling with Incomplete information." *American Journal of Political Science*, 32(2): 441–66.

Ordeshook, Peter C., and Thomas Schwartz. 1987. "Agendas and the Control of Political Outcomes." *American Political Science Review*, 81(1): 179–99.

Ordeshook, Peter C., and Mark Winer. 1980. "Coalitions and Spatial Policy Outcomes in Parliamentary Systems: Some Experimental Results." *American Journal of Political Science* 24, 4: 730–51.

Plott, Charles R. 1967. "A Notion of Equilibrium Under Majority Rule." *American Economic Review* 57: 787–806.

————. 1977. "A Comparative Analysis of Direct Democracy, Two Candidate Elections, and Three Candidate Elections in an Experimental Environment." Social Science Working Paper 457, Calif. Inst. of Technology.

————. 1978. "On the Incorporation of Public Attitudes Toward Administrative Options." In J. A. Staffa, ed., *Risk/Benefit Decisions and the Public Health*, HEW Publication # (FDA) 80–1069.

————. 1979. "The Application of Laboratory Experimental Methods to Public Choice." In C. Russell, ed. *Collective Decision Making: Applications from Public Choice Theory*. Washington, D.C.: Resources for the Future.

Rae, Douglas, and Michael Taylor. 1971. "Decision Rules and Policy Outcomes." *British Journal of Political Science* 1: 71–90.

Riker, William H. 1984. *Liberalism Versus Populism*. San Francisco: Freeman.

Salant, Steven, and Eban Goodstein. 1987. "Committee Voting Under Alternative Procedures and Preferences: An Experimental Analysis." Univ. of Michigan (mimeo).

Schofield, Norman. 1983. "Generic Instability of Majority Rule." *Review of Economic Studies* 50: 695–705.

Shepsle, Kenneth, and Barry Weingast. 1981. "Structure Induced Equilibrium and Legislative Choice." *Public Choice:* 503–19.

Wilson, Rick K. 1986. "Forward and Backward Agenda Procedures: Committee Experiments on Structurally Induced Equilibrium." *Journal of Politics* 48: 390–409.

6

Candidate Uncertainty and Electoral Equilibria

PETER J. COUGHLIN

University of Maryland
College Park

Enelow and Hinich (1990) have made it clear that the spatial theory of voting encompasses a large number of alternative models of committees and elections and deals with a large number of questions about these models. This particular essay is concerned with an important topic in the spatial theory of voting that has been addressed in a number of different references in the literature: the implications (for two-candidate elections) of candidate uncertainty about whom the individual voters in the electorate will vote for. More specifically, this chapter will concentrate on what has been learned about the implications of the presence of this type of uncertainty for the existence and location of an electoral equilibrium.

Spatial voting theorists have become interested in the implications of candidate uncertainty about voters' choices primarily because there are good empirical reasons for believing that actual candidates often *are* uncertain about the choices that voters are going to make on election day. First, candidates tend to rely on polls for information about how voters will vote, but "information from public opinion surveys is not error-free and is best represented as statistical" (Ordeshook 1986, p. 179). Second, even when economists and political scientists have developed sophisticated statistical models of voters' choices and have used appropriate data sets to estimate them, there has consistently been a residual amount of unexplained variation (see, for instance, Fiorina 1981; Enelow and Hinich 1984a, chap. 9; Enelow, Hinich, and Mendell 1986).

These circumstances have led many empirically-oriented public choice scholars to the following view, expressed in Fiorina's empirical analysis of voting behavior: "In the real world choices are seldom so clean as those suggested by formal decision theory. Thus real decision makers are best analyzed in probabilistic rather than deterministic terms" (1981, p. 155). Some theoretically-oriented public choice scholars have also adopted the same view and have developed and analyzed the theoretical properties of models in which candidates are assumed to have probabilistic (rather than deterministic)

145

expectations about voters' choices. More specifically, these theorists have carried out these studies because, as Ordeshook put it, "if we want to design models that take cognizance of the kind of data that the candidates are likely to possess, probabilistic models seem more reasonable" (1986, p. 179).

The analyses that will be discussed in detail in this essay are ones where the authors assumed that either (a) all voters vote or (b) a voter abstains if and only if he is indifferent between the two candidates. Similar assumptions were made in Hotelling's discussion of elections (1929, pp. 54–5), in Arrow's analysis of "the method of majority decision" (1951/1963, chaps. 5 and 7), in Downs's formulation of "the basic logic of voting" (1957, chap. 3), and in Black's book on committees and elections (1958). The results that will be discussed here are, therefore, ones that can be more readily compared with the results in these pioneering references on voting theory than would be the case if *both* candidate uncertainty *and* abstentions played important roles. In addition, discussing only analyses that have no (or no significant) candidate uncertainty about who will vote also has the benefit of placing the focus entirely on the implications of candidate uncertainty about the voters' choices between the candidates.[1]

The topic that this chapter is concerned with is one that I have worked on (see the earlier discussions of models with candidate uncertainty in Calvert (1986), Coughlin (1986), and Ordeshook (1986)). I will nonetheless (at least partially) resist the temptation to put my own work at "center stage" in this survey, for two reasons. First, the work by others on the topic has been of sufficient quality and quantity that my discussion of their work will easily fill an entire paper. Second, since a scholar can usually be more objective in assessing the work of others than in assessing his own work, my summaries and discussions of the work of other scholars seem to me to be of greater value. The sole exception will be a discussion of my collaborative research with Nitzan (1981a; 1981b), but this is only a partial exception (since I can claim only half of the credit for the results in those papers).

The literature on candidate uncertainty and electoral equilibria does not, unfortunately, have a uniform system of notation. I could choose to deal with this problem by using the original notation in discussing each reference. I will not, however, use that approach, because it would be cumbersome (since entirely new notation would have to be defined for each new reference) and confusing (since the same symbol would end up meaning different things in different situations). I will, instead, introduce a uniform system of notation in the next section, and then use this notation when stating the assumptions in each of the references covered in detail. Section 1 will also include their common assumptions (that is, the assumptions that are made in *all* of these references). This approach will emphasize that all the analyses can be considered within a single analytical framework. It will also facilitate comparisons and contrasts of the assumptions and results discussed here.

Candidate Uncertainty and Electoral Equilibria

Sections 2 through 7 will discuss published work that, in my view, has contributed to our current knowledge about the *implications* of candidate uncertainty about voter choices *for* the existence and location of electoral equilibria. In the conclusion (Section 8), I will briefly mention some important working papers on candidate uncertainty and electoral equilibria.

I. UNIFORM NOTATION AND COMMON ASSUMPTIONS

Each assumption made in this section, except for the assumption that will be made about the candidates' objectives, is made in all of the references discussed in detail in Sections 2–7. The alternative assumptions about the candidates' objectives that have been made in these references are discussed near the end of this section.

There are two candidates, $c = 1,2$, for a particular political office. There is a nonempty set, S, which is the strategy set for *both* candidate 1 and candidate 2. S is assumed to be a subset of a Euclidean space, E^ℓ. $\psi_c \in S$ denotes a strategy for candidate c. There is a set, N, of eligible voters. A particular individual in this set is denoted by $i \in N$. For each $i \in N$, there are two "probabilistic voting functions," $P_i^1: SxS \rightarrow [0,1]$ and $P_i^2: SxS \rightarrow [0,1]$, that are such that, for each $c \in \{1,2\}$ and $(\psi_1,\psi_2) \in SxS$, the corresponding number $P_i^c(\psi_1,\psi_2)$ is the subjective (conditional) probability for the event "i will vote for candidate c, given that $c = 1$ chooses ψ_1 and $c = 2$ chooses ψ_2" for *both* candidate 1 and candidate 2.

The expected vote for candidate c (when $c = 1$ chooses ψ_1 and $c = 2$ chooses ψ_2 is denoted by $EV^c(\psi_1,\psi_2)$. The expected plurality for candidate c at a particular pair of candidate strategies, $(\psi_1,\psi_2) \in SxS$, is denoted by $P\ell^c(\psi_1,\psi_2)$. It is assumed that each candidate's objective is to maximize his expected plurality. Accordingly, an "equilibrium" will be any pair, $(\psi_1^*,\psi_2^*) \in S \times S$, that is a Nash equilibrium for the game $(S,S;P\ell^1,P\ell^2)$. Since the game is zero-sum, this statement is (of course) equivalent to the statement that the pair must be a saddle point for $P\ell^1$.

Some of the references discussed in detail in the ensuing sections have, alternatively, assumed that each candidate's objective is to maximize his expected vote (to wit: Hinich 1977; Enelow and Hinich 1982, 1984a). Aranson, Hinich, and Ordeshook (1973), however, have established that when (as in all of the models covered in Sections 2–7) voters abstain only if they are indifferent, this assumption is equivalent to assuming that each candidate's objective is to maximize his expected plurality. That is, when indifference is necessary for abstention, a pair of strategies, $(\psi_1^*,\psi_2^*) \in S \times S$, is a Nash equilibrium in the game $(S,S;EV^1,EV^2)$ if and only if (ψ_1^*,ψ_2^*) is a Nash equilibrium in the game $(S,S;P\ell^1,P\ell^2)$.

Some of the references discussed in the ensuing sections have considered *both* what happens when each candidate is assumed to maximize his expected plurality *and* what happens under the alternative assumption that each candidate maximizes his probability of winning (to wit: Samuelson 1984; Lindbeck and Weibull 1987). In addition, fairly general assumptions that imply the equivalence of this alternative and the assumption that the candidates maximize expected plurality have been identified by Aranson, Hinich, and Ordeshook (1973), Hinich (1977), and others. What's more, (a) Samuelson (1984) shows that, under the particular conditions where he considers this alternative assumption, "maximizing expected plurality and probability of winning are equivalent objectives" (p. 313) commonly and (b) Lindbeck and Weibull (1987) establish that, under the conditions where they consider this alternative assumption, "the necessary first-order condition is the same as in the expected-plurality game" (p. 286). Hence, nothing of significance is lost by assuming that each candidate's objective is to maximize his expected plurality.

Finally, since each of the references covered in Sections 2 through 7 explicitly or (in using expected vote or probability of winning in place of expected plurality) implicitly makes all of the assumptions that have been made in this section, these assumptions will not be repeated in the ensuing sections. Rather, each time a theorem is stated, it will be understood that its premise includes *both* the assumptions that are stated before it (in the section where the theorem appears) *and* the assumptions that have been made here.

2. CANDIDATE UNCERTAINTY AND THE MEDIAN VOTER RESULT

Hinich (1977) initiated the recent research that has been done on the implications of candidates' being uncertain about whom the individual voters in the electorate will vote for. In that article, he reexamined the unidimensional Hotelling–Downs model and showed that "if there is even a small amount of indeterminateness in voter choices . . . then the general equilibrium at the median no longer holds" (p. 209). He established this result with the following three-voter example.

Example 2.1 (Hinch 1977, p. 213): Let $N = \{1, 2, 3\}$. Assume that, for each $i \in N$ and each pair $\psi_1, \psi_2 \in S$,

$$P_i^1(\psi_1, \psi_2) = 1 - P_i^2(\psi_1, \psi_2) \tag{2.1}$$

and

$$P_i^1(\psi_1, \psi_2) = P_i(|\psi_2 - x_i| - |\psi_1 - x_i|) \tag{2.2}$$

where (a) P_i is differentiable, (b) $P_i'(y) \geq 0$, $\forall y$, (c) $P_i'(y) > 0$ in some range of its argument and (d) $P_i(0) = 1/2$. Note that (2.1) implies that the candidates expect each of the three voters in N to vote. The x_i parameters in (2.2) are the voters' ideal points, and have the following values: $x_1 = -1$, $x_2 = 0$ and $x_3 = 100$. Assume that $P_1(y) = P_2(y)$, $\forall y$ and that

$$P_3(y) = \begin{cases} 1 & \text{if } y > 0 \\ 1/2 & \text{if } y = 0 \\ 0 & \text{if } y < 0. \end{cases} \tag{2.3}$$

Finally, assume that there exists an $r > 0$ such that $[0,r) \subset S$.

Hinich pointed out that, even though the *median* voter ideal point, $m = 0$, is a feasible strategy for each candidate, (m,m) is *not* an equilibrium (1977, p. 213). In particular, he noted that this conclusion follows because the assumptions in the example imply that there exists some $\epsilon > 0$ such that candidate 1 would be better off if he unilaterally changed his strategy from m to $m + \epsilon$. Hence, as Hinich (1977) put it, "this simple example shows that the median is not an equilibrium when probabilistic voting is introduced" (p. 213).

As Hinich's discussion of the example suggests (see p. 214), this unidimensional example is also one where there may be no equilibrium at all. This fact can be easily illustrated in the special case of Example 2.1, where $S = [-1, +1]$ and

$$P_1(y) = P_2(y) = \frac{1}{2} + \frac{y}{2} \tag{2.4}$$

at each possible y. Note that (2.1) and (2.4) imply that, analogous to (2.2),

$$P_i^2(\psi_1, \psi_2) = P_i(|\psi_1 - x_i| - |\psi_2 - x_i|) \tag{2.5}$$

holds for $i = 1,2$, at each pair $\psi_1, \psi_2 \in S$. Also note that (2.1) through (2.3) already imply that (2.5) holds for $i = 3$, at each pair $\psi_1, \psi_2 \in S$.

Using the fact that (2.5) holds for each $i \in N$, it follows that (under the assumptions that have been made) the corresponding two-candidate game $(S,S; P\ell^1, P\ell^2)$ is symmetric. Therefore, a particular $(v,w) \in S \times S$ is an equilibrium if and only if (v,v) and (w,w) are equilibria (see, for instance, Ordeshook 1986, p. 158). Therefore, an equilibrium exists only if there is some $w \in S$ such that $(w,w) \in S \times S$ is an equilibrium. The argument in the next paragraph will show that no such w exists, thereby establishing that there is no equilibrium.

Since (as was pointed out in Section 1) assuming maximization of expected plurality is equivalent to assuming maximization of expected vote, we will analyze the version of the two-candidate game that the simpler payoff function: $(S,S; EV^1, EV^2)$. First note that, using (2.2) and (2.3), the expected vote for candidate 1 is

$$EV^1(\psi_1, \psi_2) = P_1(|\psi_2 + 1| - |\psi_1 + 1|) + P_2(|\psi_2| - |\psi_1|)$$

$$+ \begin{cases} 1 & \text{if } |\psi_2 - 100| > |\psi_1 - 100| \\ 1/2 & \text{if } |\psi_2 - 100| = |\psi_1 - 100| \\ 0 & \text{if } |\psi_2 - 100| < |\psi_1 - 100| \end{cases} \tag{2.6}$$

at each $(\psi_1, \psi_2) \in S \times S$. Therefore, using (2.4) and the fact that $S = [-1, +1]$, the expected vote for candidate 1 is

$$EV^1(\psi_1, \psi_2) = 1 + \frac{\psi_2}{2} - \frac{\psi_1}{2} + \frac{|\psi_2|}{2} - \frac{|\psi_1|}{2}$$

$$+ \begin{cases} 1 & \text{if } |\psi_2 - 100| > |\psi_1 - 100| \\ 1/2 & \text{if } |\psi_2 - 100| = |\psi_1 - 100| \\ 0 & \text{if } |\psi_2 - 100| < |\psi_1 - 100| \end{cases} \qquad (2.7)$$

at each $(\psi_1, \psi_2) \in S \times S$. Also note that by (2.7) (or directly from Hinich's assumption that $P_i(0) = 1/2, \forall i$), we know that

$$EV^1(w,w) = 3/2, \forall w \in S \qquad (2.8)$$

The first case that will be considered is $w = 1$. By (2.7) and (2.8), $EV^1(0,1) = 2 > 3/2 = EV^1(1,1)$. Therefore, $(1,1)$ is not an equilibrium. The second case will be $w \in [1/2, 1)$. Let ϵ be any number in the interval $(0, 1 - w)$. Note that $1/2 < w + \epsilon < w + (1 - w) = 1$. Therefore $w + \epsilon$ is a feasible strategy. By (2.7) and the fact that $1/2 \le w < w + \epsilon$, we have $EV^1(w + \epsilon, w) = 1 + (w/2) - ((w + \epsilon)/2) + (w/2) - ((w + \epsilon)/2) + 1 = 2 - \epsilon$. Using (2.8) and the fact that $0 < \epsilon < 1 - w \le 1/2$, we therefore have $EV^1(w + \epsilon, w) > 3/2 > EV^1(w,w)$. Therefore, (w,w) is not an equilibrium if $1/2 \le w < 1$. As the third case, consider any $w \in [0, 1/2)$. Let ϵ be any number in $(0, 1/2)$. Note that $0 \le w + \epsilon < (1/2) + (1/2) = 1$. Therefore $w + \epsilon$ is a feasible strategy. By (2.7) and the fact that $0 \le w < w + \epsilon$, we have (as in the previous case) $EV^1(w + \epsilon, w) = 2 - \epsilon$. Using (2.8) and the fact that $0 < \epsilon < 1/2$, we therefore have $EV^1(w + \epsilon, w) > 3/2 = EV^1(w,w)$. Therefore, (w,w) is not an equilibrium if $0 \le w < 1/2$. Finally, as the last case, consider any $w \in [-1, 0)$. Let ϵ be any number in $(0, -w)$. Note that $-1 \le w < w + \epsilon < (w) + (-w) = 0$. Therefore $w + \epsilon$ is a feasible strategy. By (2.7) and (2.8) and the fact that $w < w + \epsilon < 0$, we have $EV^1(w + \epsilon, w) = 1 + (w/2) - ((w + \epsilon)/2) - (w/2) + ((w + \epsilon)/2) + 1 = 2 > 3/2 = EV^1(w,w)$. So (w,w) is also not an equilibrium if $-1 \le w < 0$. Hence, since $S = [-1, +1]$, there is *no* $w \in S$ such that (w, w) is an equilibrium. Therefore, there is no equilibrium under the assumptions that have been made.

Hinich (1977) also provided two unidimensional examples where the existence of an equilibrium is assured. The first example illustrated the fact that, when the candidates are uncertain about the voters' choices, there can be an equilibrium at the mean for the distribution of voter ideal points, rather than at the median. It also showed that the equilibrium can be "far from the median" (p. 215). The second of these examples (where an equilibrium is assured) illustrated the fact that, when the candidates are uncertain about voters' choices, there can be an equilibrium at the mode for the distribution of voter ideal points, rather than at either the median or the mean. Hinich (1977) ended with a discussion of multidimensional models, which he labeled "political games without equilibria" (p. 216).[2]

3. EQUILIBRIUM AT THE MEAN

In a subsequent article, Hinich identified conditions for multidimensional election models where "if an equilibrium exists it must be at the mean" (1978, p. 365). "Conditions for the mean position to be the political outcome [were] also presented" (1978, p. 360). The assumptions that Hinich made en route to these results will be reviewed in the next few paragraphs. Once these assumptions have been made explicit, it will be possible to state the theorems in Hinich (1978) clearly and accurately.

Hinich assumed that $S = E\ell$ (without restricting ℓ to be 1). In addition, he assumed that, for each $i \in N$, there is an ideal point, $x(i) \in S$, and an ($\ell \times \ell$), symmetric, positive-definite matrix, $A(i)$, which enter into i's evaluation of each candidate's strategy. More specifically, he assumed that they enter into the determination of a policy-related "loss" (or negative utility) associated with the winning candidate's choice of a particular $\psi \in S$. In particular, Hinich assumed that this loss is the number assigned by the following function (which depends on the "distance" between ψ and $x(i)$):

$$L_i(\psi) = M(\|\psi - x(i)\|_{A(i)}) \tag{3.1}$$

where M is a monotonically increasing function and $\|y\|_A = [y'Ay]^{1/2}$. He also assumed that, for each $i \in N$, there is a nonpolicy loss, $e_1(i)$, for i if candidate 1 is elected and a nonpolicy loss, $e_2(i)$, for i if candidate 2 is the winner.

Hinich assumed that the candidates are uncertain about the choices that the voters are going to make on election day because they are uncertain about the characteristics of the individual voters. This uncertainty was formulated by assuming that, in the minds of the candidates, "the electorate is a random sample from an infinite population with a given probability measure" – so that, in particular, "e_1, e_2, x, and A are random variables" (p. 361). The expected number of voters, n, was assumed to be independent of the strategies chosen by the candidates.

Hinich assumed that, for any given pair of strategy choices $(\psi_1, \psi_2) \in S \times S$, the probability that candidate 1 will get the vote of a particular individual i (conditional on the voter having a particular ideal point x, matrix A, and nonpolicy values e_1 and e_2) is

$$P_i^1(\psi_1, \psi_2 | x(i) = x, A(i) = A, e_1(i) = e_1, e_2(i) = e_2)$$

$$= \begin{cases} 1 \text{ if } M(\|\psi_1 - x\|_A) + e_1 < M(\|\psi_2 - x\|_A) + e_2 \\ 0 \text{ otherwise.} \end{cases} \tag{3.2}$$

That is, i will vote for candidate 1 if and only if his total loss (his policy-related loss plus nonpolicy loss) from having candidate 1 elected is smaller than his total loss from having candidate 2 elected. An analogous assumption (with 2 replacing 1 and 1 replacing 2, on the right-hand side of (3.2)) was made about the conditional probability that i will vote for candidate 2 at any particular strategy pair $(\psi_1, \psi_2) \in S \times S$. Note that, among other things, these assumptions imply that i will abstain from voting if and only if he is indifferent between the two candidates (that is, if and only if the total loss from 1 being elected is equal to the total loss from 2 being elected). Equation (3.2) can, of course, be rewritten as

$$P_i^1(\psi_1, \psi_2 | x(i) = x, A(i) = A, \epsilon(i) = \epsilon)$$

$$= \begin{cases} 1 \text{ if } M(\|\psi_2 - x\|_A) - M(\|\psi_1 - x\|_A) > \epsilon \\ 0 \text{ otherwise} \end{cases} \tag{3.3}$$

where $\epsilon = e_1 - e_2$. Hinich denoted the conditional distribution function for ϵ (given x and A) by F_ϵ. Using this notation, (3.3) leads to the conclusion that

$$P_i^1(\psi_1, \psi_2 | x(i) = x, A(i) = A) = F_\epsilon[M(\|\psi_2 - x\|_A) - M(\|\psi_1 - x\|_A)] \tag{3.4}$$

for each possible ψ_1, ψ_2, x, and A. He assumed as well that F_ϵ has a continuous density function, f_ϵ.

These assumptions imply that, at any given pair ψ_1, $\psi_2 \in S$, the expected vote for candidate 1 is

$$EV^1(\psi_1, \psi_2) = n \cdot EF_\epsilon[M(\|\psi_2 - x\|_A) - M(\|\psi_1 - x\|_A)], \tag{3.5}$$

with the expected value on the right specifically being taken with respect to the joint distribution of x and A. Using the fact that a voter abstains when (and only when) the total loss that he associates with candidate 1 is *exactly* the same as the total loss he associates with candidate 2, (3.5) leads to

$$P\ell^1(\psi_1, \psi_2) = n \cdot \{2 \cdot EF_\epsilon[M(\|\psi_2 - x\|_A) - M(\|\psi_1 - x\|_A)] - 1\} \tag{3.6}$$

at each $(\psi_1, \psi_2) \in S \times S$ (as in Hinich's equation 5 [1978, p. 364]).

In his analysis of the resulting game for the candidates, Hinich considered two models that satisfy his assumptions. The first is the "absolute value model," where it is also assumed that $M(y) = |y|$. Hinich pointed out that the absolute value model is such that, when S has one dimension, "both candidates choose the median ideal point because it is a Nash equilibrium" (p. 364). The second model that Hinich considered is the "quadratic model," where the additional assumption is (alternatively) $M(y) = y^2$. He pointed out that "in general an equilibrium does not exist for the quadratic model" (p. 366). In addition, he established the following result:

Candidate Uncertainty and Electoral Equilibria

THEOREM 3.1 (Hinich 1978, p. 365): Consider the quadratic model and assume that $f_\epsilon > 0$ with positive probability for all $(\psi_1, \psi_2) \in S \times S$. If an equilibrium exists, then both candidates choose

$$\alpha = [E\{f_\epsilon(0)A\}]^{-1}E\{f_\epsilon(0)Ax\} \tag{3.7}$$

Hinich also pointed out that if (a) $F_\epsilon(0)$ is independent of x and A and (b) x and A are uncorrelated, then α is the mean ideal point.

Building on Theorem 3.1, Hinich also established the following existence result for unidimensional election models (that is, models where $\ell = 1$):

THEOREM 3.2: (Hinich 1978, p. 368): Let $p(x)$ denote the density function of the voter ideal points. Assume that there is an interval $[a,b]$ such that $p(x) = 0$, $\forall\ x \in [a,b]$ and $p(x) > 0$, $\forall\ x \in [a,b]$. Consider the quadratic model where ϵ has a normal distribution with mean 0 and variance σ^2. There exists $\sigma_e > 0$ such that if $\sigma < \sigma_e$ then
(i) an equilibrium exists, and
(ii) (ψ_1^*, ψ_2^*) is an equilibrium if and only if $\psi_1^* = \psi_2^* = \alpha$.

At the end of the theoretical analysis in this paper, Hinich concluded: "Unless the reader is willing to accept either the quadratic or the absolute value model, it is difficult to say anything about the outcome of majority rule voting using the spatial model with the uncertainty element in it" (1978, p. 370).[3]

4. THE BINARY LUCE MODEL

Considering the implications of candidates having uncertainty about voters' choices naturally raises the more general question of how one should model expectations about individuals' choices when there is uncertainty about what the individuals will choose. As is well known, mathematical psychologists and others have carefully thought about this question (see, for instance, the survey article by Luce and Suppes 1965). As is also well known, the most famous model for such expectations is (using the terminology of Becker, DeGroot, and Marschak 1963) (see p. 43) the "Luce model," which was originally developed by Luce (1959).

When each voter is assumed to vote (and, hence, simply to be deciding whether to vote for candidate 1 or for candidate 2, rather than also deciding whether to vote), the appropriate version of Luce's model is, of course (again using the terminology of Becker, DeGroot, and Marschak 1963, p. 44), the "binary Luce model." Stated in the context of election models: the candidates use a binary Luce model for the individual voters' selection probabilities if and only if, for each $i \in N$, there exists a positive, real-valued "scaling function," $f_i(x)$, on S, which is such that

153

Peter J. Coughlin

$$P_i^1(\psi_1, \psi_2) = \frac{f_i(\psi_1)}{f_i(\psi_1) + f_i(\psi_2)} \qquad (4.1)$$

and

$$P_i^2(\psi_1, \psi_2) = \frac{f_i(\psi_2)}{f_i(\psi_1) + f_i(\psi_2)} \qquad (4.2)$$

A number of authors who have analyzed Luce models have suggested that the scaling function used to specify the selection probabilities for a particular individual could be taken to be a utility function for that individual (see, for instance, Luce and Suppes 1965, p. 335). That is, expressing this assumption in appropriate notation, $f_i = U_i$, $\forall i \in N$. Two widely used assumptions for utility functions are, of course, concavity and differentiability. Two common assumptions for election models are (a) the candidates' (common) strategy set, S, is nonempty, compact, and convex and (b) the set of voters, N, is finite. Nitzan and I established that, when the candidates use a binary Luce model for the individual voters' selection probabilities and these additional assumptions are also satisfied, the following result holds.

THEOREM 4.1 (Coughlin and Nitzan 1981a, p. 117): $(\psi_1^*, \psi_2^*) \in S \times S$ is an equilibrium if and only if both ψ_1^* and ψ_2^* maximize

$$W(x) = \sum_{i=1}^{n} \log(U_i(x)) \qquad (4.3)$$

over S.

Kaneko and Nakamura (1979, p. 432) have established that when (a) there is a distinguished alternative, $x_o \notin S$, which represents one of the worst alternatives for all individuals and (b) we set $U_i(x_o) = 0$ and have $U_i(x) > 0$, $\forall x \in S$, the objective function specified in (4.3) is a Nash social welfare function. The result in Theorem 4.1 could, therefore, also be stated as follows: A particular $\psi \in S$ is an equilibrium strategy for a candidate if and only if it is a maximum for the Nash social welfare function specified in (4.3). Nitzan and I also pointed out that this welfare maximization result directly implies (under the same assumptions):

COROLLARY 4.1 (Coughlin and Nitzan 1981a, p. 118): An electoral equilibrium exists.

and

COROLLARY 4.2 (Coughlin and Nitzan 1981a, p. 118): If at least one voter has a strictly concave utility function, then there is a unique electoral equilibrium.

Nitzan and I (1981b) also showed that results analogous to Theorem 4.1 and Corollary 4.1 hold for directional, stationary, and local electoral equilibria, even when the assumptions listed above are weakened by allowing the set of voters to potentially be infinite and by no longer requiring (a) the equivalence of scaling and utility functions, (b) concavity for the scaling functions or (c) convexity for *S*.

Samuelson (1984) subsequently studied election models in which the candidates use a binary Luce model, with the added feature that the candidates' strategies are restricted. The restrictions on the candidates' strategies were specifically included by assuming that each candidate has (a) an initial position, $w_c \in S$ and (b) a nonempty, compact, convex set, $S_c(w_c) \subset S$, of feasible options open to him. Samuelson also assumed (a) there is a nonempty, compact, Euclidean set of possible voter characteristics, (b) each scaling function is a concave function of the possible candidate strategies, (c) each scaling function is a continuous function of *both* the possible candidate strategies *and* the possible voter characteristics and (d) the electorate can be summarized by a continuous density function on the set of possible voter characteristics. He established that the resulting model has the following property:

THEOREM 4.2 (Samuelson 1984, p. 311): For each $(S_1(w_1), S_2(w_2); P\ell^1, P\ell^2)$ there exists an electoral equilibrium.

Samuelson used this result to analyze (a) a sequence of elections in which a series of opposition candidates challenged incumbents and (b) the apparent incumbency advantage that has been observed in recent congressional elections.

In light of the discussion in Section 4, a natural question is whether there are any noteworthy connections between the models to which Theorems 4.1 and 4.2 apply and models in which voters have additively separable loss functions like the ones studied by Hinich (1978). It should be noted that it has long been known that results about binary Luce models have direct implications for models in which utility/loss can be written as the sum of a nonrandom utility/loss function and a random "error" term (see, for instance, Luce and Suppes 1965, Section 5.2). The established connection between these alternative models can be used in the context of election models as follows. Suppose that (a) each voter, *i*, has a policy-related loss function, $L_i(\psi) = -log(f_i(\psi)) - b_i$ (where f_i is a positive, real-valued function on *S* and *b* is a constant), (b) analogous to (3.3), for each *i* and each $(\psi_1, \psi_2) \in S \times S$,

$$P_i^1(\psi_1, \psi_2) = \begin{cases} 1 \text{ if } L_i(\psi_2) - L_i(\psi_1) > \epsilon_i \\ \\ 0 \text{ otherwise} \end{cases} \tag{4.4}$$

and (c) ϵ_i has a logistic distribution. Then, using the argument in the proof of Luce and Suppes' Theorem 30 (1965, p. 335), it follows that the candidates are using a binary Luce model. Therefore, when the remaining assumptions for Theorem 4.1 (or Theorem 4.2) are also made, the conclusion of Theorem 4.1

(respectively, of Theorem 4.2) holds for the corresponding model with separable policy-related and non-policy voter utilities/losses.[4]

5. CANDIDATE CHARACTERISTICS

Enelow and Hinich (1982) analyzed an election model in which "non-spatial" candidate characteristics (that is, characteristics that the candidates can't alter during the election being considered) are important. The particular model that they analyzed is very similar to the one in Hinich (1978) in that, as the ensuing discussion will make clear, most of their assumptions correspond to ones that were made by Hinich en route to his existence theorem (Theorem 3.2 in Section 3). However, their existence result (Theorem 5.1 in this section) is *not* a special case for Hinich's earlier existence theorem. Thus their analysis succeeded in identifying a new sufficient condition for the existence of an electoral equilibrium.

Enelow and Hinich (1982) assumed that the (common) strategy set, S, for the candidates is such that $[0,1] \subset S \subseteq E^1$ – with the positions in S interpreted as expenditure levels on a single public-spending issue. As did Hinich (1978), they assumed that, for each $i \in N$, there is an ideal point, $x(i) \in S$, that enters into i's evaluation of each candidate's strategy. One part of the premise for Hinich's existence theorem (see Theorem 3.2) is that there is a density function, $p(x)$, for the voter ideal points such that (a) $p(x) = 0$ for x outside an interval $[a,b]$ and (b) $p(x) > 0$ inside. Enelow and Hinich (1982), by contrast, assumed that the electorate can be partitioned into two groups, $\theta = 1$ and $\theta = 2$ (with n_1 and n_2 voters, respectively), and that (a) each $i \in \theta = 1$ has the ideal point $x(i) = 0$ and (b) each $i \in \theta = 2$ has the ideal point $x(i) = 1$.

Enelow and Hinich (1982) assumed that each $i \in N$ makes a numerical assessment of the nonspatial characteristics of candidate 1 (and also the nonspatial characteristics of candidate 2), denoted by c_{i1}, (respectively, c_{i2}). This assessment was supplemented by a positive, numerical measure of the importance that i attaches to the candidates' strategies (relative to their nonpolicy characteristics), denoted by a_i. Analogous to equation (3.3), they assumed (see (4) and (6) on pp. 122–3) that, for each $i \in N$ and each pair $\psi_1, \psi_2 \in S$,

$$P_i^1(\psi_1, \psi_2) = \begin{cases} 1 \text{ if } (\psi_2 - x(i))^2 - (\psi_1 - x(i))^2 > \in_i \\ \\ 0 \text{ otherwise} \end{cases} \quad (5.1)$$

where $\in_i = (c_{i2}/a_i) - (c_{i1}/a_i)$. An analogous assumption (with 2 replacing 1, and 1 replacing 2, on the right-hand side of 5.1 and in the definition of ϵ_i) was made about $P_i^2(\psi_1, \psi_2)$. Note that in (5.1) (a) $(\psi - x(i))^2$ corresponds to Hinich's loss function (being, in particular, the special case of Hinich's quadratic model that arises when $S \subseteq E^1$ and $A = [1]$) and (b) $-c_{i1}/a_i$ and $-c_{i2}/a_i$ correspond to

e_1 and e_2, respectively, in Hinich (1978). Or, equivalently (translating this observation from "loss" terms into "utility" terms), $U_i(\psi) = -(\psi - x(i))^2$ can be thought of as a policy-related utility function for voter i and (c_{i1}/a_i) (or (c_{i2}/a_i)) can be thought of as a nonpolicy value for i if candidate 1 (respectively, candidate 2) wins the election.

In his existence theorem, Hinich (1978) assumed that the variance, σ^2, for the nonpolicy difference, ϵ, is the same for each voter. Enelow and Hinich (1982), on the other hand, assumed that the candidates believe that (a) the distribution of ϵ_i *across the group* $\theta = 1$ is normal with mean 0 and variance σ_1^2, and (b) the distribution of ϵ_i *across the group* $\theta = 2$ is normal with mean 0 and variance σ_2^2 (as the notation suggests, σ_2 need not equal σ_1.) This distributional assumption is consistent with assuming that the candidates know the nonpolicy difference for each voter and is, alternatively, also consistent with assuming that they are uncertain about the nonpolicy value for any particular voter but (nonetheless) know the distribution of the nonpolicy values across each group.

To be able to state their result clearly, Enelow and Hinich (1982) let

$$\bar{x} = [n_2 \cdot \sigma_1]/[n_1 \cdot \sigma_2 + n_2 \cdot \sigma_1]. \tag{5.2}$$

The number, $\bar{x}$, for any special case is, as they pointed out, a weighted mean ideal point (which has the property that, *if* $\sigma_1 = \sigma_2$, *then* $\bar{x}$ is the unweighted mean ideal point). Using this notation, we can state their existence result as follows.

THEOREM 5.1 (Enelow and Hinich 1982, pp. 123–4): If $\sigma_1^2 > 2 \cdot (1 - \bar{x})^2$ and $\sigma_2^2 > 2 \cdot [1 - (1 - \bar{x})^2]$,
  (i) an equilibrium exists, and
  (ii) (ψ_1^*, ψ_2^*) is an equilibrium if and only if $\psi_1^* = \psi_2^* = \bar{x}$.

This result is similar to Hinich's (1978) existence result (see Theorem 3.2) in that the conclusion is: A unique equilibrium exists and is located at a weighted mean of the voter ideal points. In addition to the differences in the underlying assumptions that were noted above, Enelow and Hinich's (1982) result also differs from Hinich's (1978) existence theorem in that (a) the sufficient condition involves lower bounds on the variances for the nonpolicy values (rather than an upper bound) and (b) the result provides precise bounds (rather than just assuring that an appropriate bound exists).

Enelow and Hinich argued that it is especially significant that the equilibrium in their election model is at a "compromise" position, rather than at the ideal point of one of the two groups. They pointed out that this property implies that (in their model) the minority group has some influence over the outcome and, therefore, there is not a "tyranny of the majority." They argued that this implication reflects an important difference between (a) representative democracy (where the citizens vote for candidates who both propose policies and have fixed characteristics that the voters care about) and (b) direct democracy (where the citizens vote solely on policies).[5]

6. CANDIDATE CHARACTERISTICS, PREDICTIVE MAPS, AND INTEREST GROUPS

Enelow and Hinich (1984a, Secs. 5.1, 5.2, and 5.4) extended their earlier analysis of election models with fixed candidate characteristics by considering cases where there are "predictive mappings" for the voters. These mappings, which are discussed in detail in Enelow and Hinich (1984a, chap. 4), allow each voter to map *from* a candidate's strategy *to* the policies he thinks will actually be adopted if the candidate is elected. The predictive mappings, therefore, allow for the possibility that voters will interpret candidates' strategies in their own individual ways, instead of simply believing that each candidate will carry out the policies that he advocates during the election.

Enelow and Hinich assumed that the candidates' strategy set is the closed interval $S = [-1/2, +1/2]$ (1984a, pp. 101–2 in Appendix 5.1). As before, they assumed that there are two groups, $\theta = 1$ and $\theta = 2$ (with n_1 and n_2 voters, respectively). They made two particular assumptions about the groups: (a) they partition the electorate and (b) for each $\theta \in \Theta = \{1,2\}$, the voters in the group have a common ideal point, $x_\theta \in E^2$, and a common predictive map,

$$w_i(\psi) = b_\theta + \psi \cdot v_\theta. \tag{6.1}$$

Enelow and Hinich specifically assumed that each predictive map goes from the unidimensional strategy adopted by a candidate to a two-component vector of "anticipated policies." Thus, for any given $(\psi_1,\psi_2) \in S \times S$, the corresponding $w_i(\psi_1) \in E^2$ (and the corresponding $w_i(\psi_2) \in E^2$) is the two-dimensional vector of policies that each person in θ thinks will actually be adopted if candidate 1 (respectively, candidate 2) is elected. Note that, since the candidates' strategies are in E^1 and the predicted policies are in E^2, the b_θ and v_θ parameters in (6.1) and (6.2) are two-component vectors, which can therefore be written as $b_\theta = (b_{\theta 1}, b_{\theta 2})'$ and $v_\theta = (v_{\theta 1}, v_{\theta 2})'$. Similarly, the common ideal point for the individuals in a given group, θ, can be written as $x_\theta = (x_{\theta 1}, x_{\theta 2})'$.

This time around, Enelow and Hinich explicitly interpreted the groups in their model as "interest groups," making the following argument for this interpretation:

The . . . homogeneous groups can be thought of as the politically salient interest groups in the electorate. Each interest group has a common set of policy concerns and looks at the candidates the same way. . . . This conception of an interest group is particularly appropriate from the point of view of the candidates. It is a common practice in campaigns to view the electorate as being composed of homogeneous issue groups. . . . This practice is a shorthand device that permits candidates to plan campaign strategies without becoming lost in the complexities of individual voter attitudes. [Enelow and Hinich 1984a, p. 83]

As before, they also assumed that each voter places a nonpolicy value on candidate 1's winning the election and a nonpolicy value on candidate 2's winning. Accordingly, analogous to equations (3.3) and (5.1), Enelow and Hinich assumed that, for each $i \in N$ and each pair $\psi_1, \psi_2 \in S$,

$$P_i^1(\psi_1, \psi_2) = \begin{cases} 1 \text{ if } \|\psi_2 - x_\theta\|_I^2 - \|\psi_1 - x_\theta\|_I^2 > \epsilon_i \\ 0 \text{ otherwise} \end{cases} \qquad (6.2)$$

where (a) $\|y\|_I^2 = y'Iy = y_1^2 + 2 \cdot y_1 \cdot y_2 + y_2^2$ (since $y \in E^2$) and (b) ϵ_i is (again) the *difference between* the nonpolicy value for i if candidate 2 is elected *and* the nonpolicy value for i if candidate 1 is elected. An analogous assumption (with the inequality on the right-hand side of 6.2 reversed) was made about $P_i^2(\psi_1, \psi_2)$ (with 1 and 2 interchanged). In addition, Enelow and Hinich assumed that the candidates believe that the distribution of ϵ_i *across a given interest group* θ is normal with mean zero and variance σ_θ^2.

The final assumption that Enelow and Hinich made (see p. 102) is that, for each group θ, there exists an upper bound, B_θ, for both $(v_{\theta 1}^1 + v_{\theta 2}^2)^{1/2}$ and $[(x_{\theta 1} - b_{\theta 1})^2 + (x_{\theta 2} - b_{\theta 2})^2]^{1/2}$ (the elements that appear in these two equations are specifically the corresponding components in the vectors v_θ, x_θ, and b_θ). The result that they established is:

THEOREM 6.1 (Enelow and Hinich 1984a, pp. 85–6, 101–2): If $\sigma_1 > 3 \cdot (\sqrt{1.5}) \cdot B_1^2$ and $\sigma_2 > 3 \cdot (\sqrt{1.5}) \cdot B_2^2$, then
(i) an electoral equilibrium exists, and
(ii) (ψ_1^*, ψ_2^*) is an electoral equilibrium if and only if $\psi_1^* = \psi_2^* =$

$$\frac{\{n_1 \sigma_1^{-1}[v_{11}(x_{11} - b_{11}) + v_{12}(x_{12} - b_{12})] + n_2 \sigma_2^{-1}[v_{21}(x_{21} - b_{21}) + v_{22}(x_{22} - b_{22})]\}}{[n_1 \sigma_1^{-1}(v_{11}^2 + v_{12}^2) + n_2 \sigma_2^{-1}(v_{21}^2 + v_{22}^2)]}. \qquad (6.3)$$

Enelow and Hinich supplemented their analysis with the following example of an election model with fixed candidate characteristics, predictive maps, and interest groups.

Example 6.1 (Enelow and Hinich 1984a, pp. 87–8): Assume that group $\theta = 1$ is twice as large as group $\theta = 2$ (that is, $n_1 = 2 \cdot n_2$). Also assume that each voter in group $\theta = 1$ has the ideal point $x_1 = (.2, .8)'$ and the predictive map

$$w_1(\psi) = \begin{bmatrix} +.3 \\ +.7 \end{bmatrix} + \psi \cdot \begin{bmatrix} +.2 \\ -.2 \end{bmatrix} \qquad (6.4)$$

159

Peter J. Coughlin

and that each voter in group $\theta = 2$ has the ideal point $x_2 = (.35, .65)'$ and the predictive map

$$w_2(\psi) = \begin{bmatrix} +.2 \\ +.8 \end{bmatrix} + \psi \cdot \begin{bmatrix} +.3 \\ -.3 \end{bmatrix} \qquad (6.5)$$

Enelow and Hinich (1984) pointed out that their result directly implies that (in their example) *if* $\sigma_1 > 3 \cdot (\sqrt{1.5}) \cdot B_1^2 = .294$ and $\sigma_2 > 3 \cdot (\sqrt{1.5}) \cdot B_2^2 = .661$, *then* there is a unique equilibrium, $(\psi_1^*, \psi_2^*) \in S \times S$, with

$$\psi_1^* = \psi_2^* = \frac{\{-.08\sigma_1^{-1} + .09\sigma_2^{-1}\}}{[.16\sigma_1^{-1} + .18\sigma_2^{-1}]} . \qquad (6.6)$$

They also pointed out that *if* one makes the further assumption that $\sigma_1 = \sigma_2$, *then* their result provides the even more precise conclusion that $\psi_1^* = \psi_2^* = .03$.

Enelow and Hinich (1984a, Sect. 5.4) also used Example 6.1 to illustrate the fact that when their sufficient condition is *not* satisfied, their model with fixed candidate characteristics, predictive maps, and interest groups *need not* have an equilibrium. They did so by (more specifically) showing that, when Example 6.1 is supplemented with the alternative assumption that $\sigma_2 = 0$ and $.06 < \sigma_1 < .12$, there is *no* electoral equilibrium. The resulting example is therefore analogous to the special case of Example 2.1 (from Hinich 1977) that was analyzed in detail in Section 2.[6]

7. REDISTRIBUTION

Lindbeck and Weibull developed a model of "balanced-budget redistribution between socio-economic groups as the outcome of electoral competition between two political parties" (1987, p. 273) in which the parties have "incomplete information as to political preferences . . . related to ideological considerations and politicians personalities" (p. 274). Since they modeled redistribution between groups, in each case where there are three or more groups, the strategy set for the parties is multidimensional. As a consequence, as with the multidimensional election models discussed in Section 4, "the presence of uncertainty is crucial for *existence* of equilibrium in [their] model" (p. 280).

Lindbeck and Weibull assumed that the set of voters, N, is finite and that each $i \in N$ has a fixed gross income, $\omega_i \in E_{++}^1$. They also assumed that the candidates have a (common) partition, $\Theta = \{1, \ldots, m\}$, of the electorate (with $m \geq 2$). Note that in what follows (as in Sections 5 and 6), the elements in Θ will be used as indices for the groups as well as to denote the sets of voters that constitute the candidates' partition.

Lindbeck and Weibull assumed that the strategies available to the candidates are vectors, $s = (s_1, \ldots, s_m) \in E^m$, of possible transfers to the members of the m groups. In addition, they assumed that each candidate must select a balanced-budget redistribution in which each individual's net income must be positive. Hence

$$S = \left\{ s \in E^m : \sum_{\theta=1}^{m} n_\theta \cdot s_\theta = 0 \ \& \ \omega_i + s_\theta > 0, \ \forall i \in \theta, \ \forall \theta \in \Theta \right\}. \quad (7.1)$$

As in many of the analyses that have already been discussed, Lindbeck and Weibull assumed that any given voter's utility for a particular candidate's election is the *sum of* his utility for the candidate's strategy *and* an additional component that reflects "other factors" that affect his preferences for the candidates. They explicitly assumed that each voter has a twice-differentiable utility function, $v_i(\omega_i + s_i)$, on his "final" (or "net") income. Using this notation, any particular i's utility function on S can be written as

$$U_i(s) = v_i(\omega_i + s_i). \quad (7.2)$$

Lindbeck and Weibull assumed that, for each $i \in N$,

$$v_i'(z) > 0 \quad \& \quad v_i^*(z) < 0, \ \forall z > 0 \quad (7.3)$$

and

$$\lim_{z \to 0} v_i'(z) = +\infty \quad \& \quad \lim_{z \to \infty} v_i'(z) = 0. \quad (7.4)$$

Analogous to (5.1) and (6.2), Lindbeck and Weibull assumed that, for each $i \in N$ and each pair $\psi_1, \psi_2 \in S$,

$$P_i^1(\psi_1, \psi_2) = \begin{cases} 1 \text{ if } U_i(\psi_1) - U_i(\psi_2) > a_i - b_i \\ \\ 0 \text{ otherwise} \end{cases} \quad (7.5)$$

where "a_i is the utility that individual i derives from other policies in party [1's] political program and likewise with b_i [and party 2]" (p. 276). They also made an analogous assumption about $P_i^2(\psi_1, \psi_2)$ (with *both* 1 and 2 *and a* and *b* interchanged on the right-hand side of (7.4) or, equivalently, with the inequality on the right-hand side of (7.4) reversed).

Lindbeck and Weibull assumed that the two parties treat a_i and b_i as random variables. More specifically, they assumed that the parties have a twice continuously differentiable probability distribution, F_i, for $b_i - a_i$. Lindbeck and Weibull additionally assumed that $f_i(y) = F_i'(y) > 0, \ \forall y \in E^1$.

The first result that Lindbeck and Weibull established provided a necessary condition for an electoral equilibrium in their model.

THEOREM 7.1 (Lindbeck and Weibull 1987, p. 278): If (ψ_1, ψ_2) is an electoral equilibrium, then

(i) $\psi_1 = \psi_2 \equiv \psi^*$, and
(ii) there exists $\lambda > 0$ such that, for each $\theta \in \Theta$,

$$\sum_{i \in \theta} v_i'(\omega_i + \psi_i^*) \cdot f_i(0) = n_\theta \cdot \lambda. \qquad (7.6)$$

Equation (7.6) is of particular significance because it is also a first-order necessary condition for maximizing the weighted Benthamite social welfare function

$$W(\psi) = \sum_{i=1}^{n} v_i(\omega_i + \psi_i) \cdot f_i(0) \qquad (7.6)$$

on the set S. Lindbeck and Weibull pointed out that, if the parties use the same party preference distribution for each voter (that is, $F_i = F_j$, $\forall i, j \in N$), then "in this special case democratic electoral competition for the votes of selfish individuals produces the same income distribution as would an omnipotent Benthamite government" (p. 278).

Lindbeck and Weibull established the following existence theorem for their model:

THEOREM 7.2 (Lindbeck and Weibull 1987, p. 280): If

$$sup\{|f_i'(t)|/f_i(t)\} \leq inf\{|v_i''(r)|/(v_i'(r))^2\}, \qquad (7.7)$$

then a unique electoral equilibrium exists.

They also drew attention to the fact that (7.7) is "more easily satisfied the larger is the degree of uncertainty" (p. 281).

Lindbeck and Weibull also examined what happens to the results stated above when additional (or alternative) features are included in their model. The particular extensions that they considered were (a) administration costs (which could vary from group to group), (b) abstentions, (c) a role for party activists who do more for a candidate than simply vote for him, and (d) (as mentioned in Section 1) each candidate's wanting to maximize his probability of winning (rather than his expected plurality). The conclusions that they arrived at were very similar (albeit not identical) to the two theorems stated above. The minor differences that result from using these alternative assumptions were discussed in detail in the corresponding sections in Lindbeck and Weibull's article.

8. CONCLUSION

As the preceding sections have made clear, during the last decade or so a tremendous amount has been learned about the implications (for two-candidate elections where voters abstain only if they are indifferent) of candidates having uncertainty about voters' choices. At the same time, however, we do not yet have definite answers about the existence and location (if existence is assured) of equilibria for *all* of the possible assumptions that could potentially be made about candidate uncertainty. As a consequence, the relation between candidate uncertainty and electoral equilibria is still a topic of lively interest.

Significant unpublished research on the topic that is at least partially by others and goes beyond what has been covered here includes Coughlin, Mueller, and Murrell (1988), Enelow and Hinich (1988), Feldman and Lee (1988), Mueller (1988, Chapter 11), and Wittman (1988). Since (a) substantial progress has been (and is continuing to be) made on understanding the relation between candidate uncertainty and electoral equilibria, (b) knowledge about the relation is cumulative, and (c) "public choice attracts so many fine scholars" (Mueller 1979, p. 270), I have no doubt that this "next wave" of research on the topic will – in turn – be followed by further work, which will provide us with even more insight into the nature of electoral competition.

ACKNOWLEDGMENTS

I gratefully acknowledge financial support provided by the General Research Board of the Graduate School of the University of Maryland at College Park and the helpful comments and suggestions provided by Jim Enelow and Mel Hinich.

NOTES

1 For discussions of analyses of election models in which, alternatively, the consequences of voters possibly abstaining are of primary concern, see Mueller (1979, pp. 100–1) or Enelow and Hinich (1984a, Section 5.3).

2 For further published discussions of the examples covered in this section, see Kramer (1978, pp. 565–7), Coughlin and Nitzan (1981a, pp. 113–5; 1981b, pp. 226–7), Austen-Smith (1983, p. 454), Enelow and Hinich (1984a, p. 103), Ledyard (1984, pp. 27 and 34), Samuelson (1984, p. 325; 1985, pp. 376–7; 1987a, p. 165; 1987b, p. 23), Blumel, Pethig, and von dem Hagen (1986, pp. 282–3), Calvert (1986, pp. 29–30 and 33–4), Sen (1986, p. 1146), Bos and Zimmerman (1987, pp. 523 and 549), Mitchell (1987, p. 153), and Morton (1987, p. 118).

3 For further published discussions of Hinich's (1978) analysis of the mean versus the median, see Coughlin and Nitzan (1981a, pp. 113–5; 1981b, p. 226), Enelow and Hinich (1982, p. 116), Austen-Smith (1983, p. 454), Ledyard (1984, p. 34), and Calvert (1985, pp. 73 and 86; 1986, pp. 33–4).

4 For further published discussions of models in which the candidates use a binary Luce model, see Austen-Smith (1983, pp. 453–4), Enelow and Hinich (1984b, p. 468), Ledyard (1984, pp. 8–9), Wittman (1984, p. 284), Calvert (1985, p. 73; 1986, pp. 35–6), Grofman (1985, p. 236), Samuelson (1985, pp. 377–9; 1987a, pp. 141–6 and 165; 1987b, p. 21), Murrell (1985, p. 426), Blumel, Pethig, and von dem Hagen (1986, pp. 282–3), Mueller (1986, p. 3), Sen (1986, pp. 1083, 1115, and 1146),

Peter J. Coughlin

Ordeshook (1986, pp. 177–9 and 491), Yinger (1986, p. 319), Bos and Zimmerman (1987, pp. 524, 533–4, and 549), Lindbeck and Weibull (1987, p. 275), Mitchell (1987, p. 153), and Morton (1987, p. 118).

5 For further published discussions of Enelow and Hinich's (1982) model with non-spatial candidate characteristics, see Austen-Smith (1983, p. 450), Enelow and Hinich (1984a, p. 103; 1984b, p. 461), Grofman (1985, pp. 231 and 236), Calvert (1986, pp. 28–9), Enelow, Hinich, and Mendell (1986, pp. 675–8 and 689–90), and Lindbeck and Weibull (1987, p. 275).

6 For further published discussions of the model covered in this section, see Enelow and Hinich (1984b, pp. 461 and 470–6), Grofman (1985, pp. 231 and 236), Calvert (1986, p. 18), Enelow, Hinich, and Mendell (1986, pp. 675–8 and 689–90), Ordeshook (1986, pp. 490–1), and Samuelson (1987, p. 164).

REFERENCES

Aranson, P., M. Hinich, and P. Ordeshook. 1973. "Campaign Strategies for Alternative Election Systems: Candidate Objectives as an Intervening Variable." In H. Alker et al., eds., *Mathematical Approaches to Politics*. Amsterdam: Elsevier, pp. 193–229.

Arrow, K. 1951. *Social Choice and Individual Values*. New York: John Wiley. (second edition: 1963)

Austen-Smith, D. 1983. "The Spatial Theory of Electoral Competition: Instability, Institutions, and Information." *Environment and Planning C: Government and Policy* 1: 439–59.

Becker, G., M. DeGroot, and J. Marschak. 1963. "Stochastic Models of Choice Behavior." *Behavioral Science* 8: 41–55.

Black, D. 1958. *The Theory of Committees and Elections*. Cambridge: Cambridge University Press.

Blumel, W., R. Pethig, and O. von dem Hagen. 1986. "The Theory of Public Goods: A Survey of Recent Issues." *Journal of Institutional and Theoretical Economics* 142: 241–309.

Bos, D., and H. Zimmerman. 1987. "Maximizing Votes Under Imperfect Information." *European Journal of Political Economy* 3: 523–53.

Calvert, R. 1985. "Robustness of the Multidimensional Voting Model: Candidate Motivations, Uncertainty, and Convergence." *American Journal of Political Science* 29: 69–95.

———. 1986. *Models of Imperfect Information in Politics*. Chur: Harwood.

Coughlin, P. 1986. "Probabilistic Voting Models." In S. Kotz and N. Johnson, eds., *Encyclopedia of Statistical Sciences*, Volume 7, New York: John Wiley, pp. 204–210.

Coughlin, P., and S. Nitzan. 1981a. "Electoral Outcomes with Probabilistic Voting and Nash Social Welfare Maxima." *Journal of Public Economics* 15: 113–21.

———. 1981b. "Directional and Local Electoral Equilibria with Probabilistic Voting." *Journal of Economic Theory* 24: 226–40.

Coughlin, P., D. Mueller, and P. Murrell. 1988. "Electoral Politics, Interest Groups, and the Size of Government." University of Maryland at College Park working paper.

Downs, A. 1957. *An Economic Theory of Democracy*. New York: Harper and Row.

Enelow, J., and M. Hinich. 1982. "Non-Spatial Candidate Characteristics and Electoral Competition." *Journal of Politics* 44: 115–30.

Candidate Uncertainty and Electoral Equilibria

———. 1984a. *The Spatial Theory of Voting*. Cambridge: Cambridge University Press.

———. 1984b. "Probabilistic Voting and the Importance of Centrist Ideologies in Democratic Elections." *Journal of Politics* 46: 459–78.

———. 1988. "A General Probabilistic Spatial Theory of Elections." SUNY at Stony Brook and University of Texas at Austin working paper.

———. 1990. "Introduction" and "The Theory of Predictive Mappings." In J. Enelow and M. Hinich, eds., *Advances in the Spatial Theory of Voting*. Cambridge: Cambridge University Press.

Enelow, J., M. Hinich, and N. Mendell. 1986. "An Empirical Evaluation of Alternative Spatial Models of Elections." *Journal of Politics* 48: 675–93.

Feldman, A., and K. Lee. 1988. "Existence of Electoral Equilibria with Probabilistic Voting." Brown University working paper.

Fiorina, M. 1981. *Retrospective Voting in American National Elections*. New Haven: Yale University Press.

Grofman, B. 1985. "The Neglected Role of the Status Quo in Models of Issue Voting." *Journal of Politics* 47: 230–7.

Hinich, M. 1977. "Equilibrium in Spatial Voting: The Median Voter Result Is an Artifact." *Journal of Economic Theory* 16: 208–19.

———. 1978. "The Mean versus the Median in Spatial Voting Games." In P. Ordeshook, ed., *Game Theory and Political Science*. New York: NYU Press, pp. 357–74.

Hotelling, H. 1929. "Stability in Competition." *Economic Journal* 39: 41–57.

Kaneko, M., and K. Nakamura. 1979. "The Nash Social Welfare Function." *Econometrica* 47: 423–35.

Kramer, G. 1978. "Robustness of the Median Voter Result." *Journal of Economic Theory* 19: 565–7.

Ledyard, J. 1984. "The Pure Theory of Large Two-Candidate Elections." *Public Choice* 44: 7–41.

Lindbeck, A., and J. Weibull. 1987. "Balanced-Budget Redistributions as the Outcome of Political Competition." *Public Choice* 52: 273–97.

Luce, R. D. 1959. *Individual Choice Behavior*. New York: John Wiley.

Luce, R. D., and P. Suppes. 1965. "Preference, Utility and Subjective Probability." In R. D. Luce et al., eds., *Handbook of Mathematical Psychology*. New York: John Wiley, pp. 249–410.

Mitchell, D. 1987. "Candidate Behavior under Mixed Motives." *Social Choice and Welfare* 4: 153–60.

Morton, R. 1987. "A Group Majority Voting Model of Public Good Provision." *Social Choice and Welfare* 4: 117–31.

Mueller, D. 1979. *Public Choice*. Cambridge: Cambridge University Press.

———. 1986. "Rational Egoism Versus Adaptive Egoism as a Fundamental Postulate for a Descriptive Theory of Human Behavior." *Public Choice* 51: 3–23.

———. 1988. *Public Choice II*. University of Maryland at College Park book manuscript.

Murrell, P. 1985. "The Size of Public Employment: An Empirical Study." *Journal of Comparative Economics* 9: 424–37.

Ordeshook. P. 1986. *Game Theory and Political Theory*. Cambridge: Cambridge University Press.

Samuelson, L. 1984. "Electoral Equilibria with Restricted Strategies." *Public Choice* 43: 307–27.

————. 1985. "On the Independence from Irrelevant Alternatives in Probabilistic Choice Models." *Journal of Economic Theory* 35: 376–89.

————. 1987a. "A Test of the Revealed-Preference Phenomenon in Congressional Elections." *Public Choice* 54: 141–69.

————. 1987b. "On the Restrictiveness of Monotonic Scalable Choice in Probabilistic Choice Models." *Mathematical Social Sciences* 14: 19–38.

Sen, A. 1986. "Social Choice Theory." In K. Arrow and M. Intriligator, eds., *Handbook of Mathematical Economics,* vol. 3. Amsterdam: North-Holland, pp. 1073–1181.

Wittman, D. 1984. "Multicandidate Equilibria." *Public Choice* 43: 287–91.

————. 1988. "Pressure Group Size and the Politics of Income Redistribution." University of California at Santa Cruz working paper.

Yinger, J. 1986. "On Fiscal Disparities Across Cities." *Journal of Urban Economics* 19: 316–37.

Note: In the period since this paper was completed (in early 1988), my working paper with Mueller and Murrell has evolved into two papers that have been accepted by *Economics Letters* and *Economic Inquiry,* Enelow and Hinich's working paper has appeared in *Public Choice* [61 (1989), pp. 461–470], Feldman and Lee's working paper has appeared in the *Journal of Public Economics* [35 (1988), pp. 205–217], Mueller's book manuscript has been published [Cambridge University Press, 1989], and Wittman's working paper has appeared in *Social Choice and Welfare* [6 (1989), pp. 275–286].

7

The Theory of Predictive Mappings

JAMES M. ENELOW
University of Texas at Austin

MELVIN J. HINICH
University of Texas at Austin

The problem of instability in social choice is often thought to be eliminated when the possible set of choices is one-dimensional, and voters have single-peaked preferences over this set. This is Duncan Black's (1958) famous median voter result. Yet, even if votes are determined solely by preferences, instability may still result. If linkages exist in the voters' minds between each possible choice along this single dimension and a future choice on other dimensions, the choice taking place in the voter's mind is multidimensional in nature. Thus, the instability that affects multidimensional social choice can afflict a social choice problem that is nominally one-dimensional. The question that arises is: Are these instabilities inevitable?

One answer is for an equilibrium point to exist in the multidimensional space, but the requirements for such an equilibrium are generally quite restrictive. A different answer comes from placing restrictions on the linkage, or *predictive mapping,* w that maps each possible choice in the nominal, one-dimensional set P of possible choices into an anticipated choice in the larger multidimensional space X. This second approach to studying stability conditions is the one taken in this essay. For each nominal contest between two elements p_A and p_B in P, the contest in the voter's mind is between $w(p_A)$ and $w(p_B)$, which are two points in X (or two probability distributions over points in X). Preference between p_A and p_B is then derived from the voter's preference between $w(p_A)$ and $w(p_B)$. What conditions on w, then, are necessary and/or sufficient to ensure that derived preferences between any p_A and p_B in P are single-peaked? Given the satisfaction of these conditions, the linkage in the voter's mind between P and X does *not* create the instabilities associated with multidimensional choice problems, and contests over elements of P will exhibit the type of stability associated with the simple, one-dimensional spatial model.

In politics, the linkage problem we have described takes many guises. We begin the next section by discussing how this problem occurs in elections. Assume candidates are known to the voters by "predictive labels" that can be represented by points in a Euclidean space, which we will call the predictive space. Each point in the predictive space is mapped by the voter into a point in a space of equal or higher dimensionality, which we will call the policy space. The point into which the predictive label is mapped is the voter's *prediction* of the policies that will result from the election of a candidate with this label.

In this setting, the stability question posed above takes the following form: What conditions on voter predictive maps are necessary and/or sufficient to ensure that preferences derived from the voter's policy predictions are single-peaked on a one-dimensional set of predictive labels?

It turns out that these conditions are helpful in understanding stability in legislative decision making. If a legislative issue can be conceived as one-dimensional, then predicting decisions on future legislative issues from a decision on a present legislative issue is generically equivalent to predicting a candidate's policies from a predictive label that belongs to a one-dimensional set.

We add one feature to the legislative model that can also be incorporated into the election model. Due to uncertainty about predictions, we represent the voter's forecast as a probability density function. If the voter's utility function is quadratic, and he maximizes expected utility, a close connection exists between the conditions that are necessary and sufficient for *point* forecasts to induce single-peaked preferences on a single predictive dimension and conditions that are necessary and sufficient for *probabilistic* forecasts to do the same.

Finally, we discuss a different probabilistic forecast model, which violates the necessary and sufficient conditions for derived single-peaked preferences on a single dimension, but show that with additional restrictions, single-peaked preferences can be obtained. We also suggest some avenues for obtaining stability results with a weaker set of sufficient conditions.

Political decision making is frequently characterized by a connection between past, present, and future decisions. What is decided today may be influenced by what was decided in the past and may influence what is decided in the future. An election between a liberal and a conservative candidate can be seen as a simple choice between candidate ideologies, but it may also be seen as a choice between two sets of future policies associated with the election of each candidate. Similarly, a legislative decision on a current issue may have a significant effect on the disposition of future issues. Likewise, the course of past elections or past legislative decisions may influence current political decision making. The theory of predictive mappings allows us to analyze these linkages and to determine their effects on the stability of social choice.

THE THEORY OF PREDICTIVE MAPPINGS

Assume two candidates, R and T, are running for election. This means that the voter must predict what he thinks would happen given the election of each candidate. To help the voter in this endeavor, suppose each candidate is identified with a predictive label, and that if P is the set of all possible labels, the elements of P can be represented as points on a single dimension. The label may be the candidate's ideology, his position on a central campaign issue, or some other indicator of his future policies. Let p_r be R's label and p_t, T's label.

Let the space of future policies be represented by a convex set X in m-dimensional Euclidean space. Voter i has an ideal point x_i in this same space, and his utility u_i for any policy vector in this space is a monotone decreasing function of distance from x_i. The voter judges candidates by his utility for their predicted positions in X.

To predict a candidate's position in X, the voter maps positions in P into positions in X. Let w_i be this mapping function for voter i, so that for any p belonging to P, $w_i(p)$ is a point in X. The voter then prefers candidate R to candidate T if and only if $u_i(w_i(p_r)) > u_i(w_i(p_t))$.

The central question posed by Coughlin and Hinich (1984) is the following: If voter preferences are defined on X, which is m-dimensional, what conditions on w_i are necessary and sufficient for *derived* voter preferences to be single-peaked on P, which is a one-dimensional set? Given the satisfaction of these conditions, we are assured by Black's (1958) median voter result that any candidate identified with the median predictive label will be undefeated in a simple majority, two-candidate election. If these conditions are not satisfied, no predictive label may be best.

The conditions on w_i that are necessary and sufficient to induce single-peaked preferences on P are either (a) w_i is constant, or (b) the range of w_i is contained in a linear interval in X and is strictly monotonic on this interval. Condition (b) is satisfied if and only if there exist vectors c_i, d_i in X and a strictly monotonic real-valued function $f_i(p)$, such that

$$w_i(p) = c_i + f_i(p)d_i \tag{1}$$

The proof of the theorem consists in showing that these restrictions on w_i imply that derived preferences on P are single-peaked. Further, a violation of any of these restrictions *allows* derived preferences on P to be nonsingle-peaked (that is, for some voter preferences on X, derived preferences on P are nonsingle-peaked).

The linear mapping model described in Enelow and Hinich (1984) satisfies condition (b) of the theorem. Assuming that the future policies of R, c_{ir}, are a linear function of R's predictive label,

James M. Enelow and Melvin J. Hinich

$$w_i(p_r) = c_{ir} = b_i + p_r v_i \tag{2}$$

Given this mapping, the derived preferences of voter i are single-peaked on P with a most preferred point

$$z_i = v_i^T A_i (x_i - b_i)/v_i^T A_i v_i, \tag{3}$$

where A_i defines the shape and orientation of i's indifference contours in X. A_i is referred to in spatial theory as i's salience matrix. The candidate identified with the median z_i is guaranteed not to lose in a two-candidate, simple majority election.

Coughlin and Hinich (1984) cited other examples of linear mapping models. One such example appears in Barr and Davis (1966), where each voter is concerned about two policy variables: x, expenditures of the local government, and r, the tax rate on the assessed value of property. If $x = r(P_1 + \ldots + P_Z)$, where P_J is the assessed value of J's property (J = 1, . . . , Z), then (x,r) is contained by the linear interval $x[1,1/(P_1 + \ldots + P_Z)]$. Consequently, voter preferences over different government expenditure levels are single-peaked.

Another example comes from Denzau and Mackay (1980). The voter cares about q_i, his consumption of a publicly provided good, and T_i, his tax bill. Let b be the budget of a government bureau. Assume that the total output of the bureau is $x = (1/m)b$, where m is the constant unit cost of producing the publicly provided good. Assume also that $q_i = a_i x$, where a_i is a constant benefit share, and that $T_i = t_i b$, where t_i is a constant tax share. Then, (q_i, T_i) is contained in the linear interval $b[a_i/m, t_i]$, and voter preferences are single-peaked over different budget levels.

PREDICTING LEGISLATIVE DECISIONS

Let us now turn to a seemingly different prediction model and show how it can be subsumed under the model discussed above. Suppose a group of legislators vote over m issues, one issue at a time, where each issue is one-dimensional. Each issue j (j = 1, . . . , m) is voted on in numerical order, and once an issue is decided, it is not voted on again. A point on a given issue is labeled an alternative on that issue, and each vote consists of a contest between two alternatives from the same issue.

Assume that legislator preferences are defined over outcomes, where an outcome is an alternative from each issue. For a legislator to determine his preference between any two alternatives y_1 and y_2 from the same issue, he must predict the alternatives on future issues that would be chosen if y_1 were adopted and the alternatives that would be chosen if y_2 were adopted. This problem gives us a setup very similar to the one we discussed above. Each issue is a predictive dimension, the alternatives of which are used to predict future issue decisions. An additional feature of this model is that forecasts can be updated after each issue is decided.

From Coughlin and Hinich (1984) we know the following: If, on any issue j, the legislator uses each alternative on issue j to forecast the decisions on issues $j + 1, \ldots, m$, the legislator's derived preferences on issue j will be single-peaked *under all forecasts* if and only if either (a) the forecast is constant, or (b) the range of the forecast is contained in a linear interval in the decision space on issues $j + 1, \ldots, m$ and is strictly monotonic on this interval.

In Enelow and Hinich (1983) and Enelow (1984), an additional feature is added to this model: The legislator is allowed to be uncertain about his prediction. Instead of a point forecast, the legislator is assumed to forecast with a probability density function. The following result is then derived: If the legislator minimizes expected quadratic loss and forecasts with a probability vector whose covariance matrix is independent of present alternatives, then legislator preferences on each issue are single-peaked if his mean forecast is linear in present alternatives.

The result is quite similar to the Coughlin–Hinich theorem. The explanation for this near-equivalence comes from observing that the expected quadratic loss function can be written as the sum of the squared mean loss and the weighted sum of the variances and covariances. More formally, if $Y_i = (Y_{i2}, \ldots, Y_{im})$ are i's forecasts on issues $2, \ldots, m$ conditional on y as the decision on issue 1, then i seeks to minimize over y

$$E[((y,Y_i) - x_i)^T A_i ((y,Y_i) - x_i)] \tag{4}$$

Similarly, we can define i's utility function as the negative of (4), in which case he seeks to maximize expected utility.

But, expanding (4), substituting $\mathrm{Var}(Y_{ij}) + [E(Y_{ij})]^2$ for $E(Y_{ij}^2)$, and $\mathrm{Cov}(Y_{ij}, Y_{ik}) + E(Y_{ij})E(Y_{ik})$ for $E(Y_{ij}Y_{ik})$, we can reexpress (4) as

$$((y,y_i) - x_i)^T A_i ((y,y_i) - x_i) + \sum_{j=2}^m \sum_{k=2}^m a_{ijk} \sigma_{jk} \tag{5}$$

where $y_i = E(Y_{i2}, \ldots, Y_{im})$ and $\sigma_{jj} = \sigma_j^2$ is the variance of Y_{ij} and σ_{jk} is the covariance of Y_{ij} and Y_{ik}.

If the variances and covariances of the Y_{ij} are independent of y, then i's preferences over the alternatives of issue 1 depend only on his utility for (y,y_i), where y_i is the vector of mean forecasts conditional on y. Consequently, by the Coughlin–Hinich theorem, if y_i is linear in present alternatives, i's preferences over the alternatives of the present issue are single-peaked.

The legislator need not make a single forecast for this result to hold. In other words, he can revise his forecast of future issue decisions after each current issue is decided. As long as the mean of the revised forecast is linear in present alternatives with a covariance matrix independent of present alternatives, preferences over the alternatives of the present issue are single-

James M. Enelow and Melvin J. Hinich

peaked. Furthermore, the most preferred alternative on each issue is a linear function of past issue decisions.

If legislator i adopts the linear mean mapping function $y_i = b_i + yv_i$, his most preferred alternative on issue 1 is

$$y^* = [(1,v_i)^T A_i x_i - (1,v_i)^T A_{-1i} b_i]/(1,v_i)^T A_i(1,v_i), \tag{6}$$

where A_{-1i} is the m x (m−1) matrix consisting of the last m−1 columns of A_i. Equations (6) and (3) are almost the same, the difference being that the legislator's utility function is defined directly over both forecasted and present decisions, while the utility function of the voter in equation (3) is defined only over future policies.

Epple and Kadane (1987) contribute a further result. Suppose all voter preferences are of the type expressed by (4) with a common A matrix. Suppose also that voter ideal points are drawn at random from a known distribution, but that x_i is known only to i. Then, by deduction, the voter's preferences over the alternatives of the present issue will be single-peaked, and his forecast of the decision on any issue yet to be decided will be linear in the decisions of issues that have been decided with a covariance matrix that is independent of the decisions that have been reached.

While the Epple–Kadane (E–K) and the Enelow–Hinich (E–H) results appear nearly the same, the two models differ in several ways. In the E–H model, predictions of future issue decisions are based on present alternatives, just as in the election model, predictions of future policies are based on the present labels of the candidates.

In the E–K model, predictions are derived endogenously. In the case of two issues, each of which is decided by majority rule, the individual knows that the decision reached on the second issue will be the median of the ideal points on the second issue, conditioned on the decision reached on the first issue. If Y_2 is this predicted decision, conditioned on y, then

$$Y_2 = \underset{i}{\text{median}} \ [x_{i2} - (a_{i12}/a_{i22})(y - x_{i1})] \tag{7}$$

But if $a_{ijk} = a_{jk}$ (there is a common set of salience weights for all individuals), then we can rewrite (7) as

$$Y_2 = -(a_{12}/a_{22})y + \underset{i}{\text{median}} \ [x_{i2} + (a_{12}/a_{22})(x_{i1})]. \tag{8}$$

The individual can therefore deduce that the decision on issue 2 will be linear in the decision on issue 1. Furthermore, since the second term on the right-hand side of (8) is independent of y, if uncertainty about the ideal points of the other voters causes this term to be a random variable, its variance will be independent of y. It follows that preferences on issue 1 are single-peaked.

The assumption of a common A matrix is equivalent to assuming that each voter has circular indifference contours (in some linear transformation of the original issue space). In this transformed issue space, the voter's forecast reduces to the median ideal point on each issue.

What if both salience weights and ideal points differ across individuals? Then, from (7), we see that the mean of Y_2 may not be linear in y and that the variance of Y_2 may not be independent of y. Suppose, for example, that one (not every) individual's utility function is $u(y, Y_2) = -(y - x_1)^2 - (Y_2 - x_2)^2$, where (x_1, x_2) is the individual's ideal point on issues 1 and 2. For preferences on issue 1 to be concave in y (and therefore single-peaked), $\partial^2 u / \partial y^2$, the second partial derivative of u with respect to y must be negative. For this example,

$$\partial^2 u / \partial y^2 = -1 - (\partial y_2 / \partial y)^2 - (y_2 - x_2)(\partial^2 y_2 / \partial y^2)$$
$$- \partial^2 \sigma^2 / 2 \partial y^2 < 0 \tag{9}$$

where y_2 is the mean and σ^2 is the variance of Y_2.

If y_2 is linear in y and the variance of Y_2 is independent of y, then the third and fourth terms on the right-hand side of the equality drop out and the second partial derivative is negative. But, if the third and fourth terms do not drop out, then the second partial derivative may be positive.

If both salience weights and ideal points differ across individuals, it is unclear how much information the individual can derive about the characteristics of Y_2. The E–H approach is to cut this Gordian knot by assuming that the individual acts as if the linear-mean, independent-covariance assumption were true (even if it is not). If information about Y_2 is fragmentary, it is reasonable to assume that the individual uses a least-squares approach to estimating Y_2.

The linear-mean, independent-covariance conditions can be derived from a different starting point. Suppose, before any voting takes place, that the individual's forecasts of the decisions on issues 1, . . . , m are described by a *multivariate normal* distribution. Then, after any set of issues has been decided, the individual's forecasts on the remaining issues, given this actual set of decisions, will also be multinormal, with a mean vector that is linear in the decisions that have been reached and a covariance matrix that is independent of these fixed values.

To understand this result, return to the case of two issues and assume, before any voting takes place, that the forecast variable $Y = (Y_1, Y_2)$ is bivariate normal with mean vector (y_1, y_2) and covariance matrix Σ, where σ_1^2 is the variance of Y_1, σ_2^2 is the variance of Y_2, and σ_{12} is the covariance of Y_1 and Y_2.

Now, suppose that the actual decision reached on issue 1 is z_1. What is the individual's *conditional* forecast on issue 2 given that $Y_1 = z_1$? The answer is a normal density whose expected value is

$$E(Y_2|z_1) = y_2 + (\sigma_{12}/\sigma_1^2)(z_1 - y_1) \qquad (10)$$

and whose variance is

$$Var(Y_2|z_1) = \sigma_2^2 - \sigma_{12}^2/\sigma_1^2. \qquad (11)$$

These results can be found in most multivariate statistics texts, such as Morrison (1967). Note that the expected value of Y_2 given z_1 is linear in z_1 and that the variance of Y_2 given z_1 is independent of z_1.

The conditional density can depend on a conjecture about the decision on issue 1 rather than a realization. The individual can make a forecast on issue 2 given each of a set of possible decisions on issue 1. In this case, (10) and (11) imply that the individual's preferences on issue 1 are single-peaked. Thus, we see that the assumption of a multinormal forecast variable implies single-peaked preferences on each of the issues that is decided.

A BINARY PREDICTION MODEL

In Enelow and Hinich (1987a and b) and Enelow (1988), a different prediction model is constructed. Once again, the goal is to provide (sufficient) conditions for preferences on a one-dimensional issue to be single-peaked. In this model the mean forecast is nonlinear in present alternatives, and the variance of the forecast variable depends on the alternative being considered.

Assume an individual must define his preferences over a one-dimensional set of alternatives, where each alternative y may be put up for a vote, or series of votes, and either accepted or rejected by one or more voting bodies. This setup is similar to Romer and Rosenthal's (1978, 1979) school budget model. An individual may propose a \$50 raise in salary, but it is up to the boss (or a set of bosses) to decide whether he gets the \$50 or nothing. If a committee must reach a decision about which alternative to propose, then single-peakedness of the preferences of the committee members over the alternatives that may be proposed guarantees that a best alternative exists for the committee, if majority rule is used to decide which of any two alternatives is better to propose.

For simplicity, assume that a single voting body accepts or rejects any given proposal y. If y is rejected, a status quo alternative z takes effect. Let $G(y)$ be i's forecast of the probability that y will be accepted, and $F(y) = 1 - G(y)$ be i's forecast of the probability that y is rejected. Then, if i's utility function $u(y) = -(y - x_i)^2$, i seeks to maximize

$$L(y) = -(y - x_i)^2 G(y) - (z - x_i)^2 F(y) \qquad (12)$$

But, an alternative expression for $L(y)$ can be derived in terms of the mean and variance of the discrete random variable Y, where $G(y)$ is the probability that Y equals y and F(y) is the probability that Y equals z. Setting z = 0, for computational convenience, an equivalent expression is

$$L(y) = - (yG(y) - x_i)^2 - y^2G(y)F(y), \qquad (13)$$

where yG(y) is the mean and $y^2G(y)F(y)$ is the variance of Y.

Unless G(y) is a constant, the mean of Y is not linear in y. Furthermore, the variance of Y is not independent of y. Therefore, we cannot make use of the Enelow–Hinich extension of the Coughlin–Hinich theorem to show that preferences over different y are single-peaked.

Does this mean that L(y) is not a single-peaked function? Not necessarily. Recall that linearity of the (mean) forecast is necessary in the sense that nonlinearity *allows* for the possibility that derived preferences are nonsingle-peaked. In fact, without additional restrictions, single-peakedness of L(y) cannot be guaranteed. But if f(y) is the density of F(y), the following two additional conditions are sufficient for the single-peakedness of L(y): For all y such that G(y) > 0,

(1) u(y) ≥ u(z).
(2) f(y)/G(y) is increasing in y.

Condition (2) will be satisfied by any density that can be expressed as f(y) = exp(− g(y)), where g is a convex function. Such densities include the normal, exponential, gamma, binomial, poisson, beta, and others. Utility can be any concave function, and not just the negative quadratic.

To provide an example, suppose G(y) = 1 − y for all y in [0,1]. Then the mean of Y is $y - y^2$ and the variance of Y is $y^3 - y^4$. The mean is a quadratic function of y, and the variance is a 4th degree polynomial in y, violations of either the Enelow–Hinich or Coughlin–Hinich conditions. Nevertheless, if x_i = 1 and z = 0, u(y) = $- (y - 1)^2$, f(y)/G(y) = 1/(1 − y), and both (1) and (2) above are satisfied. L(y) is single-peaked over all y in [0,1], with a maximum at y* = .42.

If, on the other hand, either (1) or (2) is violated, L(y) may be nonsingle-peaked. As one example, suppose u(y) = $1/4 - (y - 1/2)^2$ and G(y) = 1 − 2y/3 for y in [0,3/2]. If z = 0, then for 3/2 > y > 1, u(z) > u(y), so condition (1) above is violated. L(y) = u(y)G(y) + u(0)F(y) = $(y - y^2)(1 - 2y/3)$ changes direction twice between y = 0 and y = 3/2, so L(y) is nonsingle-peaked.

It is interesting that conditions (1) and (2) are sufficient for the single-peakedness of L(y) under more complicated decision procedures. For example, if there are m voting bodies that decide whether to accept or reject y, suppose y is adopted only if each voting body accepts y. If these voting bodies reach decisions in serial fashion, the decision of any voting body may be conditioned on the decisions reached by the voting bodies that acted previously. Conditions (1) and (2) are still sufficient for L(y) to be single-peaked. Condition (2) now applies to every f/G, where both f and G are subscripted by voting body j and decision history h_{j-1}.

FURTHER EXTENSIONS

We see that certain relaxations of the Coughlin–Hinich/Enelow–Hinich conditions are possible without destroying single-peakedness of individual preferences over a one-dimensional set of predictive elements. In the case of the binary prediction model, however, additional assumptions are required to avoid nonsingle-peakedness.

Are further relaxations possible? The prediction model of Enelow and Hinich (1981) suggests another possibility. In this model, the predictive elements are a one-dimensional set of policies used to "predict themselves." The idea is similar to one used by Austen-Smith and Riker (1987), where the "policy space" is distinguished from the "outcome space." In a legislative setting, this distinction may be caused by uncertainty about how policies will be implemented. In an electoral setting, the distinction may be caused by any factor that affects the translation of a candidate's policy position during the campaign into a policy outcome after the campaign is over. In either case, the voter believes that what he selects (the choice) may not be what he gets (the outcome).

As in the Enelow–Hinich legislative prediction model, the forecast of the policy outcome is a probability density function, although the forecast is a mapping from the policy issue into itself, rather than into a different policy issue. The essential difference between these two models, though, is that the variance of the forecast variable *is* dependent on the predictive elements of the model. Formally, if y is a policy alternative and Y is the forecast of the policy outcome that will result if y is chosen, then the variance of Y is a function of y. Furthermore, y is the mean of Y so that, on average, what the voter selects is what he gets (that is, on average, the policy is "faithfully" executed).

As before, we seek sufficient conditions for individual preferences to be single-peaked over the predictive elements of the model (in this case, policy alternatives). If utility over policy *outcomes* is described by the negative quadratic function used throughout this essay, we can express the expected utility of any Y in terms of its mean and variance, as we did in expression (13). Thus,

$$u(Y) = -(y - x_i)^2 - \sigma_Y^2 \qquad (14)$$

Consider three policy alternatives $y_1 = 1$, $y_2 = 2$, and $y_3 = 3$, with associated forecast variables Y_1, Y_2, Y_3. Let $x_i = 1$. Then, assume that $\sigma_{Y1}^2 = \sigma_{Y3}^2 = 0$ and $\sigma_{Y2}^2 = 4$. Then, if i prefers y_j to y_k if and only if $u(Y_j) > u(Y_k)$, i prefers y_1 to y_2 and y_3 to y_2, which are not single-peaked preferences over these policy alternatives.

Clearly, therefore, σ_Y^2 cannot be any old function of y. But consider the quadratic function $\sigma_Y^2 = r + ty^2$, which is assumed by Enelow and Hinich

The Theory of Predictive Mappings

(1981). Letting $y = 0$ be a status quo policy alternative, predictive uncertainty is a marginally increasing (if $t > 0$) or decreasing (if $t < 0$) function of the difference between the considered policy alternative and the status quo. Substituting this function for σ_Y^2 in equation (14), the second derivative of $u(Y)$ with respect to y is $-2(1 + t)$. For $t > 0$, $-2(1 + t) < 0$, so individual preferences are concave (and so single-peaked) in y. For $t < 0$, the same result is obtained if $t > -1$. Furthermore, given the satisfaction of the second-order condition, the most preferred policy alternative $y^* = x_i/(1 + t)$.

Focusing on the case where $t > 0$, we see that if the variance of Y is a marginally increasing quadratic function of the difference between a considered policy alternative and the status quo, then preferences over policy alternatives are single-peaked. This result generalizes to our legislative prediction model. Rewrite expression (5), the negative of the legislator's objective function, as

$$((y, y_i) - x_i)^T A_i ((y, y_i) - x_i) + \sigma^T D_i \sigma + 2 \sum_{j=2}^{m-1} \sum_{k=j+1}^{m} a_{ijk} \sigma_{jk} \qquad (15)$$

where D_i is a diagonal matrix composed of the diagonal elements of A_i and $\sigma^T = (0, \sigma_2, \ldots, \sigma_m)$ is the vector of standard deviations of the Y_{ij} ($j = 2, \ldots, m$). If σ_{jk}, the covariance of Y_{ij} and Y_{ik}, is independent of y for $j \neq k$, but $\sigma_j^2 = r_j + t_j y^2$ for $j = 2, \ldots, m$ then individual preferences are single-peaked over y, the predictive elements of the model.

CONCLUSIONS

We have discussed a broad class of predictive mapping models, stressing necessary and sufficient conditions for derived preferences to be single-peaked over a one-dimensional set of predictive elements. When such conditions hold, what appears to be a multidimensional choice problem is equivalent to choosing over a one-dimensional set of alternatives with a "best" element in this set from the standpoint of social choice.

Predictive mapping models have wide applicability to problems of group decision making. In elections, the voter may be seen as choosing between the predicted policies he associates with the election of each candidate. In legislative settings, the voter may also use present alternatives to predict future alternatives. One extension of the electoral model that we have not discussed is the evaluation of candidates by their past policies. This is known in the political science literature as *retrospective* voting.

The question raised by Epple and Kadane (1987) is the extent to which forecasts can be made endogenous to the model. They have shown that under certain conditions, the voter can deduce a forecast that is linear in past decisions with covariance matrix independent of past decisions. As they are aware, Denzau and Mackay (1981) have shown that if voters make "perfect forecasts," due to complete information about all voters' preferences over all issues, voter preferences over present alternatives may be nonsingle-peaked if voter salience matrices differ.

177

James M. Enelow and Melvin J. Hinich

We have shown that if prior beliefs are described by a multinormal distribution, then voter preferences on each issue will be single-peaked if possible decisions on the present issue are used to predict future issue decisions. This result follows because the conditional distribution of future issue decisions is multinormal, with a mean vector linear in past issue decisions and a covariance matrix independent of these fixed values.

It remains an open question whether the linear-mean, independent-covariance result can be obtained under other types of imperfect voter information. Models in which voters make systematic forecasting errors need not be dismissed out of hand. While unfashionable in economics, such models have proved fruitful in psychological studies of decision making.

REFERENCES

Austen-Smith, D., and W. Riker. 1987. "Asymmetric Information and the Coherence of Legislation." *American Political Science Review* 81: 897–918.

Barr, J., and O. Davis. 1966. "An Elementary Political and Economic Theory of the Expenditures of Local Governments." *Southern Economic Journal* 33: 149–65.

Black, D. 1958. *Theory of Committees and Elections*. New York: Cambridge University Press.

Coughlin, P., and M. Hinich. 1984. "Necessary and Sufficient Conditions for Single-Peakedness in Public Economics Models." *Journal of Public Economics* 25: 161–79.

Denzau, A., and R. Mackay. 1980. "A Model of Benefit and Tax Share Discrimination." *Journal of Public Economics* 13: 341–68.

———. 1981. "Structure Induced Equilibrium and Perfect Foresight Expectations." *American Journal of Political Science* 25: 762–79.

Enelow, J. 1984. "A Generalized Model of Voting One Issue at a Time with Applications to Congress." *American Journal of Political Science* 28: 587–97.

Enelow, J. 1988. "A Bayesian Analysis of a Class of Multi-Stage Decision Problems." *Journal of Conflict Resolution* 32: 759–72.

Enelow, J., and M. Hinich. 1981. "A New Approach to Voter Uncertainty in the Downsian Spatial Model." *American Journal of Political Science* 25: 483–93.

———. 1983. "Voting One Issue at a Time: The Question of Voter Forecasts." *American Political Science Review* 77: 435–45.

———. 1984. *The Spatial Theory of Voting: An Introduction*. New York: Cambridge University Press.

———. 1987a. "Optimal Decision Making When the Shapes and Locations of Voter Preference Curves Are Unknown." *Economia delle scelte pubbliche* 3: 161–70.

———. 1987b. "Uncertainty and the New Institutionalism: The Existence of a Structure Induced Equilibrium." Delivered at the 1987 meetings of the Public Choice Society, Tucson, AZ, March 1987.

Epple, D., and J. Kadane. 1987. "Sequential Voting with Endogenous Voter Forecasts." Carnegie-Mellon University (unpublished).

Morrison, D. 1967. *Multivariate Statistical Methods*. New York: McGraw-Hill.

Romer, T., and H. Rosenthal. 1978. "Political Resource Allocation, Controlled Agenda and the Status Quo." *Public Choice* 33: 27–44.

Romer, T., and H. Rosenthal. 1979. "The Elusive Median Voter." *Journal of Public Economics* 12: 143–70.

8

Multicandidate Spatial Competition

GARY W. COX

*University of California,
San Diego*

The classical spatial model, first formulated by Hotelling (1929), focused on competition between two agents (interpreted either as business firms or political parties). Although competition between more than two agents was considered soon thereafter (for example, Chamberlain 1933), only in the last decade or so has sustained attention been paid to the multiagent case. This essay surveys the results of this attention, especially as regards competition between political parties or candidates for political office.

Broadly speaking, the literature divides into two streams: those works analyzing multi-item agendas, and those works dealing with elections in which more than two candidates or parties are competing. I shall focus on the second topic: models of multicandidate (or multiparty) electoral competition.

An increasingly important distinction among such models is that some models attempt to endogenize the number of candidates, letting the model predict what the equilibrium number should be, while others take the number of competitors as exogenously given. In other words, some models allow entry, while others do not. Because Chapter 2 by Shepsle and Cohen covers the question of entry, I shall focus here on no-entry models. Such models are of course necessary parts of the more elaborate entry models, but they are also of interest on their own: The no-entry assumption accurately describes the situation of candidates in a race after the filing deadline (for getting names onto the ballot) has passed. It is true that the possibility of write-in campaigns exists, but it is also true that such campaigns are usually of negligible importance. No-entry models should therefore be useful in investigating the incentives of candidates in the post-filing stage of the campaign.

All the models investigated here share a common spatial approach. Each typically assumes a unidimensional policy space, although some – to be noted – have straightforward multidimensional extensions. Each involves $m \geq 3$ candidates who compete for $\kappa \geq 1$ positions. Candidates are assumed to compete for the position(s) available by advocating one of the feasible policies. Voters are assumed (a) to possess single-peaked spatial preferences with unique ideal points (sometimes further constrained to be symmetric); (b) to vote deterministically, not probabilistically; and (c) to vote sincerely, not strategically. Each model posits a particular electoral formula, which specifies both the voting options available to voters and how votes are counted. Each then characterizes equilibrium strategies for candidates: Will candidates converge on some (centrally located) point, as in the well-known median voter result? Will they disperse over the policy space and, if so, how widely?

The discussion is organized first by district magnitude (κ, the number of positions to be filled) and second by electoral formula. That is to say, I consider single-member districts first, separately investigating multicandidate competition under various possible electoral formulae (such as plurality rule, approval voting, and Borda's rule). Next, I consider multimember districts, again separately investigating competition under various electoral institutions (to wit, various proportional representation and plurality-based rules). Both district magnitude and electoral rules affect the character of competition, as will be seen.

SINGLE-MEMBER DISTRICTS

This section investigates models that pertain to elections held in single-member districts (for which $\kappa = 1$). The chief distinction between these models regards the electoral formula (or class of electoral formulae) used. Here, attention will be limited to four: plurality rule, scoring rules, approval voting, and Condorcet completion procedures.

Plurality rule

The political interpretation of spatial models goes all the way back to Hotelling, who thought his results explained not just the close physical proximity of competing business firms on Main Street but also the ideological similarity of the Republican and Democratic platforms in 1928. Hotelling was also the first to consider the multiagent case, although only as regards firms. He speculated that the tendency to "cluster unduly" near the center of the market would persist, even if more than two firms were competing (Hotelling 1929, p. 55).

Soon thereafter, Chamberlain (1933, Appendix C) disputed Hotelling's view, arguing that "as soon as there are three [firms], the one who is caught between the other two will move to the outer edge of the group, and a series of such moves, always by the one left in the center, will disperse the group." Chamberlain's general conclusion was that, as "the number of sellers increases, they may group in twos . . . but any group of three or more would be broken up in the manner already described [so that] for fairly large numbers, the distribution approximates closely the ideal which maximizes the convenience of the buyers." He mentions in a footnote the political implication of his argument: "Where there are more than two parties, a dispersion takes place analogous to that of the sellers on the line."

Chamberlain's conjectures regarding mutiagent spatial competition were not fully formalized until the mid-1970s. In the interim, there was a dearth of research. The vast bulk of research in spatial economics has complicated the early models by introducing simultaneous price competition, a feature that really has no political analog. Among the work that does not introduce price competition, Lerner and Singer (1937, pp. 176–82) have an important early statement, and Downs (1957, pp. 122–32). Lipsey (1963, p. 255–6), and Tullock (1967, pp. 54–5) have brief informal conjectures, but not until Eaton and Lipsey (1975) is the multiagent case dealt with rigorously. Their model is worth exploring at some length.

First, it should be noted that Eaton and Lipsey are primarily interested in the economic implications of their model. Here, I shall reinterpret their assumptions and findings in terms of electoral competition. Put briefly, Eaton and Lipsey make the following assumptions in their basic model:

(1) The policy space is a closed, bounded, and connected subset of the real line, which they normalize to be the [0, 1] interval.

(2) Every voter has symmetric and strictly single-peaked preferences over the policy space (and thus has a unique ideal point).

(3) The distribution of voters' ideal points is uniform across the [0, 1] interval.

(4) Every voter votes (no abstention).

(5) Every voter votes sincerely (that is, in light of assumption 2, for the candidate whose platform is closest to the voter's ideal point).

(6) There are m candidates who seek to maximize the share of the vote they garner by adopting a platform in [0, 1].

(7) Candidates may reposition themselves without cost.

(8) There is zero-order conjectural variation. That is, each candidate estimates the payoff to relocating on the hypothesis that his or her competitors will remain at their current positions.

Eaton and Lipsey define an *interior* candidate as one who has opponents both to the left and to the right, and *peripheral* candidates as those who are not interior. Two candidates are said to be *paired* if they are positioned at the same point in policy space.

Qualitatively, Eaton and Lipsey's results agree with Chamberlain's. They do prove that peripheral candidates are paired in equilibrium, and this result does reflect Hotelling's original insight: Whenever a candidate is positioned so that all his competitors are to the right (or to the left), he will move toward them (because the no-abstention assumption means that he will not lose votes on the side without competitors, while he will gain votes from the side with competitors). Nonetheless, despite this partial reflection of Hotelling, none of the

Gary W. Cox

equilibria that Eaton and Lipsey investigate have more than two candidates bunched at a single location and, overall, candidates are dispersed fairly widely over the ideological spectrum – just as Chamberlain conjectured.

These last two results have been stated and proven more formally by later work. Denzau, Kats, and Slutsky (1985), working with the same model (expect that they investigate both candidates who seek to maximize their vote share and those who seek to minimize their rank of finish in the poll), prove that no multicandidate equilibrium can have more than two candidates bunched at a single position. The logic of this result reflects Chamberlain's response to Hotelling: Whenever three or more candidates get "too close" together, the middle ones are "squeezed" and thereby motivated to move; this prevents convergence of more than two candidates and ensures a certain amount of overall dispersal.

The amount of dispersal guaranteed has been specified more precisely by Cox (1987a). Cox's model is addressed primarily to political rather than economic phenomena and consequently relaxes a few of the assumptions made in the economic models. In particular, assumptions (2), (3), and (6) are replaced by the following, less restrictive assumptions:

(2') Voters have single-peaked but not necessarily symmetric preferences (the assumption of symmetry being reasonable in economic models but unnecessarily restrictive in electoral models).

(3') The distribution of voter ideal points is continuous but not necessarily uniform (uniformity being a restrictive assumption in either model).

(6') Each candidate has an "admissible" objective, but not all candidates need have the same objective (the class of "admissible" objectives including Eaton and Lipsey's maximization of vote share, maximization of plurality, and some others).

The point of allowing different candidates to have different goals is that, in multicandidate contests, some may seek a "respectable" finish, or a second-place finish, rather than believing they can attain a first-place finish. With assumption (6'), the model partially allows for such possibilities.[1]

Cox finds that previous results are robust to the changes he makes: Peripheral candidates are still paired in equilibrium, and it is still true that no equilibrium has more than two candidates bunched. In addition, he demonstrates that any multicandidate equilibrium must be noncentrist in the sense that some candidate(s) will be positioned outside the interquartile range of voter ideal points (or on the boundary of this range). Moreover, if candidates all seek to maximize their vote shares, then it can be shown that equilibrium requires that some candidate(s) be positioned outside the range $(Q[1/m], Q[(m-1)/m])$, where $Q[\alpha]$ is the αth percentile of the distribution of voter ideal points (and m is the number of candidates).

The political meaning of this result, and the previous "no more than two bunched" result, boils down to this: In multicandidate elections held under the plurality system, the desire of candidates to win election does not provide them with a clear and consistent incentive, as it does in the two-candidate case, to move to the middle of the political spectrum. Multicandidate equilibria, when they exist, are decidedly noncentrist in the sense that candidates are dispersed fairly widely relative to the distribution of voters.[2]

The importance of these results may of course be tempered if they are not robust to modification of the more stringent assumptions underpinning them or if multicandidate equilibria simply fail to exist. The latter possibility is not too worrisome if assumption (3) – which posits a uniform distribution of voter ideal points – is retained. In this case, equilibria exist for a variety of assumptions concerning candidate motivation (Eaton and Lipsey positing vote-share maximizers, Denzau, Kats and Slutsky adding rank-of-finish minimizers, Cox adding plurality maximizers and others). If the distribution of voter ideal points is allowed to be nonuniform, however, equilibria are rarer. Eaton and Lipsey, in a model that replaces (3) with (3') but is otherwise the same as their basic model, find that there are no equilibria for any number of candidates greater than two if the distribution of voter ideal points is strictly monotonic increasing from each end of the political spectrum to a single mode. Thus, for example, a truncated normal distribution would not support any multicandidate equilibria. They also prove that, if the voter distribution is not uniform over any range, then a necessary condition for equilibrium is that the number of candidates does not exceed twice the number of modes. More generally, Eaton and Lipsey's work supports (I conjecture) the following conclusion: If, for a particular voter distribution, there exists a multicandidate equilibrium, then an arbitrarily small change in the voter distribution can always be made such that no multicandidate equilibrium exists for the changed distribution. If true, *this means that multicandidate equilibria are just as rare in one dimension as are two-candidate equilibria in many dimensions.*

Despite the rareness of multicandidate equilibria, however, they are worth studying for much the same reasons that two-candidate equilibria are worth studying, even in multidimensional spaces. First, it is relatively easy to re-establish two-candidate equilibria by assuming that voters are probabilistic rather than deterministic; moreover, the qualitative features of deterministic and probabilistic equilibria are substantially the same (I consider the difference between weighted means and medians – both measures of central tendency – to be relatively small for purposes of political interpretation). It seems likely that the same would be true of multicandidate equilibria.

Second, in two-candidate models, the disequilibrium dynamics turn out to reflect many of the same features that are highlighted in equilibrium (see, for example, Kramer 1977). The same has been shown to be true for multicandidate models by Eaton (1972) and Eaton and Lipsey. In particular, they identify a tendency for pairs of candidates to bunch in "local clusters" and for larger groups to disperse, as Chamberlain described.

Figure 8.1. An example of equilibrium with four candidates in two dimensions. Two candidates are located at A, the center of the right rectangle, and two at B, the center of the right rectangle. The distribution of voters is uniform over the larger rectangle (the union of the left and right rectangles).

Third, important features of equilibrium behavior in two-candidate models are preserved when one looks at weaker behavioral requirements, such as that candidates avoid playing dominated strategies. This is the gist of two-candidate research focusing on the uncovered set (McKelvey 1976; Miller 1977; Cox 1987b). The same is true regarding multicandidate models (Cox 1989), although in the particular case of plurality rule the results are weak.

Assuming, then, that multicandidate equilibria are worth investigating, even if they rarely exist, the question arises as to whether the particular qualitative results emphasized above are robust to alterations in the key assumptions. Except in the case of assumption (5), regarding sincere voting, the answer appears to be affirmative.

Assumption (1). If multidimensional models are considered, the problem of nonexistence may be exacerbated. Eaton and Lipsey speculate, and Shaked (1975) shows, that no equilibrium exists in two dimensions when there are three candidates competing, regardless of the voter distribution. The three-candidate case is similarly anomalous in one dimension, however, so Shaked's result does not distinguish between the one- and many-dimensional cases. Moreover, equilibrium can be concocted with *four* candidates in two dimensions, as Figure 8.1 illustrates. Thus, it is not yet clear that multicandidate equilibira will be significantly rarer in multidimensional spaces than they are in one-dimensional spaces. In any event, the same reasons for studying equilibria that obtain in one-dimensional models also obtain in multidimensional models. There may be as yet no work involving probabilistic voters, but Eaton and Lipsey have found that the dynamics of disequilibrium in many-dimensional models are similar to those in the simpler models.

Assumption (4). The "no-abstention" assumption was first relaxed in two-candidate models by Smithies (1941) and in three- and four-candidate models by Hinich and Ordeshook (1970). In both cases, the main effect of allowing abstention is to deter candidates from converging.

Assumption (7). The assumption of costless spatial mobility has yet to be modified in multicandidate models. It seems unlikely that adding a cost to mobility would destroy any equilibria that existed in a costless world, but it might create more bunched equilibria if the cost were sufficiently high.

Assumption (8). Virtually all spatial models, regardless of the number of candidates, assume zero-order conjectural variation (or ZCV). Among multicandidate models, the only exceptions are Eaton and Lipsey, who consider a kind of first-order conjectural variation that I will not consider (see Shepsle and Cohen), and Chamberlain. Chamberlain offered an interesting if brief conjecture about equilibrium with three candidates (assumptions (1)–(7) retained): "For three sellers, the outcome seems to be that two of them, say A and B, would be located at the quartile points and the third, C, at any point between them."

This conjecture is clearly false under ZCV: If candidate A moved toward C, he would lose no votes on his left (because there is no abstention), and he would gain some votes on his right (from voters situated between the first quartile and C's position). Nonetheless, Chamberlain seems clearly to have had some sort of first-order conjectural variation in mind: "if we suppose either A or B to move towards the center in order to enlarge his [vote share], his place would promptly be taken by C." This idea can be fleshed out as follows. Define a *move* as any change in spatial location, a *countermove* as any move by one firm immediately after that of another, and a *harmful* countermove as one that improves the vote share of the countermover while reducing the vote share of the original mover below his pre-move share. If one assumes that a candidate will move only if (a) his move increases his vote share and (b) no harmful countermove exists, then it can be proven that the situation described by Chamberlain is an equilibrium.[3]

Essentially the same equilibrium (two firms at the quartiles, the third somewhere in between) has been suggested by Lipsey (1963, p. 255) as a model of collusion and elaborated by Palfrey (1984) as a model of sequential entry. No work has been done with Chamberlain's type of conjectural variation for larger numbers of candidates, but it seems likely that equilibria in this case would continue to exhibit significant dispersion of candidates.

The incentive of candidates in many-sided contests to disperse is thus robust against a number of alterations in the behavioral assumptions underpinning the analysis. The key to this dispersal is the phenomenon of "squeezing" identified by Chamberlain, where a candidate caught between two others garners only a tiny vote share as these others move closer together. The candidate in the middle is squeezed because, under the assumptions of the model, he gets no votes from voters from whom he is separated by an opponent. Only if this feature of the model is altered can convergence of more than two candidates occur.

Assumption (6). This feature might be altered if voters are strategic. Consider, for example, three candidates all positioned at the median of a one-dimensional voter distribution. If voters are sincere, each candidate has an incentive to move slightly to the left (or right). For, the two candidates who

Gary W. Cox

remain at the median will split a bit more than half the voters, for an expected vote share slightly in excess of one fourth, while the mover will have a share slightly less than half. If voters are strategic, however, then perhaps the majority of voters who prefer the two candidates at the median will coordinate on just one of them, thereby defeating the mover – and destroying the incentive to move in the first place.

Another way that convergence can reemerge in equilibrium is if voters have more than one vote to cast or the voting rule is somehow changed. This possibility is investigated in the next few subsections.

Scoring rules

This subsection investigates the nature of candidate incentives under a generic scoring rule, following Cox (1987a). Under a scoring rule, each voter submits a strict rank ordering of the m candidates. The candidate ranked first receives s_1 votes, the candidate ranked second receives s_2 votes, and so on. Different scoring rules have different values of $s = (s_1, \ldots, s_m)$ and these values may change with the number of candidates, but all are such that $s_1 > s_m$ and $s_k \geq s_{k+1}$ for $k = 1, \ldots, m - 1$. The candidate with the most votes wins.

A wide variety of different voting methods fall under the general heading of scoring rules. These can be classified into three broad categories based on the incentives they give to candidates. The first category – *first-place rewarding rules* – can be described as follows. Let the average number of votes awarded by a particular scoring rule when there are m candidates be

$$s(m) = \frac{1}{m} \sum_{k=1}^{m} s_k$$

and consider the number $c(s,m) = [s_1 - s(m)]/[s_1 - s_m]$. This number compares two terms: (a) the drop in votes that a candidate suffers if he falls from first in some voter's ranking to an average ranking ($s_1 - s(m)$); and (2) the drop in votes that a candidate suffers if he falls from first to last in some voter's ranking ($s_1 - s_m$). When $c(s,m) > 1/2$, the drop in votes from top to average is "large" relative to the top-to-bottom drop. Getting an average amount of votes may not be much better than getting the fewest possible. Thus, scoring rules with $c(s,m) > 1/2$ (for $m \geq 3$) present candidates with an incentive to make sure that they place first or high in as many voters' rankings as possible. The starkest example of this is the scoring rule with $s = (1, 0, \ldots, 0)$, for which $c(s,m) = (m - 1)/m$; this rule awards a vote only for first place and is essentially equivalent to the plurality rule.

Another class of scoring rules – the *last-place punishing rules* – has $c(s,m) < 1/2$ (for $m \geq 3$). For these rules, the drop in votes from top to average is small relative to the top-to-bottom drop, so that an average amount of votes

186

may be almost as good as getting the most possible. The incentive under these rules is to avoid placing last or very low in voters' rankings. The best example of such a rule is the one for which s = (0, . . . , 0, −1) and c(s,m) = 1/m; this rule awards a negative vote for last place and is essentially equivalent to negative voting.[4]

The final class of scoring rules is *intermediate* and is defined by the condition c(s, m) = 1/2 (for m ≥ 3). These rules provide a more symmetric drop in votes as a candidate falls in a voter's ranking. The best-known example is Borda's method of marks, defined by s = (m − 1, m − 2, . . . , 0). Under the Borda rule, the fall from first place to second in a voter's ranking is just as painful, in terms of votes lost, as the fall from second to third, or third to fourth, or (m − 1)th to mth.

The main result on scoring rules concerns convergent Nash equilibrium. A Nash equilibrium is *convergent* if all candidates adopt the same position. Again letting Q[α] be the αth percentile of the distribution of voter ideal points – that is, the point in [0, 1] such that a proportion α of all voters' ideal points lie at or to the left of it – convergent equilibria under a generic scoring rule can be characterized as follows:

THEOREM I (Cox 1987a) For a given scoring rule, s, and number of candidates, m ≥ 2, the situation in which every candidate adopts the position x is a Nash equilibrium if and only if Q[c(s, m)] ≤ x ≤ Q[1 − c(s, m)].

This theorem, which has a straightforward multidimensional extension, says that if all candidates adopt a position sufficiently central in the voter distribution, then the resulting situation will be in equilibrium. If there are just two candidates, then –since c(s, 2) = 1/2 for all scoring rules – only the situation in which both candidates position themselves at the median of the voter distribution can be in equilibrium. For m > 2, the result depends on the particular subclass of scoring rule:

1. First-place rewarding rules. For these rules, c(s, m) > 1/2 and 1 − c(s, m) < 1/2 if m ≥ 3. Thus, for m ≥ 3, no x exists that satisfies Q[c(s, m)] ≤ x ≤ Q[1 − c(s, m)], and no convergent equilibria exist.

2. Intermediate rules. For these rules, c(s, m) = 1/2 if m ≥ 3. Thus, the unique convergent equilibrium is the situation in which all candidates adopt the median voter's position, Q[1/2].

3. Last-place punishing rules. For these rules, c(s, m) < 1/2 if m ≥ 3. Thus, if all candidates adopt some point in the (non-empty) interval [Q[c(s, m)], Q[1 − c(s, m)]], the resulting situation is in equilibrium.

The reemergence of convergent equilibria – where more than two candidates are bunched at a single location – is driven by the fact that candidates need not be ranked first in voters' rankings in order to get significant number of votes from them (at least in the case of intermediate and last-place punishing rules). This means that candidates caught between two others are not "squeezed" as badly as they are under the plurality rule, which removes or mitigates the tendency to disperse identified by Chamberlain.

It is interesting to note that the idea that candidates can receive votes from relatively "distant" voters has a natural economic analog: consumers may make more than one purchase, and have some chance of buying from firms other than the closest one. A 1985 paper by Papageorgiou and Thisse has exploited just this point to partially reestablish Hotelling's principle of minimum differentiation.

Nonconvergent equilibria are more difficult to characterize for a generic scoring rule. But what we know gibes with the results on convergent equilibria. First, for plurality rule, where no convergent equilibria exist, we have already seen that nonconvergent equilibria do exist and can be characterized. Second, for negative voting, where multiple convergent equilibria exist, there are no nonconvergent equilibria. It seems likely that all first-place rewarding rules are like plurality rule and have nonconvergent equilibria, and that all last-place punishing rules are like negative voting and do not have nonconvergent equilibria, but these questions are open.

Approval voting

Approval voting is a method of voting in multicandidate elections in which citizens may vote for as many candidates as they wish, but cannot cumulate, that is, cast more than one vote for a given candidate. In recent years, approval voting (or AV) has been promoted by its advocates as "the election reform of the 20th century" (Brams 1980, p. 105), largely on the strength of certain desirable theoretical properties.

One argument in particular urged by advocates of AV concerns the fate of centrist candidates in multicandidate plurality elections. To take the example of presidential primaries, the possibility of victory by "extremist" candidates is viewed as an inherent problem with the current plurality method of election:

It is indeed unfortunate for the voters when the winner in an election is in fact a weaker candidate than one or more of the losers! This paradoxical result most often occurs when two or more moderate candidates split the centrist vote, allowing a more extremist candidate to eke out a victory with only minority support. It is precisely this shortcoming of our system that seems in part responsible for the presidential nomination of Barry Goldwater by the Republican party in 1964, and the nomination of George McGovern by the Democratic party in 1972. Although each nominee had vociferous minority support within his party, each was a disaster to his party in the general election. [Brams and Fishburn 1983, p. 3]

Brams and Fishburn argue that AV offers a "simple, practicable solution to this defect in our election system," since centrist voters can support more than one candidate.

The idea that approval voting will favor centrist candidates – and thereby promote centrist candidacies – receives some support from the main formal result on electoral equilibria under AV. This result is based on a model incorporating assumptions (1), (2'), (3'), (4), (5), (6'), (7), and (8) and pertains to convergent equilibria:

THEOREM 2 (Cox 1985, 1987a) In an approval election with $m \geq 3$ candidates, each having an admissible objective, the unique convergent Nash equilibrium is the situation $(Q[1/2], \ldots, Q[1/2])$ where all candidates adopt the position of the median voter.

The possibility of convergence under AV, as was the possibility of convergence under a generic scoring rule, is linked to the fact that a candidate need not be ranked uniquely first in a voter's estimation in order to receive a vote from him. The importance of this can be readily seen. Suppose, for expositional ease, that all voters have symmetric preferences and that there is a uniform distribution of voter ideal points along $[0, 1]$. If m candidates are positioned at $1/2$ and one candidate alone moves to $1/2 + 2\epsilon$, then *all* voters at or to the left of $1/2 + \epsilon$ will vote for *all* $m - 1$ candidates at $1/2$; because these voters constitute a majority, there is no incentive to move.

As with scoring rules, less is known about nonconvergent equilibria under AV. It has been shown (Cox 1985) that there are no nonconvergent equilibria under AV if $m = 3$, but no more general result exists.

Condorcet procedures

One of the most widely accepted normative criteria for evaluating voting systems was first enunciated by the Marquis de Condorcet in the eighteenth century. Put simply, Condorcet's principle is that, if a candidate can beat each of his opponents in a head-to-head contest, then any fair system should elect that candidate. Candidates who can beat each of their opponents in pairwise competition are known as Condorcet winners. Voting systems that choose such candidates, when they exist, and then complete the rules of election by specifying an outcome in the absence of a Condorcet winner, are called Condorcet (completion) procedures. A simple example is that proposed by Duncan Black: Choose the Condorcet winner, if there is one; otherwise use the Borda method.

The main result on Condorcet procedures – in a model using assumptions (1), (2'), (3'), (4), (5), (7), (8) and (6''): candidates seek to maximize the probability that they will win the election – is as follows:

THEOREM 3 (Cox 1987a) In an election with $m \geq 3$ candidates held under a Condorcet procedure, probability maximizing candidates have a dominant strategy to adopt $Q[1/2]$, the median of the distribution of voter ideal points.

Gary W. Cox

This result follows because Condorcet procedures essentially disaggregate multicandidate contests into a series of two-candidate contents. If a candidate can defeat each of his or her opponents head-to-head, he or she wins overall; but the dominant strategy to defeat another candidate in a two-candidate contest is of course the median voter's position.

This "disaggregating" effect of Condorcet election procedures also means that Theorem 3 is robust in much the same way that the median voter result is robust. For example, substituting (6) for (6″) just makes the result a bit more difficult to prove, without altering its substance much. More important, a multidimensional "extension" of Theorem 3 exists much like Miller's (1977) "extension" of the median voter theorem: For a subclass of Condorcet procedures (those that depend only on the majority preference relation), it can be shown that all candidates' undominated strategies lie in the uncovered set, regardless of the dimensionality of the policy space (Cox, 1989).

2. MULTIMEMBER DISTRICTS

Electoral districts with magnitudes greater than one are in use throughout the world. These districts are compatible with a variety of electoral systems that, for present purposes, can be classified as plurality-based and proportional.

Plurality-based electoral systems

Plurality-based systems allocate the positions at stake in a κ member district to the top κ vote-getters. They are generalizations in this respect of the ordinary plurality rule in single-member districts. Where they differ, both with the simpler rule and among themselves, is in the voting options available to voters. These can be classified into three broad categories: the bloc vote, the cumulative vote, and the limited vote.

1. The bloc vote gives each voter as many votes as there are seats to be had. Each voter can cast up to κ votes in any fashion desired, except that no more than one vote can be cast for any given candidate (no cumulation). In some bloc-voting systems (such as that currently used in Arizona for elections to the lower state house), partial abstention is allowed: The voter need not cast all of his or her votes. Thus, for example, a voter in a three-member district might legally choose to vote for only one candidate, or for only two, rather than for three. Other bloc-voting systems (such as those in the United States governed by so-called "anti-single shot" provisions) outlaw partial abstention: the voter must vote for exactly κ candidates.

2. Cumulative voting, like bloc voting, gives voters as many votes as there are seats to be filled. It differs in that voters can "cumulate" their votes; that is, they can give more than one vote to a given candidate if they wish. No cumulative vote system of which I am aware allows partial abstention, per-

haps because allowing such an option would not really alter voter or party strategies much (as it can in the case of block or limited voting). The cumulative vote was at one time used in Illinois state legislative elections and is still used widely in corporate elections and local elections.

3. The limited vote is just like the block vote except that each voter has fewer votes to cast than there are seats to fill. The limited vote has been used in English parliamentary elections and is currently used in Japanese national elections and elsewhere. The possibility of a limited cumulative vote exists but, as far as I know, such a system is not in use.

There is little work on any of the plurality-based systems as regards the nature of spatial competition between candidates. MacRae and Sawyer (1962) provide a game-theoretic analysis of some aspects of *party* competition under the cumulative vote, and Kap-Yun (1981) has a similar piece on party competition under the limited vote. Both of these works focus on the question of how best to allocate a fixed amount of voter support among several candidates from the same party (in order to maximize the number of seats the party wins).

Greenberg and Shepsle (1987) look at the most limited of limited vote systems – those in which voters have only one vote to cast. They ask whether there is a way to position κ candidates so that no $(\kappa + 1)$st candidate could enter and beat one or more of the established candidates. Their answer – described more fully Chapter 2, this volume – is that, for any κ, there exist voter distributions in which the entry of a $(\kappa + 1)$st candidate cannot be deterred. It is likely that this result would generalize for other plurality-based systems, but no one has yet demonstrated this.

Cox (1984a) addresses the question of spatial location in the special context of double-member districts ($\kappa = 2$) operating under bloc voting without partial abstention. The model he uses employs essentially the same assumptions as does the model of Eaton and Lipsey, with assumption $(3')$ substituted for (3), so that the distribution of voter ideal points is not required to be uniform, and assumption $(6')$ substituted for (6), so that candidates need only have an admissible objective. In this model, it can be shown that, if there are three candidates, then any situation in which all three adopt a position x is in equilibrium if $x \in [Q[1/3], Q[2/3]]$; and that, if there are four candidates, then the unique Nash equilibrium is the situation in which all candidates adopt the median voter's position. More generally, it can be shown that:

THEOREM 4 (Cox 1984) In a κ-member district operating under the bloc vote without partial abstention, the situation in which $m > \kappa$ candidates adopt the same position, x, is in equilibrium if and only if $x \in [Q[(m - \kappa)/(m)], Q[\kappa/m]]$.

The possibility of convergence in multimember districts stems, as it did in the case of scoring rules, from the fact that candidates sometimes need not fear being "squeezed." Because each voter has κ votes, all of which he must use, being between two other candidates is not necessarily a bad thing. In

0		A	B	C	D	E	F	G		1

Figure 8.2. A seven-candidate contest in a four-seat district operating under the
bloc vote without partial abstention.

fact, if $m \leq 2\kappa$, then candidates located in the center of the distribution of
candidates are advantaged.

To see this, consider Figure 8.2. This figure displays the positions of seven
candidates (labeled A, B, C, D, E, F, and G) competing in a four-seat district.
Note that candidates A, B, and C are cut off from the voters between G and 1
(that is, they receive no votes from this area) because four candidates are
closer to these voters than are A, B, and C. Similarly, candidates E, F, and G
are cut off from the voters between 0 and A. Only candidate D receives a vote
from every voter, because he is at least fourth-closest to every voter. Thus, a
central location is an advantage, rather than a disadvantage, when there are
sufficiently many votes per voter relative to candidates.

If $m > 2\kappa$, however, then the advantage of being centrally located among
candidates disappears, and the disadvantage – in the form of squeezing –
reappears. In Figure 8.2, for example, if $\kappa = 3$ instead of 4, then candidate D
gets no votes from either the [0, A] region or the [G, 1] region; as the
candidates bunch closer together, this provides D with a clear incentive to
disperse. More generally, note that in Theorem 3, $m > 2\kappa$ implies $Q[(m - \kappa)/m] > Q[\kappa/m]$, which says that no convergent equilibria exist.

A similar result holds for limited vote systems without partial abstention: if
v is the number of votes per voter, and $v < \kappa < m$, then x is a convergent
equilibrium if and only if $Q[(m - v)/m] \leq x \leq Q[v/m]$. As $v = \kappa$ in the case
of the bloc vote, a reasonable summary of both results is as follows: In block-
vote or limited-vote systems without partial abstention, if the number of
candidates exceeds twice the number of votes per voter, then no convergent
equilibria exist; it is expected that candidates will disperse. On the other hand,
if the number of candidates equals or falls short of twice the number of votes
per voter, then convergent equilibria exist in an interval centered on the
median.

If one assumes that the number of candidates will always exceed the
number of seats available ($m > \kappa$), then a necessary condition for a limited
vote system to have any convergent equilibria is that the number of votes per
voter exceed half the district magnitude ($v > .5\kappa$). Thus, "severely limited"
limited vote systems ($v \leq .5\kappa$), such as that considered by Greenberg and
Shepsle, never have convergent equilibria.

Proportional Representation Systems

Most of the world's democracies elect their national legislatures by one version or another of proportional representation. Nonetheless, there is still a dearth of spatially based research into the workings of PR systems.

The primary exceptions to this generalization are two papers by Sugden (1984) and Greenberg and Weber (1985). Both papers deal with a particular version of PR: the uniform quota. Under this system, an arbitrary quota is fixed, and a seat is awarded for every quota of votes that a party receives (each voter casting one vote). In Weimar Germany, for example, the quota was 60,000, so that anything from 60,000 to 119,999 votes got one seat, anything from 120,000 to 179,999 votes earned two seats, and so on (Hoag and Hallett 1926, pp. 412–14).

Neither Sugden nor Greenberg and Weber deal directly with the question of how a fixed number of parties might competitively position themselves under the uniform quota system, but both deal with related questions. Sugden focuses on the voters, rather than the candidates, and investigates the nature of the core, as do spatial models of committee behavior. That is, he asks whether there exists an n-tuple of votes, one for each of n voters, such that no coalition of voters could, by unilaterally changing their votes, achieve an outcome they all prefer to the outcome that would result if they did not change.

Outcomes, in this case, are sets of elected candidates. For example, in a district with 100 voters, a quota of 20, and 6 candidates – A, B, C, D, E, and F – the possible outcomes can be described as follows: (a) no one is elected (perhaps A through E get 18 votes each and F gets 10); (b) exactly one of the candidates is elected (c) exactly two of the candidates are elected; . . . ; (f) exactly five of the candidates are elected.

Voter preferences over outcomes are defined by Sugden lexicographically:

Each voter has a strict preference ordering on S, the set of candidates. A voter's preferences between [outcomes] are derived lexicographically from his preference between candidates; that is, a voter prefers [outcome] A_1 to [outcome] A_2 if and only if either (*i*) after ignoring all those candidates who are common to A_1 and A_2, the most preferred candidate in A_1 is preferred to the most preferred candidate in A_2 or (*ii*) A_2 is a proper subset of A_1. [Sugden 1984, p. 34]

This is not a standard assumption in spatial theory. Nonetheless, it resembles standard assumptions in important ways. The usual procedure is to make an assumption both about voter preferences among candidates (for example, that each voter prefers candidates closer to some given ideal point in a unidimensional policy space) and about how votes relate to these preferences (such as that voters are sincere). Sugden does in fact make the usual assumption of the first kind, assuming that voter preferences among candidates are single-peaked and that candidates' and voters' positions can be represented on

a line. But he does not attempt to link preferences among candidates directly
to votes, because he construes the ultimate objects of choice to be sets of
candidates. Thus, he does not assume, as a more conventional analysis might,
that voters simply vote for the candidate whose spatial position is closest to
their ideal points. Nonetheless, the assumption that Sugden does make comes
close to implying the same thing. For, that voters prefer A_1 to A_2 if the best in
$A_1 - A_2$ is better than the best in $A_2 - A_1$ means that they always stand ready
to vote for a candidate who is closer to their ideal point than any currently
available one, if they can find a quota who will also vote for such a candidate.
This is similar in analytic impact to the more usual assumption.

Sugden's main result concerns a uniform quota election with *n* voters and
quota q held in a district of magnitude κ. Since, for a given *n* and q, anywhere
from zero to [*n*/q] candidates might be elected,[5] the notion of district magnitude is less clear than in other electoral systems. Here, it will be understood
that the district magnitude, κ, equals the maximum number of seats that could
be allocated to the district, given *n* and q; this number is just [*n*/q], the
number of full quotas contained in *n*. The procedure Sugden envisions allo-
cates to each district a certain number of seats, κ, and then sets the quota to
ensure that no more than κ seats will be awarded. For purposes of mathematical tractability, Sugden assumes that q = $(n + 1)/(\kappa + 1)$ (which entails
that $(n + 1)/(\kappa + 1)$ be an integer). Given this assumption, which he shows to
be inessential to the main thrust of the result, he proves:

THEOREM 5 (Sugden 1984) In a uniform quota election with *n* voters and
quota q held in a district of magnitude κ, the outcome in which κ = [*n*/q]
candidates are elected, positioned at the κ points Q[q/*n*], Q[2q/*n*], . . . ,
Q[κq/*n*], is a core point.

One interpretation of this result is that, were κ candidates to adopt the positions indicated and were all voters to vote for the closest candidate, then (a) all
κ candidates would be elected; and (b) no coalition of voters could unilaterally
change their votes to produce an outcome that they preferred.

This latter clause means not only that no voter coalition could improve the
outcome by voting for some other candidate among the κ mentioned, but also
– and more important – that no coalition could nominate and vote for a new
candidate, or group of candidates, and thereby improve the outcome. This is
tantamount to saying that no potential candidate could find a successful platform to run on, were there already κ candidates, positioned as indicated in the
theorem.

A quite similar result, based on more standard assumptions, is reached by
Greenberg and Weber. They investigate the number of parties that can be
supported in equilibrium under a uniform quota system and assume (a) that
parties will enter if and only if they can capture at least a quota; (b) that votes
will vote for the party whose spatial position they most prefer; and (c) that

voters have single-peaked preferences along a single dimension. They find that there is always a positioning of c candidates, where $c \leq \kappa = [n/q]$, such that no single new candidate could enter and capture a quota. If $q < n/2$, they find that such a positioning must always be such that at least one party is at or to the left of $Q[q/n]$ and at least one party is at or to the right of $Q[(n - q + 1)/n]$. The reason is straightforward: Were no party at or to the left of $Q[q/n]$, one could then enter at $Q[q/n]$ and earn a quota; a similar argument pertains regarding $Q[(n - q + 1)/n]$. (Note that, given Sugden's assumption $q = (n + 1)/(\kappa + 1)$, so $n - q + 1 = \kappa q$, $Q[(n - q + 1)/n] = Q[\kappa q/n]$, and the Greenberg/Weber result partially coincides with Sugden's.)

Both Sugden and Greenberg and Weber find a considerable dispersion of candidates in their models, similar to the dispersion found in models of multicandidate competition under the plurality rule (see earlier subsection). The driving force behind this dispersion is largely the same as that in the plurality models. What most distinguishes the plurality and PR models is the behavioral assumption made about candidates. In the plurality models, a fixed number of candidates are typically assumed to maximize their vote share or plurality; in the PR models, a "no-entry" condition – more stringent in Sugden's model, more transparent in Greenberg and Weber's – constitutes the chief behavioral assumption.

The "no-entry" conditions emphasize that candidates must position themselves, not just in competition with other current entrants but also in competition with those who might enter. Nonetheless, both "no-entry" conditions are consistent with standard assumptions about candidate and voter motivation. In Greenberg and Weber's model, for example, a potential candidate will enter if he can find a position that will earn him a quota of votes (all voters voting sincerely). This is something like assuming that potential candidates maximize their probability of election.

Given the population of election-seeking candidates (potential and current), both the plurality rule and PR models find a dispersion of candidates. The reason is that in both types of model, voters have only one vote and vote sincerely. This means that the area from which a candidate receives votes is bounded on his left and right by his closest competitors to the left and right. Hence, in both models, the phenomenon of squeezing occurs, which provides the incentive for dispersal.

SUMMARY

This essay has reviewed the nature of multicandidate competition under a variety of electoral systems. The chief distinction between these various systems is that some provide consistent centrist incentives, in the sense that they have convergent equilibria at the center (median) of the voter distribution, while others possess no convergent equilibria, centrist or otherwise, and give candidates an incentive to spread out fairly widely over the political spectrum. The key features determining whether an electoral system will encourage centrist candidacies or not are the number of votes per voter; the degree to which voters are encouraged or required to cast some of their votes for candidates who rank second, third, or lower in their personal rankings; and the number of candidates.

In general, fewer voters per voter, less encouragement for voters to support their second and lower preferences, and more candidates lead to greater dispersion. Thus, systems in which voters have only one vote – such as plurality rule in single-member districts, the Greenberg–Shepsle version of the limited vote in multimember districts, or the uniform quota version of PR – give election-seeking candidates an incentive to disperse over the political spectrum. So also do scoring rules in which most of the points are awarded to the top places. In contrast, systems that give voters many votes – such as approval voting in single-member districts or the bloc vote in multimember districts – promote centrist candidacies.

The key to this result is relatively straightforward. When voters have few votes, relative to the number of candidates competing, it is bad news for a candidate to be centrally located within a tight cluster of candidates. Imagine, for example, a situation in which voters have three votes and there are ten candidates. If a candidate, say A, is situated with three opponents close-by on each side, he is in trouble. Most voters on either side of A will find three candidates closer to them than is A; because they have only three votes to cast; this means that A's vote total will be meager. The general result in v-vote systems is that clusters of more than $2v$ candidates cannot be supported in equilibrium.

This result holds regardless of the district magnitude. For example, the equilibrium conditions for plurality rule in single-member districts are the same as those for the Greenberg–Shepsle version of the limited vote in multimember districts. The number of seats to be awarded may well affect the number of parties or candidates competing, but it does not affect the size of candidate clusters in equilibrium.

ACKNOWLEDGMENT

This research was partially supported by the National Science Foundation (SES - 8811022).

NOTES

1 Another reason to allow different candidates to have different objectives is simply to make the results more general. It is standard practice to prove results for the largest

class of voter preferences possible; it is equally sensible to allow for as broad a class as possible of candidate motivations.

2 It should be added that the nature of these equilibria is often such that all candidates have an equal probability of victory, so that not only are there noncentrist candidates but there may also be noncentrist victors.

3 Suppose that A is at 1/4, C at 1/2, and B at 3/4. A's current vote share is 3/8. If A moves toward C and C counters by moving to 1/4, then A's vote share will fall to 1/4, while C's increases to 3/8. Thus, A will not move under the conjectural variation assumption stipulated in the text.

4 Negative voting is a system in which each voter has one vote to cast against the candidate of his or her choosing. Either the votes are negative and the candidate with the highest (least negative) total wins, or the vote are positive and the lowest total wins (as in golf). See Brams 1977.

5 The notation [x/y] stands for the greatest integer less than or equal to x/y.

REFERENCES

Brams, Steven. 1977. "When Is it Advantageous to Cast a Negative Vote?" In R. Henn and O. Moeschlin, eds., *Mathematical Economics and Game Theory.* Berlin: Springer-Verlag.

––––––. 1980. "Approved Voting in Multi-Candidate Elections." *Policy Studies Journal* 9: 102–8.

Brams, Steven, and Peter Fishburn. 1983. *Approval Voting.* Boston: Brikhauser.

Chamberlain, Edward. 1933. *The Theory of Monopolistic Competition.* Cambridge: Harvard University Press.

Cox, Gary W. 1984a. "Electoral Equilibrium in Double-Member Districts." *Public Choice* 44: 443–51.

––––––. 1984b. "Notes on Electoral Equilibria in Multimedia Districts." University of California at San Diego (unpublished).

––––––. 1985. "Electoral Equilibrium Under Approval Voting." *American Journal of Political Science* 29: 112–8.

––––––. 1987a. "Electoral Equilibrium Under Alternative Voting Institutions." *American Journal of Political Science* 31: 82–108.

––––––. 1987b. "The Core and the Uncovered Set." *American Journal of Political Science* 31: 408–22.

––––––. 1989. "Undominated Candidate Strategies Under Alternative Voting Rules." *Mathematical and Computer Modelling* 12: 451–60.

Denzau, Arthur, Amoz Kats, and Steven Slutsky. 1985. "Multi-Agent Equilibria with Market Share and Ranking Objectives." *Social Choice and Welfare* 2: 37–50.

Downs, Anthony. 1957. *An Economic Theory of Democracy.* New York: Harper & Row.

Eaton, B. C. 1972. "Spatial Competition Revisited." *Canadian Journal of Economics* 5: 268–77.

Eaton, B. C. and Richard Lipsey. 1975. "The Principle of Minimum Differentiation Reconsidered: Some New Developments in the Theory of Spatial Competition." *Review of Economic Studies* 42: 27–50.

Greenberg, Joseph, and Kenneth Shepsle. 1987. "The Effect of Electoral Rewards in Multiparty Competition with Entry." *American Political Science Review* 81: 525–38.

Greenberg, Joseph, and Shlomo Weber. 1985. "Multiparty Equilibria Under Proportional Representation." *American Political Science Review* 79: 693–703.

Hinch, M., and P. C. Ordeshook. 1970. "Plurality Maximization vs. Vote Maximization: A Spatial Analysis with Variable Participation." *American Political Science Review* 64: 772–91.

Hoag, C., and G. Hallett. 1926. *Proportional Representation.* New York: Macmillan.

Hotelling, Harold. 1929. "Stability in Competition." *Economic Journal* 39: 41–57.

Kap-Yun, Lee. 1981. "Two Analytic Aspects of the Japanese Political Party System: Leadership Formation and Candidate Endorsement." Yale University (unpublished).

Kramer, Gerald. 1977. "A Dynamical Model of Political Equilibrium." *Journal of Economic Theory* 16: 310–34.

Lerman, A. P., and H. W. Singer. 1937. "Some Notes on Duopoly and Spatial Competition." *Journal of Political Economy* 45: 423–39.

Lipsey, Richard. 1963. *An Introduction to Positive Economics.* London: Weidenfeld and Nicolson.

MacRae, Duncan, and J. Sawyer. 1962. "Game Theory and Cumulative Voting in Illinois: 1902–1954." *American Political Science Review* 56: 936–46.

McKelvey, Richard. 1976. "Covering, Dominance, and Institution-Free Properties of Social Choice." *American Journal of Political Science* 30: 283–314.

Miller, Nicholas. 1977. "Graph-theoretical Approaches to the Theory of Voting." *American Journal of Political Science* 21: 769–803.

Palfrey, Thomas. 1984. "Spatial Equilibrium with Entry." *Review of Economic Studies* 51: 139–56.

Papageorgiou, Y. Y., and J.-F. Thisse. 1985. "Agglomeration as Spatial Interdependence Between Firms and Households." *Journal of Economic Theory* 37: 19–31.

Shaked, Avner. 1975. "Non-existence of Equilibrium for the Two-Dimensional Three-Firms Location Problem." *Review of Economic Studies* 42: 51–6.

Shepsle, Kenneth, and Ronald Cohen. 1989. "Multiparty Competition, Entry, and Entry Deterrence in Spatial Models of Elections." This volume.

Smithies, Arthur. 1941. "Optimum Location in Spatial Competition." *Journal of Political Economy* 49: 423–39.

Sugden, Robert. 1984. "Free Association and the Theory of Proportional Representation." *American Political Science Review* 78: 31–43.

Tullock, Gordon. 1967. *Toward a Mathematics of Politics.* Ann Arbor: University of Michigan Press.

9

The Setter Model

HOWARD ROSENTHAL

Carnegie Mellon University

Political processes that involve voting are invariably subject to an element of agenda control.[1] Predictions about the outcomes of these processes can be made only if we specify (a) the preferences of the agenda setters, (b) the preferences of the voters, (c) institutional constraints on the process–the rules of the game, (d) the behavioral rules used by voters (are they sincere-myopic or sophisticated–forward looking), and (e) the information structure of the game.

What has come to be known as the monopoly model or setter model (Romer and Rosenthal 1978, 1979a) puts enormous, restrictive structure on the political process. In this essay, I limit the discussion to this model and its extensions. The first part of the essay analyzes the case of a single issue (a budget) under complete (and perfect) information. Dynamic as well as static analysis is covered. The second part treats effects of both simple uncertainty and strategic uncertainty that allows for learning. The third part summarizes empirical evidence that bears on the model. The essay contains some new work on the dynamics of agenda setting with sophisticated voters in a complete information environment and on learning by agenda setters under incomplete information; the basic thrust, however, is directed at providing a review.

THE SETTER MODEL WITH COMPLETE INFORMATION

The setter model was developed in the context of budgeting decisions. Motivated by Niskanen (1971), Romer and Rosenthal made several simplifying assumptions. First, the agenda setter was assumed to be an individual whose goal is to maximize the total budget. Second, voter preferences were single-peaked over budget levels. Single-peaked preferences for three voters are illustrated in Figure 9.1. The top of a voter's curve represents the voter's ideal point. The median of the three ideal points is the ideal point of voter B. The model obviously also applies to one-dimensional contexts other than budgets if the agenda setter always prefers more to less on the dimension. Third, the

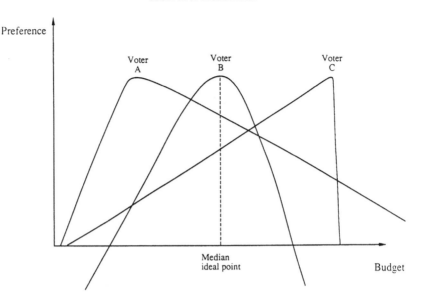

Figure 9.1. Three voters with single-peaked preferences.

institutional structure allowed the setter to confront the voter with an all-or-none, take-it-or-leave-it proposal. "Leave it" means accepting a prespecified reversion or status quo budget. Since there is only one vote, voting will be sincere (Ordeshook 1986, p. 82); a voter will vote for the reversion if and only if she prefers it to the setter's proposal. Finally, there is full information in the basic setter model.

Both the setter and the voters know the value of the proposed budget and the reversion budget. The setter knows the preferences of all voters. (Whether voters know the preferences of other agents is irrelevant, given the assumption of a take-it-or-leave-it vote.)

The structure of the basic setter model leads to an important qualitative relationship between the reversion level and the budget. To see the relationship, first consider the case where the reversion equals the median of voters' ideal points. While the setter would like a higher budget, the median voter and all voters with ideal points below the median prefer the reversion to all higher budgets. Consequently, the setter cannot propose a higher budget that defeats the reversion. The budget is simply the reversion. The argument extends directly to all reversions that are higher than the median ideal point; the budget is the reversion.

Now turn to the more interesting situation where the reversion is less than the median ideal point. Let us begin by considering the median voter. When the reversion is below her ideal point, she will, backed into a take-it-or-leave-

200

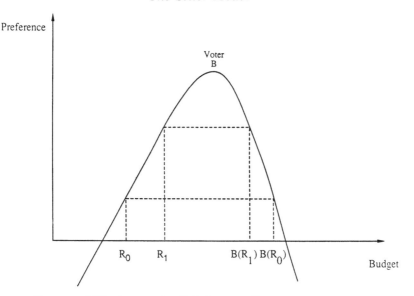

Figure 9.2. With a low reversion [R_0], the voter will approve a budget [$B(R_0)$] that is greater than the highest budget she will approve [$B(R_1)$] with a larger reversion [R_1].

it choice, approve some budgets that are higher than the reversion. The range of budgets she will approve stretches from the reversion to a budget that is higher than her ideal point. When, as in Figure 9.2, the reversion is R_1, she will approve all budgets up to and including $B(R_1)$, the budget that is at the same level of preference as R_1. If the reversion were lower than R_1, say R_0 in Figure 9.2, the voter would approve a still higher expenditure shown as $B(R_0)$. As the reversion gets lower, the setter can effectively use the threat of a bad leave-it position to get voters to approve higher expenditures.

What the exact expenditure level will be is easy to see in the very special situation where all voters' preference curves are identical except for the location of the ideal point. In this case, when the reversion is R_0 and the setter proposes $B(R_0)$, the median voter and all voters with ideal points above the median will support the proposal, while all voters below the median will vote against. A proposal larger than $B(R_0)$ will fail because voters at or below the median will oppose, while a smaller proposal would not be consistent with budget-maximization by the setter. So the budget will be $B(R_0)$. Similarly, the result is $B(R_1)$ when the reversion is R_1. In general, the budget is (weakly) decreasing in the reversion for reversions less than the median. (See Figure 9.3.) If all preferences are symmetric about ideal points, the inverse relationship is linear. The budget, B, equals $2I - R$, where I is the median ideal point and R is the reversion.

201

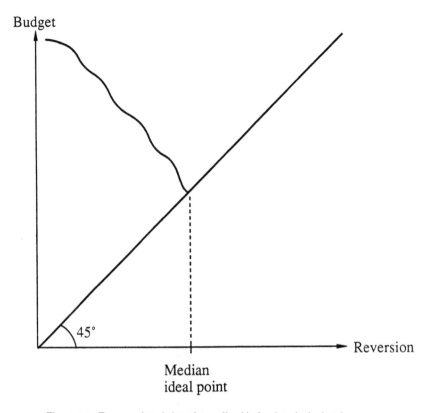

Figure 9.3. For reversions below the median ideal point, the budget increases as the reversion falls. For reversions above the median, the budget equals the reversion.

If voter preferences have different "shapes" as well as different ideal points, as in Figure 9.1, the qualitative relationship illustrated in Figure 9.3 still holds. As the reversion falls, "leave it" gets worse for at least the median and all voters with higher ideal points, so a majority will approve increasingly large budgets. In this more general case, however, the setter can no longer base his calculation of a budget-maximizing proposal solely on the preferences of the median voter. In the monopoly story, a voter is pivotal if she is the median voter in terms of the distribution of the largest budgets voters would approve given a specific reversion. As Figure 9.4 illustrates, this pivotal voter is not always the voter with median ideal point.

The Setter Model

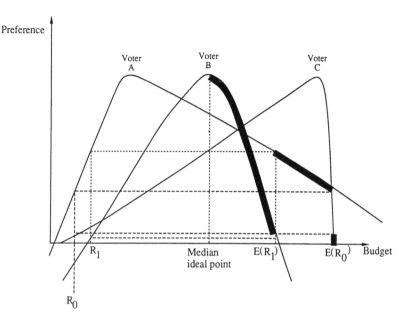

Figure 9.4. Who the pivotal voter is depends on the reversion. For reversions no greater than R_0, voter C is pivotal. For reversions between R_0 and R_1, voter A is pivotal. For reversions between R_1 and the median ideal point, voter B, the median voter, is pivotal.

Agenda Setters That Are Not Maximizers

Budget-maximization by the agenda setter is obviously a key element of the monopoly model. If this assumption is relaxed while all others are maintained, the results are modified in a very obvious manner, as shown by Arthur Denzau and Robert Mackay (1983). Assume the agenda setter's ideal point is greater than the median. Consider three ranges: (a) Reversions sufficiently small that a proposal greater than the setter's ideal point will pass. (b) Intermediate reversions. (c) Reversions greater than the setter's ideal point.

In ranges (a) and (c), the setter simply proposes his ideal point. In range (b), the result is identical to the outcome for budget-maximizing setters. Thus, the absence of maximizing behavior simply attenuates the results for the budget-maximizing world. Of course, if the setter has an ideal point below the median or is a budget-minimizer, the analysis completely reverses (see Figure 9.5).

Denzau and Mackay placed their analysis in the context of legislative decision making in which the setter represented a congressional committee or its chairman and the voters the full legislative body. The take-it-or-leave-it

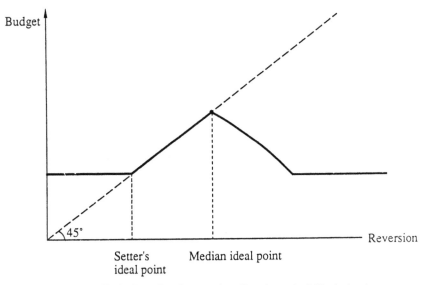

Figure 9.5. The budget when the setter is a "low demander." The budget is
never less than the setter's ideal point.

vote corresponded to a stylized closed rule under which the committee could
prevent amendments to its bill.

Denzau and Mackay continued their analysis to contrast the closed rule
with an open rule under which amendments are permitted. The setter, however, still has the option to impose the reversion: bottle up the bill in committee. Were the setter to permit voting under an open rule, the median voter's
ideal point would emerge. So the setter has a choice between keeping the
gates shut (that is, accepting the reversion) and moving to the median voter's
ideal point. In this binary choice situation, the setter simply opts for his better
outcome. If the setter is maximizing a budget, the budget will simply be the
higher of the reversion and the median ideal point. The open versus closed
rule contrast is thus valuable for illustrating how much the setter gains from
his ability to make a take-it-or-leave-it offer.

The richness of the institutional setting offered by the U.S. Congress has in
fact resulted in a small cottage industry of agenda models, initiated by Kenneth Shepsle and Barry Weingast (1981).[2] For example, in addition to the
open-closed distinction made by Denzau and Mackay, Thomas Gilligan and
Keith Krehbiel (1986) also consider a modified rule where an additional agent
(such as the leader of the majority party) can propose an alternative (an
amended bill) to the committee bill. In other words, the amendment goes
against the committee bill, with the winner then being voted on against the

status quo. The model can readily be solved by the backward induction method. For every bill proposed by the committee, one can find the amendment that maximizes the additional agent's utility. With this knowledge, the committee, which moves first, can find its optimal bill (or elect to close the gates).

Indeed, as long as there is a prespecified sequence of agents who can propose amendments, it is straightforward to solve for an optimal action for the initial "setter." (Of course, if the median voter is in the sequence, this voter's ideal point will be the outcome, unless the gates are closed.)

It is unfortunate that solving out for policies under open or closed rules or various intermediate, modified rules, is only a very initial step in our theoretical understanding of legislative agenda-setting. Committees in fact operate under substantial uncertainty as to the rule under which a bill will be considered (Gilligan and Krehbiel 1986). Consideration of uncertainty regarding rules is an important research topic that has been addressed only recently (Gilligan and Krehbiel 1989).

Intertemporal Dynamics

Another critical assumption in the basic setter model is that the situation is a "one-shot game." Today's decision has no implications for tomorrow's relationship between the setter and the voters. The lack of temporal dependence can be characterized by the statement that the reversion is assumed to be exogenous. (Recall that the setup is one where everyone has full information, so there is no concern for learning. It is also assumed that voters act in terms of preference as specified; that is, the setter need not be concerned with "protest" voters in the future.)

In some institutional contexts (such as Oregon school referenda prior to 1987; see Romer and Rosenthal 1979a, 1982a and b, 1983b), an exogenous reversion is appropriate. But typically (as is now the case in Oregon and most other states holding school referenda), the reversion is endogenous. A typical reversion rule would be for next year's revenue to be this year's spending, in real (inflation-adjusted) dollars per student. In such a situation, known as permanent levy, the setter faces a potential trade-off: getting high spending today may result in lower revenues tomorrow.

Daniel Ingberman (1985) characterized the trade-off under permanent levy in the context of a setter with a fixed tenure in office who faces myopic voters (voters who treat each period as a one-shot game). It is easy to illustrate that there are circumstances where the setter will do other than use his one-shot strategy. For example, let the setter serve for four years, all voters have symmetric preferences, the first reversion be 500, and the sequence of inflation-adjusted median ideal points be 1000, 1500, 1750, 2000. (A possible scenario: between years one and two, a large, industrial facility is added to the tax base. The other intervals have "normal" increases from increases in real income.) If the setter plays his one-shot strategy, he gets $B = 2I - R = 2(1000) - 500 = 1500$ in the first year. As 1500 then becomes the year two reversion, the setter also gets 1500 in year two. In years three and four he gets 2000. The four-year budget totals 7000.

If, instead, the setter uses the reversion in year one, he gets only 500. But in all subsequent years, he gets 2500, for a total budget of 8000. If the setter does not discount the future too heavily, he will use this second *reculer pour mieux sauter* strategy.

Which type of strategy should be more common? To answer this question, we must introduce some additional concepts and notation. Ingberman assumes that there is a unique pivotal voter for all reversions. This voter has ideal point I_t at time t. Let $\lambda_t \equiv I_t - I_{t-1}$ define the change in the ideal point from $t-1$ to t. In our example, we had $\lambda_2 = 500$, $\lambda_3 = \lambda_4 = 250$. The voter's preferences are characterized by a parameter θ. If $\theta = 1$, preferences are symmetric. Let $B(R_t)$ be the largest proposal the voter will accept, and let $R_t < I_t$.

$$\text{If } B(R_t) - I_t \gtreqless I_t - R_t \qquad \theta \gtreqless 1$$

Thus, if $\theta > 1$, the voter prefers an increase above her ideal point to a decrease of equal magnitude. For example, in Figure 9.4, voter A has $\theta > 1$, while voter C has $\theta < 1$. Finally, we define β as the setter's discount factor.

Now Ingberman showed that,

if $\theta\beta \leq 1$ and the sequence of λ_t is non-decreasing, the setter's optimal strategy is the sequence of one-shot strategies.

Now if (a) the budget B is measured in real terms, (b) the voter has a constant income elasticity of demand, and the real income of the median voter is growing at a nondecreasing rate, the condition on the λ will be satisfied, ceteris paribus. Economic analysis assumes $\beta < 1$. Therefore, in "normal" situations, the condition of Ingberman's theorem will hold as long as preferences don't deviate "too" far from symmetry in the sense that positive departures from the ideal point are preferred to negative departures of equal magnitude ($\theta > 1$).

Under the conditions of his theorem, Ingberman also shows an important corollary. If the initial reversion under permanent levy is equal to the fixed reversion of a basic setter model, the budget is higher in every time period under the fixed-reversion regime. This result may relate to why states such as Colorado, New York, and Oregon (the latter only in 1987) have now adopted permanent levy regimes for school referenda.

Ingberman's results relate to the case of what we may characterize as a prospering community, one with increasing λ_t values. What happens in a "decaying" community where all the λ_t are negative? In this case (for any β

and θ), it is clearly optimal for the setter to use a sequence of one-shot strategies. In the first period, the setter receives his one-shot budget. This becomes the reversion and is the budget for all future periods. Indeed, if $R_1 <$ I_1 under these conditions, permanent levy expenditures equal those of a fixed-reversion regime in the first period and exceed them in subsequent periods. In other words, although permanent levy checks the rise of expenditures under prosperity, it prevents reducing expenditures in times of decay.

Whether there is "prosperity" or "decay," however, budget-maximizing setters under permanent levy will, if preferences are not too asymmetric, behave as in the original one-shot model. Only in exceptional cases, where an initial large increase (λ) in ideal point is followed by smaller increases, will it be necessary to consider the possibility of more complex dynamic strategies.

To summarize the results on permanent levy, the strategic nature of the basic setter model is, on the whole, surprisingly robust to the important institutional dynamics introduced by Ingberman. Of course, since endogenous reversions will typically differ from fixed exogenous reversions, actual policy outcomes will differ under the two regimes.

The Ingberman model nonetheless contains an important asymmetry in assumptions. While setters are forward-looking, voters are myopic. It is interesting to ask what happens when voters have the same acumen as the setter. After all, for some agenda forms, sophisticated voting limits the possibility for agenda control (Ordeshook 1986, pp. 271–81). For example, in a multidimensional setting with Euclidean preferences and amendment agendas, an agenda setter facing myopic voters can, typically (absent a median in all directions), move from any status quo point to any other point in the space (McKelvey 1976). But with sophisticated voters, it is not possible to move outside of a subset of the Pareto optimals, the uncovered set (Shepsle and Weingast 1984).

For agenda setting where the ideal point of the pivotal voter is dynamic, the results are exactly the reverse of this standard folklore.[3] Sophistication hurts the voter. The intuition is simple. When the voter has foresight, the setter can confront the voter with a threat pertaining to the entire "supergame" rather than with a series of smaller, one-shot threats. The voter would like the setter to believe she can't see ahead! (The voter would also like to misrepresent her preferences.)

A simple two-period example illustrates the general point. Assume a permanent levy setup with $I_1 = 4$, $I_2 = 12$, $R_1 = 2$, and β = 1 for the voter. Let the voter have quadratic preferences. Under myopia, we can use Ingberman's theorem and the symmetry of quadratic preferences to find $B_1 = 6$, $B_2 = 18$. But consider what would happen if the voter rejected the setter's proposal at t=1. We would then have $B_1 = 2$, $B_2 = 22$. The voter's utility can be calculated as $-(4 - 2)^2 - (12 - 2)^2 = -104$.

Now if the setter proposes $B_1 = B_2 = 14$, the voter also obtains -104. So when the voter looks ahead, $B_1 = 14$ will pass. The setter obtains a two-period budget of 28 as against 24 under myopia. Even if $\beta < 1$, the setter can gain, although B_1 will be less than 14.

Notice also that voter foresight allows the setter to move expenditure into earlier time periods. In the example, relative to myopia, four units in period 2 are sacrificed to gain eight in period 1. Consider then what happens if setters have limited tenure in office. In the example, assume there are two setters, each of whom serves for one period. The initial setter can still get 14 in period 1, leaving the successor with a smaller budget than the successor would obtain under myopia. The gains to setters from voter foresight will accrue to the initial setter.

Introducing both permanent levy and voter foresight shows that dynamics are important: We can no longer lean on the one-shot, exogenous reversion models to calculate period-by-period policies. Yet, the spirit of the initial model is reinforced. Voter foresight enhances the setter's monopoly power and permits larger and earlier expenditures.

UNCERTAINTY MODELS

In this section, we treat three types of uncertainty models in increasing order of complexity. In the first, the setter has *complete* information about voter preferences but does not know which voters will actually vote. In the second, the setter has complete information about voter preferences, but voters have incomplete information about the characteristics of the reversion. In the last, there is a reversal of roles. Votes know the proposal and the reversion, but the setter has incomplete information about voter preferences.

Turnout Uncertainty with a Single Proposal

The simplest form of turnout uncertainty was treated by Romer and Rosenthal (1979a). Let's start with the situation where the setter can make a single take-it-or-leave-it proposal. He knows the preferences of each voter, but each voter votes only with fixed probability r^4. As a result, the pivotal voter in the "sample" represented by the election may not have the true median $B(R)$, denoted $\hat{B}$. The setter cannot simply pass a proposal p with $p = \hat{B}$. Instead, there is a probability distribution denoted $Pr(p)$ that gives the probability that a proposal p will pass. *Without loss of generality, take the reversion to be zero.* Assume the setter maximizes the expected budget, denoted Π. The setter then must solve

$$\max_{p} \Pi = pPr(p) \tag{1}$$

Two important cases should be considered:

1. Median ideal point ≤ 0. In this case, under certainty, the budget equals the reversion. Nonetheless, with uncertain turnout the setter can take a gamble. The worst he can do is lose and get zero. But if he makes a proposal greater than zero, there is some chance (< 0.5) that it will pass. So when reversions are high relative to the median, the setter is guaranteed to have a higher expected budget when turnout is uncertain.

2. Median ideal point > 0. The intuition for this case is given by the extreme situation where all voters have ideal points greater than the reversion. Assume the setter makes his certainty proposal. Since half the population of voters has $B(0)$ below $\hat{B}$, when turnout is random, the probability that $p = \hat{B}$ passes is about $1/2$. So the expected budget is only about $1/2$ the certainty budget. Now if the setter picks p slightly below $\hat{B}$, the probability of passage will increase. In fact, unless r is very small or the number of voters is very small, a small change in p will bring the probability close to 1.0. In other words, by picking a proposal below the certainty budget, the setter will maximize his expected budget. Here, in effect, because the setter isn't protected by a reversion that is high (relative to the median), the setter, rather than gambling on a lucky turnout draw, will gladly trade a reduction in his proposal for an increased chance of passing.

There is one proviso. If there were, for example, one voter with an unusually high $B(0)$, the setter might propose this and hope for the rare event where only this voter showed at the polls. So increased proposals might occur if there were enough weight in the tail of the distribution of the $B(0)$ points. Romer and Rosenthal (1979a) show that a very weak condition on the tail rules out this possibility. Proposals should be lower than certainty proposals.

For those cases where the median ideal point is greater than zero but some voters have ideal points below zero, the proposal and the expected budget may or may not fall below the certainty budget (see Figure 9.6).

Turnout Uncertainty with Multiple Proposals

Under many state school referenda rules, the setter has multiple attempts available to pass the annual budget. To illustrate, consider the case where three tries are allowed. The setter's expected budget is

$$\Pi = p_1 Pr(p_1) + p_2[1 - Pr(p_1)]Pr(p_2) + p_3[(1 - Pr(p_1)][(1 - Pr(p_2)]Pr(p_3) \tag{2}$$

Finding the optimal p_1, p_2, and p_3 is a straightforward dynamic programming problem. Romer and Rosenthal (1979a) show that (a) the proposal sequence is decreasing ($p_3 < p_2 < p_1$), and (b) the last proposal equals the proposal that would be made if there were only one shot. Consequently, having multiple attempts makes the setter better off–he can gamble more

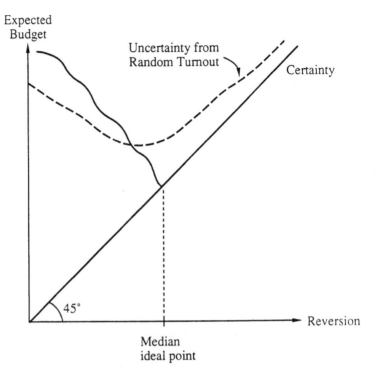

Figure 9.6. For reversions much below the median ideal point, the expected budget under random turnout is less than the budget with full turnout. For reversions above the median, the expected budget exceeds the certainty budget.

often. I show below that the setter also makes a sequence of decreasing proposals and benefits from having multiple attempts in settings where voters are strategic players.

Incomplete Information

Up to this point, the discussion has assumed that all agents had complete information about the decision problem. In particular, all agents were presumed to know the indirect utility levels that voters associated with both the reversion and the proposal. Of course, the complete information assumption is not very realistic. Agenda setters, particularly in settings with large electorates, are unlikely to be fully informed as to the structure of voter preferences. On the flip side, voters are likely to be uncertain as to how utility levels will reflect either maintaining the reversion or adopting some proposed new expenditure.

The Setter Model

Several recent papers have addressed these alternative, complementary models of how incomplete information alters the agenda setter's problem. The first paper to apply the developing literature on incomplete information models to the setter problem is by Sanford Morton (1988),[5] who looked at the situation where the setter had incomplete information about voter preferences. The alternative track of imperfectly informed voters was pursued by Thomas Gilligan and Keith Krehbiel (1987, 1988, 1989), and by Jeffrey Banks (1988). Gilligan and Krehbiel cover a complex set of institutional scenarios; their important work cannot be treated within the scope of this essay. Thus, I begin with the Banks model, since it represents a relatively simple illustration of an incomplete information model.

Imperfectly Informed Voters

In the Banks model, the indirect utility functions of all voters are assumed identical except for the location of the ideal point, thus reducing the problem to the interaction between the setter and a voter with median ideal point. Banks works with quadratic preferences, but I find it more instructive to consider a voter with "tent" preferences, shown in Figure 9.7. Without loss of generality, the units of measurement can again be chosen so that the pivotal voter's ideal point is 0. Thus, an outcome B results in a voter utility of $-|B|$. The setter's utility is given by B.

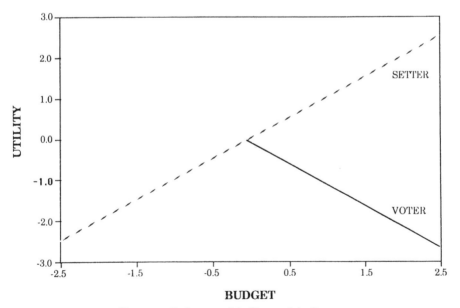

Figure 9.7. Preferences of the Voter and the Setter

We now come to the fundamental difference between the Banks model and the Romer–Rosenthal setup. In Romer–Rosenthal, both the setter and the voter had complete information about the nature of the reversion. In contrast, Banks assumes that the setter knows the *voter's* preferences about the reversion, but that the voter does not![6] The voter is assumed to know only that the reversion is a random variable α, drawn from a continuous distribution on $[\underline{\alpha},\bar{\alpha}]$.

School budget referenda in the state of New York (Romer, Rosenthal, and Munley 1987) represent a real-world situation that is close to the Banks scenario. In the event of a failed referendum, the school board may impose a "contingency" budget that is disclosed only after the referendum.

I now discuss equilibrium behavior in the Banks model in terms of four exhaustive and mutually exclusive cases. I will simply analyze the equilibrium that is best for the setter.[7]

Case 1. All possible reversions above the ideal point ($\underline{\alpha} \geq 0$). The outcome here will simply be that $B = R$, the actual reversion value. This follows immediately from recognizing that proposals below $\underline{\alpha}$ are dominated strategies for the setter and that rejecting all proposals $\geq \underline{\alpha}$ dominates for the voter.

Case 2. All possible reversions below the ideal point ($\bar{\alpha} \leq 0$). In this case, the proposal and the budget are the absolute value of the expected value the voter assigns to the reversion, that is, $-E(\alpha)$. That is, we have a "pooling" equilibrium where, regardless of the true value of R, the setter proposes $-E(\alpha)$. It is clear that the voter will accept this proposal since it gives him a utility of $E(\alpha)$, equal to his expected utility if he rejects it.

Note that the setter's proposal cannot be used to send the voter a credible signal of the true value of the reversion. If the true value is below $E(\alpha)$ and the setter makes a proposal higher than $-E(\alpha)$, the voter will reject it. The voter, after all, recognizes that if he accepts this higher proposal, then the proposal will also be made by setters with reversions above $E(\alpha)$. *As (a) the voter's incomplete information concerns his own preferences, (b) the voter and the setter are in a pure conflict situation for B>0, and (c) if the reversion is revealed, the setter's utility is decreasing in α whereas the voter's is increasing, no communication by the setter is credible.*[8] Indeed, the conflict situation also implies that setter communications other than the proposal will also not be believed by the voter.

Case 3. Reversions above and below the ideal point and $E(|\alpha|) \geq \bar{\alpha}$. This case is very similar to Case 2. The proposal and the budget are both the expected value of the absolute value of the reversion, $E(|\alpha|)$. Again this quantity represents the voter's ex ante expected utility from the reversion. The logic of the "pooling" equilibrium is identical to Case 2; indeed, note that in Case 2, $-E(\alpha) = E(|\alpha|)$. Nevertheless Case 2 and Case 3 differ, in a key way, in the nature of the payoff to the setter. In Case 2, the setter obtains the negative of the expected value of the reversion. It is as if the setter were playing a complete information game with the voter, with the lottery over reversions replaced by the expected reversion. In contrast, in Case 3, the setter obtains more than the negative of the expected value, since $E(|\alpha|) > -E(\alpha)$. The intuition for this contrast is that in Case 3 the voter faces a lottery for which he is risk-averse, whereas in Case 2 the voter was risk-neutral over the range of reversions. Because of the risk aversion in Case 3, the setter is able to "sell insurance" to the voter as well as threaten the voter with the reversion lottery.

Case 4. Reversions above and below the ideal point and $E(|\alpha|) < \bar{\alpha}$. In this case, the complete pooling equilibrium breaks down. The reason is easy to see. Setters with actual reversions above $E(|\alpha|)$ will prefer the reversion to proposing $E(|\alpha|)$. Thus, not all setters can be counted on to make a common proposal. Consider, however, the point p* defined by:

$$p^* = E(|\alpha|) \text{ given } \underline{\alpha} \leq \alpha < p^* \qquad (3)$$

An equilibrium results if a setter with a reversion not greater than p* proposes p* and a setter with a reversion above p* make any proposal not less than the reversion and if voters accept only those proposals not greater than p*. Given the setter's strategy, the voter's strategy is a best response since $-$ p* is the expected utility of the reversion given a proposal of p*. Thus, this last case gives us a mixture of the behavior in Cases 1 and 3. For low actual reversions there is pooling, with the setter benefiting from the risk aversion of the voter. For high reversions, the reversion results.

Having characterized the (most favorable to the setter) equilibrium in the context of incompletely informed votes, we now proceed to compare the results to those of the complete information setting. In all four Cases, the budget is weakly monotone increasing in the reversion, whereas in the complete information model, the budget is weakly monotone decreasing for reversions below the median ideal point.

As an illustration, consider α uniformly distributed on $[-1, +1]$. This distribution makes Case 4 applicable. Routine calculation shows p* $= \sqrt{2} - 1$. Using this result, we graph, in Figure 9.8, the outcome versus the actual reversion over the interval $[-1, +1]$, and we also show the corresponding (complete information) relationship when the voter knows the reversion ex ante. The contrast is evident.

This important contrast serves to complement our previous results on how uncertain turnout affects the setter model. The earlier results pertained to a model where the setter had incomplete information on voter preferences as a result of purely random turnout variations. In the context of that model, it is easy to construct examples where the plot of the *expected* budget versus the reversion is similar to that for the incomplete information model in Figure 9.8.

On the other hand, an entirely different perspective on the incomplete versus

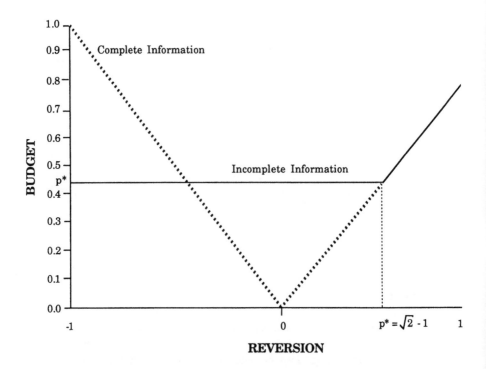

Figure 9.8. Comparison of the Budget-reversion relationship under complete and incomplete information. For actual reversions below p*, under incomplete information, setters pool and propose p*. For greater reversions, the budget equals the reversion. The graph is for the case where the reversion is uniform on [−1, +1].

complete comparison is given by examining the results from an ex ante perspective. What is the expected budget before either the voter or the setter know the value of the reversion? Consider a family of distributions that are identical up to a mean shift. How does the expected budget vary as the mean is increased? In Cases 2 and 3, which have the mean below the median ideal point, we get the standard result that the expected budget is decreasing in the mean reversion. Likewise in Case 1, where the mean is above the median ideal point, we get the standard result that the expected budget is increasing in the mean reversion. By continuity, in Case 4, the expected budget must initially be decreasing and ultimately increasing in the mean reversion.

In Figure 9.9, the ex ante expected budget is plotted as a function of the mean of a uniform distribution of width 2 and of another of width 4. Several points are worth noting.

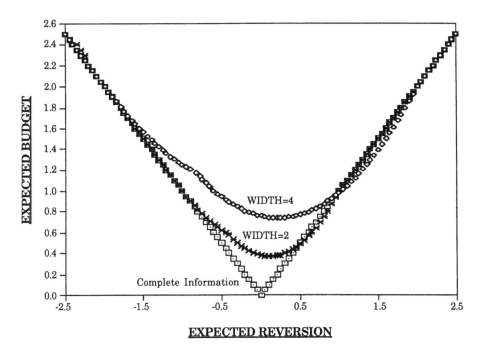

Figure 9.9. The ex ante reversion-budget relationship in the Banks model for uniform distribution. Except for very high expected reversions, increased uncertainty (width) benefits the setter.

1. The qualitative V-shaped nature of the complete information story is preserved; the original model is robust to incomplete information as it appears in the Banks model.

2. For expected reversions below the ideal point, increasing uncertainty makes setters better off–their insurance business increases.

3. If one used Banks's quadratic preferences rather than "tent" preferences, the qualitative picture would be the same. The major distinction is that with quadratic preferences, the incomplete information curve would also lie above the complete information line for Case 2 since, with quadratic preferences, the voter's global risk aversion implies that the setter can also sell insurance even when the reversion is known to be below the ideal point. (The budget becomes $\sqrt{E(\alpha^2)}$, which is greater than $E(|\alpha|)$.)

4. In contrast, for utility functions with a risk-acceptant range, part of the Figure 9.9-type curve below the median would lie below the complete information curve. Nonetheless, one would continue to have the qualitative relationship of a "V-shape."

5. The smallest expected budget does not occur when the mean reversion is at the median ideal point, but when the mean is somewhat greater than the median. [For the distribution of width 2, the mean with minimum expected budget is given by $(3-2\sqrt{2})/(3-\sqrt{2})$.]

6. There is a range of reversions above the median where ex ante setters' expected budgets are (slightly) lower than they are in the complete information setting. This range occurs for a subset of Case 4 distributions. The intuition for this result (which also relates to observation 5) is direct. Only some types of setters in Case 4 are in the insurance game. Those with reversions above p* are simply going with the reversion. The "defection" of the high α types lowers the budget that can be obtained by pooling types. The defection effectively signals to the voters that they should reject high proposals that might otherwise be made by low α types As the expected reversion increases, the gains from the insurance business are more than canceled by the defection problem.

7. From this ex ante perspective, one obtains an interesting contrast with the Romer–Rosenthal uncertain-turnout model. In the turnout model, for very low reversions, we have seen that the setter is worse off than with no uncertainty, whereas, for reversions above the median, the setter is always better off. In the Banks model, this qualitative relationship is, roughly speaking, reversed. The setter is never worse off for expected reversions below the median and may be worse off for expected reversions above the median. The reversal in the qualitative relationship lies precisely in the fact that the setter is informed in the Banks model and uninformed in the turnout model.

Imperfect Information About Voter Preferences

We have already characterized the setter's problem when there is complete information about voter preferences. The largest proposal a voter will approve is given by B(R). The setter's proposal, p, is then just $\hat{B} \equiv$ median B(R). In realistic settings, $\hat{B}$ is unknown to the setter. The setter can be thought of as assigning a probability distribution, $F(\hat{B})$, over the various possible values of this unknown median.

When the setter can hold but a single vote or referendum, voters have a dominant strategy of voting for their preferred alternative, p or R. Because there is but a single election, there is no opportunity for learning by the setter. Thus, the setter has a simple maximization problem. Again without loss of generality, let the reversion be zero. The setter then picks p to solve the following problem:

$$\max_{p} \Pi = p \cdot (\text{Probability p passes}) = p \cdot [1 - F(p)] \tag{4}$$

As long as the support of $F(\hat{B})$ is finite, there is a solution to this problem.[9]

For example, if $F(\hat{B})$ is uniform on $[0,1]$, the setter picks $p = 1/2$ for an expected budget of $\Pi = 1/4$.

The analysis gets more interesting and more tricky when the setter is allowed to alter his proposal and call for one or more revotes in the case of a failed proposal. In this case, which is common in school budget referenda in the United States,[10] the setter has the opportunity to acquire information about voter preferences as the sequence of referenda proceeds. On the other hand, voters have incentives that may cause them to vote strategically in the sense that they may vote against p, even if p gives higher utility than R. One possible reason for voting against a current proposal is to hold out to extract a lower proposal from the setter on a future round; another possible reason is to conceal information from the setter, to prevent the setter from learning about voter preferences. Before exploring the strategic interaction between the voters and the setter, it will be instructive to see how the setter behaves when voters are nonstrategic.

Initially assume that, when confronted with a proposal, p, the voter always votes for p if p gives her at least as much utility as the reversion, R. Assume further that the setter first has the option of adopting R or making a proposal p_1. If this first election passes, p_1 becomes the budget. *Most important, the setter does not have the option of asking for a revote if it turns out that, from his viewpoint, the initial proposal was too small.* In contrast, if p_1 fails, the setter may then propose p_2. This last proposal then becomes the budget, unless it also fails, in which case the budget is the reversion.

Both to simplify the presentation and to consider the most interesting case, assume the setter is certain that he can get a budget higher than the reversion. Since we continue to assume the reversion is zero, we thus have $F(0) = 0$. Moreover, assume that there exists a finite upper bound H such that $F(H) = 1$ and that there are voters for whom $B(R) > H$. That is, if the setter proposes H, H will fail for sure, but the vote against H will not be unanimous.

We now turn to two interesting subcases. In the first, with one election the setter can learn the value of $\hat{B}$. In the second, the first election increases the setter's information, but some uncertainty remains.

Case 1. Setter can learn $\hat{B}$. As an example of the first case, assume that the setter knows that the distribution of the individual B(R) is uniform on an interval of width 4 but does not know the mean of the interval. He knows only that the mean is uniform on $[0,1]$. If the setter proposes 1.1 and gets 40 percent of the vote, he can infer that $\hat{B} = 0.7$. (If $\hat{B}=0.7$, the voters are distributed on $[-1.3,2.7]$, and 40 percent of the voters are above 1.1.)

More generally, when the setter can learn $\hat{B}$, optimal policy for the setter is simply to pick a proposal that guarantees the first election will be lost and then behave exactly as a Romer–Rosenthal complete information setter by picking

$\hat{B}$ in the second round. The logic for this result is simple. If the proposal p_1 has a strictly positive probability of passage, the setter will obtain $\hat{B}$ when the proposal fails but $p_1 < \hat{B}$ if the proposal passes. So a guaranteed loss on the first round strictly dominates, in terms of expected budget, all proposals with some probability of passage. In our example, if the setter guarantees a loss by proposing 1.1, his Π is $E(\hat{B}) = 0.5$. Having the extra round has benefited the setter; recall that with only one round $\Pi = 0.25$.

Note that the above argument extends readily to settings where, as is common practice in American school finance elections, multiple referenda are possible. If M tries are available and N < M tries suffice to produce complete information on $\hat{B}$, the setter will use the first N electrons to extract this information and then propose $\hat{B}$. The result is robust. A setter who is risk-averse but prefers bigger budgets to smaller ones will behave in the same manner as a risk-neutral setter. A non-budget-maximizing setter of the De-nzau-MacKay type will also extract all the information (or obtain his ideal point on an early round). The only reason for setters not to gain full information on $\hat{B}$ in this case would be if holding referenda were costly; here the setter would need to trade off the benefits of information against the costs of gathering information.

Case 2. Setter cannot learn $\hat{B}$. This case is quite distinct in its behavioral implications from Case I. Typically, the setter's inability to learn the precise value of $\hat{B}$ results in some positive probability that the budget will pass on each try. This can be shown by considering the limiting case where the only information a setter gains from a failed proposal is that $\hat{B}$ is less than the proposal.[11] In other words, failing a proposal simply causes Bayesian updating where the posterior $G(\hat{B}) = F(\hat{B})/F(p)$, for $\hat{B} \le p$.

With this simple form of updating, the backward induction argument is straightforward. When the setter has two attempts, given that his first proposal p_1 failed, he will choose p_2^* to solve:

$$p_2^*(p_1) = \underset{p_2}{\text{argmax}}\ p_2[1 - G(p_2|p_1)] \tag{5}$$

That is, in the last period, the setter acts exactly as he would if there were only one period, except that he operates with the updated distribution $G(\bullet)$. In the first period, the setter chooses p_1 to maximize his expected budget:

$$\underset{p_1}{\text{max}}\ \Pi = p_1[1 - F(p_1)] + p_2^*(p_1)[1 - G(p_2^*|p_1)]F(p_1) \tag{6}$$

The first term in the above expression is the first period proposal times the probability of passage in the first period. The second term is the second period proposal times the probability of passage times the probability of failure in the first period. (Recall that, if both proposals fail, the budget is zero.) To return to our example of a [0,1] uniform distribution on $\hat{B}$, some simple manipulations show that the setter will choose $p_1 = 2/3$ and $p_2 = 1/3$. The expected budget is 0.39.

Several observations are in order. First, having more than one opportunity obviously benefits the setter, even when the setter's updating is limited to truncating budgets greater than the previous failures. Second, the setter is no longer going to fail all but the last proposal but will choose a decreasing series of proposals, all of which have some chance of passage. Indeed, by continuity, such decreasing will also be observed in some situations where the setter can carry out a more complex form of updating.[12] Third, Case 2 appears more consistent with empirical observation, since many first proposals pass. Fourth, the decreasing sequence of proposals that one generally observes empirically (Romer and Rosenthal 1979a) is consistent both with uncertainty where truly no learning is possible, as in the Romer–Rosenthal random turnout model, and with uncertainty where learning occurs.

Sophisticated Voters

Having explored the setter's optimization problem when he is presented with the opportunity to learn from the behavior of "naive" voters, we turn to the more complicated analysis of the situation that arises when the voters become strategic, or sophisticated, players. This situation has been elegantly addressed by Morton (1988).

Because sophisticated voters look ahead as if they were evaluating lotteries, their risk preferences become important. Like Banks, Morton models voters as having quadratic preferences, which he parameterizes as:

$$U(B) = \tau B - B^2 \tag{7}$$

The parameter τ discloses the voter's "type" and represents the largest budget the voter will approve when the reversion is, as assumed, 0. That is, $\tau = B(0)$. With quadratic utility, a lottery over expenditures gives rise to an expected utility of $\tau\mu - \mu^2 - \sigma^2$, where μ is the mean of the lottery and σ^2 is the variance.

In this situation, what do we mean by strategic voter behavior? On the surface, one might think that voters would be better off if a majority adopted the strategy of *always* voting against first proposals, thus strategically eliminating the setter's opportunity to learn and reducing the expected budget to its value when the setter has only one shot. Such strategies are Nash equilibria, but they are "bogus" (Ordeshook 1986, p. 137) in that they involve using weakly dominated strategies. For example, such strategies call for voters to vote against even those proposals that are equal to their ideal points. A more natural type of equilibrium to investigate, as suggested by Morton (1988), is a cutpoint equilibrium where there is a critical value τ^* such that voter types with $\tau > \tau^*$ support an initial proposal, and those with $\tau < \tau^*$ reject it.[13]

Case 1 with Sophistication. When we have cutpoint equilibria, if the setter were able to learn $\hat{B}$ under naive voting, he will be able to learn it from cutpoint voting. While τ^* will no longer be p_1, as is the case for naive voting, the setter will still be able to map from the observed vote to the true value of $\hat{B}$. Note that sophisticated voters are aware that the electorate will always get an offer it can't refuse on the second round. As a result, voters, being strategic in the sense of Farquharson (1969), realize that the initial vote on p_1 is really a vote between p_1 and a lottery over potential second-period proposals from the setter. Sophistication rules out any immediate consideration of the reversion. Consequently, a voter will vote against the initial proposal if and only if

$$\Delta = U(p_1) - EU(p_2) < 0. \tag{8}$$

Assume p_1 given and some candidate cutpoint τ^*. We have

$$\begin{aligned}
\Delta(p_1, \tau^*) &= U(p_1) - EU(p_2 | \hat{B} < \tau^*) \\
&= [\tau p_1 - p_1^2] - [\tau \mu^* - \mu^{*2} - \sigma^{*2}],
\end{aligned} \tag{9}$$

where the "*" denotes truncation consistent with τ^*. That is, in forming his expected utility of the second proposal, the voter takes into consideration that the second proposal surely can be at most τ^*.[14] (Recall that $\tau = B(0)$ for the voter. Then, if the voters with $\tau \leq \tau^*$ are a majority, $\hat{B} \leq \tau^*$.)

From the setter's viewpoint, it is critical whether τ^* is at least p_1. When the cutpoint is greater than the proposal, more people vote against the proposal than if they were voting naively. As Figure 9.10 illustrates, in this case the setter's lottery when he picks a proposal that always fails dominates any lottery with a proposal that has some possibility of passage. So if there is a "protest" vote, the setter will always opt to lose the first election and adopt $\hat{B}$ on the second round. *If $\tau^* \geq p_1$, the budget under sophisticated voting is identical to the budget under naive voting.*

When some proposals lead to cutpoints that are less than the proposal, we cannot rule out, as Figure 9.11 indicates, the setter choosing to pick an initial proposal that would have some chance of winning. When is this possible? Note that if we ignore the variance term in (9), Δ is negative for a voter with $\tau = p_1$ if $\tau^* = p_1$, so in fact we would have to have $\tau^* > p_1$. Therefore, to have $\tau^* < p_1$, the variance term, which reflects voter risk aversion, must be relatively large.

The preceding analysis can be illustrated by returning to our uniform [0.1] example. Note that (a) cutpoints above 1.0 guarantee failed proposals and (b) the variance of the uniform distribution is $1/12$. Therefore $\mu^* = (1/2)\tau^*$ and $\sigma^{*2} = (1/12)\tau^2$. We thus have:

$$\begin{aligned}
\Delta(p_1, \tau^*) &= U(p_1) - EU(\hat{B} | \hat{B} < \tau^*) \\
&= \tau p_1 - p_1^2 - (1/2)\tau + 1/4 - 1/12 \qquad\qquad \tau^* \geq 1
\end{aligned}$$

Probability

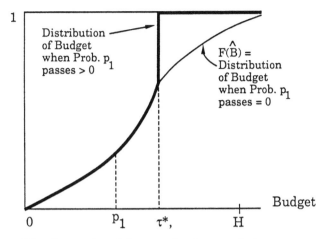

Figure 9.10. When the cut point, τ^*, is greater than the proposal, the setter loses the opportunity to obtain a budget greater than τ^*. The setter always obtains a higher expected budget by making a proposal that is certain to fail.

Probability

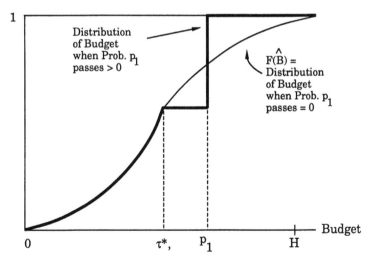

Figure 9.11. When the cut point, τ^*, is less than the proposal, the setter can have a budget of p_1 even if $\hat{B}$ is less than p_1.

221

$$= \tau p_1 - p_1^2 - (1/2)\tau^*\tau + (1/4)\tau^{*2} + (1/12)\tau^{*2} \quad \tau^* < 1 \quad (10)$$

We know that the setter will not make a proposal below $1/2$, for if the setter makes a proposal that is guaranteed to lose, his expected budget is $1/2$, as established in the section on naive voting. In turn, one can verify that Δ is increasing in τ for proposals greater than $1/2$; in other words, cutpoints will be consistent with voters below the cutpoint rejecting the proposal. To compute the cutpoint for a given proposal, we set $\tau = \tau^*$ in (10), equate Δ to zero, and solve. This gives,

$$\tau^*(p_1) = 3p_1 [1 - \sqrt{1/3}] \simeq 1.27 \, p_1, \tau^* < 1 \quad (11)$$

It then follows that $\tau^* > p_1$ for any proposal that might pass. The setter will thus always choose to lose the first election. In our example, sophistication changes voting behavior but not the final budget. Situations where the final budget would be changed in the presence of sophisticated voting seem unlikely; I have been unable to construct an example of such a situation. If sophisticated voting affects the interaction between the voter and the setter, it is more likely to be in situations where the setter cannot learn the value of $\hat{B}$.

Case 2 with Sophisticated Voting. As shown in Morton (1988), analysis of sophisticated voting with partial learning is a highly complex matter; general results are not available. Morton has, however, solved the uniform [0,1] model for the limiting case, considered above for naive voting, where the setter's only updating is restricted to knowledge that his first proposal failed. Sophisticated voters now realize that if the cutpoint is τ^*, the second-period proposal will be $\tau^*/2$ and that this proposal will pass with probability $1/2$. The indifference condition at the cutpoint then becomes:

$$\Delta = U(p_1) - 1/2 \, U(p_2)$$
$$= \tau^* p_1 - p_1^2 - \tau^{*2}/4 + \tau^{*2}/8 = 0. \quad (12)$$

Morton solves for the setter's optimal p_1, and finds $p_1 = 0.61, \tau^* = 0.72, p_2 = 0.36$. Again, we have a decreasing sequence of proposals; this time, however, sophisticated voters have forced the setter to moderate his initial proposal over what it would have been for naive voters. Indeed, the setter's expected budget is roughly 0.30, less than the 0.39 expected from naive voters in the same conditions but still better than the 0.25 that results when the setter has only one shot. Morton's example shows a situation where sophisticated voting can attenuate the increased expenditures that are likely to result when agenda setters are allowed to ask for multiple revotes.

Case 1 Reconsidered: The Pivotal Voter Calculus. In Morton's analysis of Case 1, the situation where the setter could learn $\hat{B}$ with one proposal, voters based their decisions on a comparison of the current proposal, p_1, to the lottery of the potential proposals that could result if the proposal failed. In contrast, one can interpret the Case 2 analysis as assuming that each voter acts as if he were pivotal in the first-period election.[15]

To apply the pivotal concept to Case 1, consider what happens if the first-period election ends in a tie. Typically, tied referenda go against the proposal. Thus, the pivotal voter is the voter with the highest τ among the "No" voters. Since the setter has learned the distribution of preferences, he can make his second proposal equal to the τ of the pivotal voter and pass in the second period. So if a voter believes she is pivotal in the first election, she should vote against any proposal greater than her τ. When all voters act this way, we have $\tau^* = p_1$. Consequently, it is optimal for the setter to make a proposal that will always fail. Thus, if we impose the pivotal voter calculus, we are guaranteed that naive and sophisticated behavior lead to the same outcome. Sophisticated behavior becomes relevant only when the setter has a high degree of uncertainty, as in Case 2.

EMPIRICAL ANALYSIS OF THE SETTER MODEL

Circumstantial Evidence

In the field of public finance, the major alternative hypothesis to the setter model is the median voter model. Following early work by James Barr and Otto Davis (1966), a large literature developed with econometric specifications that were more-or-less "derived" from the median voter model.[16] The most common specification, which originated with Theodore Bergstrom and Robert Goodman (1973) was to perform a log-linear regression with expenditures as the dependent variable. The key independent variables were median income and median tax price. The tax price variable was, given the key role of the property tax in local finance, defined as the ratio of median housing value to the total assessed value in the community. A variety of socio-demographic variables were also included, partly to get a handle on specification error.

Testing the median voter model is beset by two key methodological problems. The first is simply that when demand is determined by two characteristics—such as income and property wealth—the characteristics of the median demander will generally not correspond to the medians of the two characteristics.[17] the second is that, even were it appropriate to regress on median income and median tax price, significant results would not provide strong support for the median voter model. One must confront both the "multiple fallacy": the log-linear regression cannot identify whether expenditures are at the level of median demand or at twice or some other multiple of that demand and the "fractile fallacy"—the log-linear regressions do not test the median against other fractiles of the distributions of the characteristics (Romer and Rosenthal 1979b). Indeed, regressions for Oregon school districts indicate that substituting any decile of the income distribution from the 2nd through the 8th gives a fit comparable to the median (Romer and Rosenthal 1982a).

Despite these methodological difficulties, the "median voter" studies in local public finance have provided substantial circumstantial evidence that agenda setting or some other form of institutional structure matters in local decision-making. Even after the inclusion of a bevy of auxiliary variables, price and income elasticities for municipal expenditures vary widely across American states.[18] There is also substantial variation in elasticities between municipalities that have had "reformist" changes, such as city-manager systems, and those that have not.[19] Similarly, in Switzerland, the median voter model appears to apply better to municipalities with direct democracies than to municipalities with representative democracies.[20]

Description of the Institutional Context in Oregon

To develop more than circumstantial evidence to support the setter model, Romer and Rosenthal and colleagues began a series of studies of school operating budgets and budget referenda in Oregon and, later on, New York.

Through the mid-seventies, the school finance system in Oregon presented several features that provided an excellent setting for studying the basic setter model.

i. Unless changed in a separate voter referendum, the reversion was of the exogenous type in the sense that the budget voted did not affect reversions in future years.

ii. One important component of the reversion was $L_t = (L_{1916})(1.06)^{t-1916}$, where L_t represents the (nominal) budget that could be spent from local property tax revenues in year t, and L_{1916} represents what the district spent in 1916. There was one important exception to the "1916" rule; if a district had been formed by merger subsequent to 1916, $L_t = 0$. Thus, many of the reversions were very low.[21] In contrast, some other districts, most notably Portland, had had substantial expenditures in 1916 and had experienced enrollment declines. In these cases, L_t was substantial. Consequently, there was substantial variation in the reversion, the key variable in the setter model.

iii. A school district could elect not to hold a budget referendum and to operate solely with its reversion budget.

iv. A school district was permitted a fixed, small (approximately six, the exact number being subject to change by the state legislature) number of attempts to pass an operating budget each year. The amount requested could be revised upward or downward after each failed attempt. *However, a passed budget could not be amended and subjected to a revote.*

v. Once every two years, a school district could call a special referendum where it could propose a change in the reversion. Like the operating budget, the proposed change had to be approved by a simple majority.

vi. About one quarter of each district's budget was represented by a lump sum grant from the state government. Another part of the budget came from a lump sum grant from county-level Intermediate Education Districts. These grants were close to zero in some counties, substantial in others. Both amounts could be treated as part of the reversion.

Evidence from Setter Proposals and Spending

From (iii) and (i), there is an immediate prediction under the simple setter model. Those districts not holding elections should have reversions above the median ideal point. Consequently, spending in those districts should equal the reversion. In fact, in the sixty-four cases where districts did not hold elections or failed to pass an election between 1970–71 and 1976–77, all but $300,000 of the available $946,200,000 in reversion monies were spent. Thus, reversion districts basically spend all of the reversion. We would observe this level of spending in a median voter model only in the very unlikely event that all the reversion districts had reversions extremely close to the ideal point of the median voter.

Events in Portland, by far Oregon's largest school district, provided a particularly informative illustration of the extent to which expenditures may have exceeded the median ideal point. For several years prior to 1971, Portland had not held a referendum and had just gone with the reversion. In such a situation, one might expect that an agenda setter—budget-maximizing or median voter implementing—might have experienced a decay in information that would lead it to undertake a learning process of the Morton type. It is not surprising that the Portland school board went to the voters in 1971 for a 13 percent increase in the locally financed portion of the budget. On each of three attempts, the proposed increase was defeated by overwhelming margins. Even the last attempt, when the increase was trimmed back to 11 percent, failed by a 63–37 margin. Unlike a median-seeking agenda setter, the board failed to make a substantial cut after this expression of voter sentiment.

Another manifestation of direct conflict between the setter and the pivotal voter is provided by observations of the use of the institutional feature (v) which provided for changes in the (nominal) reversion level. Note that, under the simple, complete information, setter model, expenditures are at or above those desired by the pivotal voter. Thus, ceteris paribus, any change in the reversion that would lead to a higher budget for the setter would make the pivotal voter worse off. It is, therefore, not surprising that attempts to change the reversion were rarely made and that the few attempts that were made were almost always defeated by the voters (Romer and Rosenthal 1982a).

The lump sum form of state aid (vi) made it possible to investigate an additional source of conflict between the setter and the voters. When aid is lump sum, the setter has an unambiguous interest in withholding from the

Howard Rosenthal

voters information about the amount of aid. There are two motivations. First, even in a straight median voter story, perceived state aid will lead to less total spending than unperceived. Under standard economic assumptions regarding income effects, voters will treat perceived state aid as fungible and divert part of the grant to non-education expenditures by lowering local taxes. In contrast, a budget-maximizing setter would fully spend any unperceived grant. Second, agenda setting gives the setter an added interest in limiting voter awareness of lump-sum grants. Since grants represent a portion of the reversion, unperceived grants make for lower reversions and higher total expenditures (Romer and Rosenthal 1980).

Empirical evidence about the effect of the lump-sum grants was provided by Filimon, Romer, and Rosenthal (1982). They estimated that only 3 percent of the grant sums were "perceived" and that the failure to perceive the grants increased spending by about 30 percent. An interesting counterpoint to these findings was provided by Romer, Rosenthal, and Munley (1987), who investigated New York (for 1975) where school budgets were also subject to referenda but the aid took the form of closed-end matching grants. With this form of grant, the setter's interest in withholding information is ambiguous, since he wants the voters to know that the price effect of the match has made education cheaper (Romer and Rosenthal 1980). It is not surprising, therefore, that Romer, Rosenthal, and Munley did not find strong perception effects with the New York data.

While the above set of observations is largely consistent with the simple setter model, the fact that proposals frequently fail—for example, 42 of 111 first proposals failed in Oregon in 1971–72—suggests that some uncertainty is present. Indeed, in Oregon, a few schools have actually closed for several months because voters failed to approve an operating budget.

When budgets are rejected by the voters, one almost invariably observes a non-increasing sequence of proposals. How do we interpret this observation in terms of the various uncertainty models we have considered? Failed proposals seem likely to result from uncertainty that confronts the setter rather than the voter. Thus, I confine the discussion to the random turnout model of Romer and Rosenthal and the Bayesian learning model of Morton.

The key observation for discriminating between models of setter uncertainty is that while proposal sequences are non-increasing, proposals are frequently unchanged from one round to the next and, when cuts are made, they tend to be relatively small fractions of the budget (Romer, Rosenthal, and Ladha 1984). This leads us to rule out both random turnout and setter learning with naive voters as models that are sufficient to account for the observations. Those models all predict a strictly decreasing sequence of proposals.

In contrast, when voters are sophisticated, increased proposals become possible. Consider equation (11). An optimal first proposal for the setter is $p_1 = 0.8$, since $\tau^*(0.8) = 1.02$, which guarantees that the proposal loses. Since

226

$\hat{B}$ is equally likely to be anywhere between 0 and 1, 20 percent of the second proposals will be expected to be higher than the initial proposals. This very low form of uncertainty embodied in Case 1 presents, however, two problems when confronted with the data. First, in Case 1, first proposals should always fail. Second we should expect a good deal of variability in second proposals relative to first proposals, with unchanged proposals being a purely knife-edge condition. On the other hand, at the other extreme, Case 2 first proposals can pass, but the sequence will be strictly decreasing. One can conjecture, however, that in the less tractable intermediate forms of uncertainty, rejection of a first proposal could lead to a second proposal quite close to the original. In such an environment, the referendum institution would acquire a ritualistic appearance. Voters are given a number of occasions to express their dissatisfaction, but, in the end, the setter gets (at least close to) what was originally requested. Thus, while uncertainty may be partly responsible for failed referenda, leading to a sequence of elections, losing an election results in, at most, only a slight cut in the budget.

The impact of uncertainty may be more manifest in the overall level of the budget, embodied in the setter's first proposal. Romer and Rosenthal (1982a) found that the V-shaped relationship between reversion and budget was only partly supported in Oregon.[22] They estimated a reversion-budget relationship with a discontinuity at a threshold level hypothesized to be a reversion point below which the schools would actually have to close. For the very low reversions below the threshold (estimated at $206 per student), the setter's threat may have been particularly effective, since voters would lose the custodial, as well as the educational, value of the school system. Indeed, the 41 districts below the threshold had expenditures that averaged about 15 percent more, per student, than districts just above the threshold. Above the threshold, they estimated a linear budget-reversion relationship for all districts holding elections. By the simple setter model theory, the slope of this relationship should have been negative. In fact, it was weakly, but significantly, positive (see Figure 9.12). Such a relationship might conceivably arise under any of the uncertainty models treated here.

Evidence from Voting Results

In this section, we have so far used observations on proposals and budgets to examine the setter model. This model also has implications for what will be observed in aggregate voting behavior given that the setter has picked an optimal proposal in an expenditure referendum. Literally taken, the simple model says the setter should pick this proposal to win by exactly one vote.[23] Given some uncertainty about turnout, the setter should, for reversions below the median ideal point, typically aim for slightly more than 50 percent of the vote.[24] In "aiming" the setter has to take account of voters' indirect prefer-

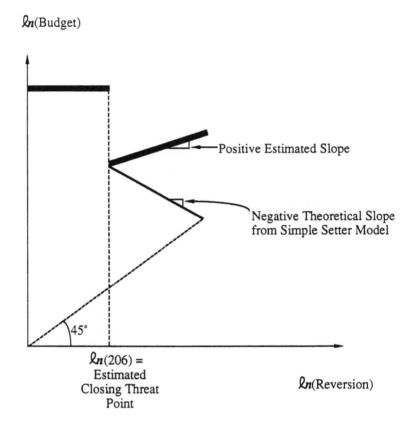

Figure 9.12. The Estimated Budget-Reversion Reversion Relationship (Net of State Aid) for Oregon School Districts in the 1971–72 School Year.

ences for education. In turn, these preferences reflect income, tax price, children per household, and other variables used in cross-sectional studies by social scientists. Because the setter "takes out" the effects of these variables in "aiming," we should find that the level of "Yes" voting in a cross-section of districts holding elections should appear as random variation about a mean level, statistically unrelated to income, price, or other exogenous variables.

In studying Oregon school referenda, Romer and Rosenthal (1982b) found evidence consistent with the "take-out" prediction. In particular, variables that were significant in the estimated equation for spending had no predictive power in the equation for voting.

In one respect, this support for the setter model was fortuitous. Because census data on income and housing were unavailable for smaller school districts, the Oregon study was confined to a subset of relatively large school districts. But Romer and Rosenthal (1983b) and Hansen, Palfrey, and Rosenthal (1987) later reported that smaller districts tended to pass their budgets with majorities well above 50 percent. The data thus suggest that the pure budget-maximizing version may be appropriate only in jurisdictions where the presence of either established bureaucracies or free-riding by citizens may lead to agenda setters that are not representative of the population. Elsewhere, the agenda setter may choose to limit spending à la my earlier discussion of the Denzau–Mackay model.

The findings of Romer and Rosenthal that exogenous variables are taken out by the setter was confirmed in a study of Michigan school districts by Rothstein (1988) and another of New York by Romer, Rosenthal, and Munley (1987).[25]

In the New York study, size played a key role, similar to that found in Oregon. But once a district lost an election—a fairly strong indication of a budget-maximizing setter, the percent voting "Yes" on second and later tries averaged only slightly over 50, regardless of size. Thus, even some relatively small jurisdictions may have budget-maximizing setters.

Evidence from the Relationship Between Voting and Spending

The central observation about local school spending is that spending appears responsive to well-known demand determinants, principally income and tax price, and to an institutional factor, the reversion. The central observation about voting, at least for relatively large districts, is that referenda tend to be approved by only slightly larger than 50-50 splits and that the determinants of spending have no impact on the level of the vote.

How do these two sets of observations tie together? If the setter makes an "error" by proposing a budget larger than that called for by the spending equation, he should receive fewer votes than the "target." Conversely, small proposals should be received relatively favorably. (Note that the spending equation can be taken as approximating the setter's optimal proposal, based on the characteristics of his jurisdiction as he seeks to attain the "target" called for by the voting equation.) Thus, a final prediction of the model is that the covariance between the spending equation and the voting equation should be negative. This prediction was supported in both the Oregon study and the New York study.

CONCLUSION

In this essay, I have reviewed the theory of unidimensional agenda setting. The theory can lead to strong predictions about observables when the preferences of the agenda-setter are known. Empirical analysis suggests that re-

Howard Rosenthal

source allocation is indeed affected by the agenda-setting process in addition to the preferences of the citizenry.

In the course of my research with Thomas Romer, I have noticed that our results tend to be espoused by conservatives who believe that government spending is excessive. Indeed, we have occasionally been labeled "Leviathan" theorists. After all, haven't we argued that spending will exceed the ideal point of the median voter?

I have two reactions to this simplistic reading of ideology into basic scientific research.

First, nothing is normatively sacred about the median voter's ideal point. For example, the setter model was applied (Romer and Rosenthal 1983a) to a simple economy where government's role was limited to setting an externality (pollution) tax. For this economy, it can be shown that, when a "median" voter exists, the "median" of preferred tax rates is, except for knife-edges, not the Pigovian welfare-optimizing tax. In this context, majority rule, even if it has an equilibrium, is not a good process for making decisions. In contrast, a reversion mechanism with an endogenously selected setter will enact the appropriate tax.

Second, a key point drawn forth in the externality example is that voting decisions are based not only upon preferences re the externality but also upon the redistributive implications of the system of taxation. These redistributive implications are what lead to the nonoptimality of majority rule. With regard to local finance of education, the empirical focus of this essay, then, it is appropriate to be concerned not only about the distortion of voter preferences in the selection of a point above the median but also about all the other distortions. These include a tax system, often based on the property tax, zoning restrictions, and household selection of residence based on spending levels. In this broader context, it becomes complicated and problematic to argue that reversion mechanisms lead to excessive spending. Casual comparison with Western Europe and Japan certainly does not suggest that the local systems of primary and secondary education represent a crown jewel of American federalism.

In summary, caution should be exercised in drawing normative conclusions from the setter model. Caution is especially in order given the infancy of the theoretical and empirical research on agenda-setting as a positive model of government.

ACKNOWLEDGMENTS

I thank Jeff Banks, Jim Enelow, Mel Hinich, Dan Ingberman, Susanne Lohmann, John Londregan, Sandy Morton, and Tom Palfrey for discussion or comments. I owe a special debt to Tom Romer, who set an agenda I followed for several years. Any mistakes are mine.

NOTES

1 See the literature spanned by Farquharson (1969), McKelvey (1976), Shepsle and Weingast (1984), and Ordeshook and Palfrey (1988).

2 See Inman (1987) and Khrebiel (1988) for reviews of this literature.

3 The results on sophistication are original to this essay but reflect a suggestion of Susanne Lohmann and several conversations with Daniel Ingberman.

4 The assumption of a common probability is not critical. What is critical is that each voter's probability is independent of the setter's actions.

5 Morton's paper circulated for several years before publication.

6 Treating the case where the voter had incomplete information about the reversion and the proposal would be an interesting extension of the Banks model.

7 See Banks (1988) for detailed discussion of the equilibrium selection issue.

8 I am indebted to Jeff Banks and Tom Palfrey for this interpretation.

9 Morton (1988) points out that the solution is unique under standard "regularity" assumptions concerning the hazard rate. Enelow and Hinich (1987) consider the situation where, in a legislative context, the setter's proposal must pass several bodies, such as committees and the two houses of a bicameral legislature. In their model, there is a distinct F(•) for each body. They show, under surprisingly general assumptions about probability distributions and the setter's utility function, that the setter also has a unique optimal proposal in this more general setting.

10 See Hamilton and Cohen (1974).

11 See Morton (1988) for a more detailed discussion of uninformative priors.

12 Morton (1988) points out that the dynamic programming analysis of these more complex situations is likely to be very difficult.

13 Cutpoint equilibria are now fairly common in political theory. Palfrey and Rosenthal (1985) and Ordeshook and Palfrey (1988) illustrate other applications of cutpoint analysis.

14 Morton (1988) errs in using the unconditional distribution of $\hat{B}$ at this point. In correcting this error, I arrive at sharply different conclusions.

15 The importance of the pivoting assumption is more important in Morton's general analysis of the situation where the setter cannot learn $\hat{B}$ than in the limiting case where updating is limited to truncation. A pivotal voter calculus applied to a sequence of votes also appears in Ordeshook and Palfrey (1988).

16 Romer and Rosenthal (1979b) provide a review and bibliography of research through, roughly, 1978.

17 This aggregation problem is set forth in Bergstrom and Goodman (1973). Filimon (1979) presents an "impossibility" theorem that shows that median-by-median characteristics will be the appropriate specification only under knife-edge conditions.

18 Bergstrom and Goodman (1973).

19 Farnham (1985).

20 Pommerehne (1978).

21 As reversions also included other revenues [see (vi) below], reversions were rarely zero; nonetheless, many reversions in (1971) were only a few hundred dollars per student, amounts far from adequate for operation of a school district. For details, see Romer and Rosenthal (1982a).

22 See Romer et al. (1987) for discussion of why a similar test was inappropriate for the New York data.

23 This statement assumes no two voters have exactly the same ideal point.

24 Note that in a median voter model, the setter would "aim" for 50 percent only

when the reversion equaled the median ideal point. Otherwise, the vote should exceed 50 percent. Moreover, when reversions are above the median, proposals should be for less than the reversion.

25 Rothstein places a somewhat different interpretation on his results since some variables are statistically significant at conventional levels. The important finding, however, is that the overall R^2 for the vote equation is only on the order of 0.11, higher than Romer and Rosenthal (1982b) but still very low. The statistical significance is partly a matter of methodological differences and partly a matter of Rothstein's working with 384 observations versus Romer and Rosenthal's 111.

REFERENCES

Banks, Jeffrey. 1988. "Monopoly Agenda Control and Asymmetric Information." University of Rochester (mimeo).

Barr, James, and Otto A. Davis. 1966. "An Elementary Political and Economic Theory of Expenditures of Local Governments." *Southern Economic Journal* 33: 149–65.

Bergstrom, Theodore C., and Robert P. Goodman. 1973. "Private Demands for Public Goods." *American Economic Review* 63: 180–96.

Denzau, Arthur, and Robert Mackay. 1983. "Gatekeeping and Monopoly Power of Committees: An Analysis of Sincere and Sophisticated Behavior." *American Journal of Political Science:* 740–761.

Enelow, James M., and Melvin J. Hinich. 1987. "Uncertainty and the New Institutionalism: The Existence of a Structure-Induced Equilibrium." (mimeo).

Farnham, Paul G. 1985. "Form of Government and the Median Voter: A Disaggregated Analysis." Georgia State University (mimeo).

Farquharson, Robin. 1969. *Theory of Voting.* New Haven: Yale University Press.

Filimon, Radu. 1979. "Aggregation and the Allocation of Public and Private Goods." Ph. D. dissertation, Carnegie Mellon University.

Filimon, Radu, Thomas Romer, and Howard Rosenthal. 1982. "Asymmetric Information and Agenda Control: The Bases of Monopoly Power in Public Spending." *Journal of Public Economics* 17: 51–70.

Gilligan, Thomas W., and Keith Krehbiel. 1986. "Rules, Subjurisdictional Choice, and Congressional Outcomes: An Event Study of Energy Taxation Legislation in the 93rd Congress." Social Science Working Paper No. 594. Pasadena: California Institute of Technology.

———. 1987. "Collective Decision-Making and Standing Committee: An Informational Rationale for Restrictive Amendment Procedures." *Journal of Law, Economics, and Organization* 3: 287–335.

———. 1988. "Collective Choice Without Procedural Commitment." Stanford: Hoover Institution Working Paper in Political Science, P-88-8.

———. 1989. "Asymmetric Information and Legislative Rules with a Heterogeneous Committee." *American Journal of Political Science* 33: 459–490.

Hamilton, Howard D., and Sylvan K. Cohen. (1974. *Policy Making by Plebiscite: School Referenda.* Lexington: D. C. Heath.

Hansen, Steven, Thomas R. Palfrey, and Howard Rosenthal. 1987. "The Relationship Between Constituency Size and Turnout: Using Game Theory to Estimate the Cost of Voting." *Public Choice* 52, 15–33

Ingberman, Daniel. 1985. "Running Against the Status Quo: Institutions for Direct Democracy and Allocations Over Time." *Public Choice* 146: 19–44.

Inman, Robert P. 1987. "Markets, Government, and the 'New' Political Economy." In Alan Auerbach and Martin Feldstein, eds., *Handbook of Public Economics*, vol. 2.

Krehbiel, Keith. 1988. "Spatial Models of Legislative Choice." *Legislative Studies Quarterly* 13: 259–319.

McKelvey, Richard D. 1976. "Intransitivities in Multidimensional Voting Models and Some Implications for Agenda Control." *Journal of Economic Theory* 12: 472–82.

Morton, Sanford. 1988. "Strategic Voting in Repeated Referenda." *Social Choice and Welfare* 5: 45–68.

Niskanen, William. 1971. *Bureaucracy and Representative Government*. Chicago: Aldine-Atherton.

Ordeshook, Peter C. 1986. *Game Theory and Political Theory*. New York: Cambridge University Press.

Ordeshook, Peter C., and Thomas R. Palfrey. 1988. "Agendas, Strategic Voting, and Signaling with Incomplete Information." *American Journal of Political Science* 32: 441–66.

Palfrey, Thomas R., and Howard Rosenthal. 1983. "Voter Participation and Strategic Uncertainty." *American Political Science Review* 79: 62–78.

Pommerehne, Werner W. 1978. "Institutional Approaches to Public Expenditures: Empirical Evidence from Swiss Municipalities." *Journal of Public Economics* 7: 225–80.

Romer, Thomas, and Howard Rosenthal. 1978. "Political Resource Allocation, Controlled Agendas, and the Status Quo," *Public Choice* 33: 27–44.

———. 1979a. "Bureaucrats vs. Voters: On the Political Economy of Resource Allocation by Direct Democracy." *Quarterly Journal of Economics* 93: 563–87.

———. 1979b. "The Elusive Median Voter." *Journal of Public Economics* 12: 143–70.

———. 1980. "An Institutional Theory of the Effect of Intergovernmental Grants." *National Tax Journal* 33: 451–8.

———. 1982a. "Median Voters or Budget Maximizers: Evidence from School Expenditure Referenda." *Economic Inquiry* 20: 556–78.

———. 1982b. "An Exploration in the Politics and Economics of Local Public Services." In D. Bos et al., *Public Production, Zeitschirft fur Nationalokonomie/Journal of Economics* Supplementum 2: 105–26.

———. 1983a. "A Constitution for Solving Asymmetric Externality Games." *American Journal of Political Science* 27: 1–26.

———. 1983b. "Voting and Spending: Some Empirical Relationships in the Political Economy of Local Public Finance." In G. Zodrow, ed., *Local Provisions of Public Services: The Tiebout Hypothesis After 25 Years*, New York: Academic Press 165–82.

Romer, Thomas, ed., Howard Rosenthal, and Krishna Ladha. 1984. "If at First You Don't Succeed: Budgeting by a Sequence of Referenda." In H. Hanusch, ed., *Public Finance and the Quest for Efficiency*. Detroit, Wayne State University Press, pp. 87–108.

Romer, Thomas, Howard Rosenthal, and Krishna Ladha. 1984. "If at First You Don't Succeed: Budgeting by a Sequence of Referenda." In H. Hanusch, ed., *Public Finance and the Quest for Efficiency*. Detroit, Wayne State University Press, pp. 87–108.

Romer, Thomas, Howard Rosenthal, and Vincent Munley. 1987. "Economic Incentives and Political Institutions: Spending and Voting in School Budget Referenda." NBER Working Paper #2406.

Rothstein, Paul. 1988. "State Aid to Schools in the Interjurisdictional Spending and Voter Behavior Models." St. Louis: Washington University (mimeo).

Shepsle, Kenneth, and Barry Weingast. 1981. "Structure-induced Equilibrium and Legislative Choice." *Public Choice* 37: 503–520.

———. 1984. "Uncovered Sets of Sophisticated Voting Outcomes with Implications for Agenda Institutions." *American Journal of Political Science* 28: 49–74.

Author Index

Allais, M., 62
Aranson, P., 61, 147–48
Arrow, K., 146
Aumann, R., 3
Austen-Smith, D., 5, 14, 18, 27–28, 37–39, 41, 51, 56, 163–64, 176

Banks, J. S., 5, 13–14, 18, 27, 37–38, 41, 211–12, 215, 219, 230–31
Barr, J., 170, 223
Beard, C., 58
Becker, C., 58, 153
Bergstrom, T. C., 223, 231
Berl, J., 107–8, 110–11, 137
Black, D., x, 1, 12–14, 46, 101, 146, 167, 169, 189
Blumel, W., 163
Bos, D., 163–64
Boulding, K., 40
Bowen, H. R., x
Brams, S. J., 42, 188, 197
Brock, T. C., 56
Bush, G., 40

Calvert, R. L., 27, 56, 146, 163, 164
Caplin, A., 4
Chamberlain, E., 179–83, 185, 188
Cohen, R. N., 5, 6, 35, 37, 179, 185
Cohen, S., 231
Collier, K., 119
Coughlin, P., 3, 7–8, 146, 154, 163, 169–71
Cox, G. W., 4–6, 8, 42, 103, 182–84, 186–87, 189–91

d'Aspremont, C., ix
Davis, O., 1, 2, 30, 40, 99, 101, 170, 223
de Condorcet, M., 189
Degroot, M., 2, 101, 153
Denzau, A., 20, 42, 52, 170, 177, 182–83, 203–4
Downs, A., 1, 2, 15, 17, 27, 39, 41, 46, 146, 181
Dukakis, M., 40

Eaton, B. C., 6, 17–23, 28–29, 32, 36, 38–42, 181–85, 191
Eavey, C., 61, 109
Enelow, J. M., 3–4, 8, 52, 56, 100, 102, 145, 147, 156–60, 163–64, 166, 169, 171, 174, 176, 230–31
Epple, D., 172, 177

Farnhan, P. G., 231
Farquharson, R., 2, 53, 220, 231
Feld, S. L., 46
Feldman, A., 163, 166
Ferejohn, J., 5, 13, 46, 53
Filimon, R., 226
Fink, E., 56, 58
Fiorina, M., 5, 13, 100, 104–5, 107–9, 119, 127, 135, 137, 145
Fishburn, P., 188
Froelich, N., 61

Gabszewicz, J. J., ix
Gasmi, F., 5
Gilligan, T., 204–5, 211
Goldwater, B., 188

Goodman, R., 223, 231
Goodstein, E., 107, 127
Greenberg, J., 4, 6, 27, 28
Greenberg, M., 31–35, 37–38, 42–43, 191–95
Grether, D., 62, 131
Grey, P., 119
Grofman, B., 46, 163–64

Hagen, O., 62
Hallett, G., 193
Hamilton, H. D., 231
Hammond, T. H., 50
Hansen, S., 229
Hay, D. A., 24, 39
Hinich, M., 1–4, 8, 30, 40–41, 56, 99–102, 145, 147–53, 155–60, 163–64, 166, 169–71, 174, 176, 184, 230–31
Hoag, C., 193
Hoffman, E., 140
Hotelling, H., ix, 1, 6, 15–21, 23–24, 26, 28–30, 33, 41, 146, 179–82, 188

Ingberman, D., 205–7, 230–31
Inman, R. P., 231
Isaak, M., 131

Jackson, H., 48
Jacobson, G. C., 14

Kadane, J., 172, 177
Kahneman, D., 61
Kaneko, M., 154
Kap-Yun, L., 191
Kats, A., 20, 42, 182–83
Kernell, S., 14
Key, V. O., 119
Khrebiel, K., 231
Kiewiet, D. R., 14, 52
Koehler, D. H., 52
Kormendi, R., 127–28, 133–34
Kramer, G., 2, 5, 46, 100, 102, 112, 121, 134–35, 163, 183
Krehbiel, K., 204–5, 211
Kreps, D. M., 43

Ladha, K., 126–32, 135, 226
Ledyard, J., 3, 5, 163
Lee, K., 163, 166
Lerman, A., 181
Levine, M., 6, 51, 53, 103
Lindbeck, A., 148, 160–62, 164
Lipsey, R., 6, 17–23, 28–29, 32, 36, 38–42, 181–85, 191
Lohmann, S., 230, 231
Londregan, J., 230
Losch, A., 36
Luce, R. D., 153–55, 163

Mackay, R., 170, 177, 203–4
MacRae, D., 191
Magnuson, W., 48–49, 51
Mansbridge, J. J., 59–60
Marschak, J., 153
Maschler, M., 3
McGovern, G., 188
McKelvey, R., 2–5, 7, 13, 46, 53, 109, 112–19, 121–27, 130, 134, 136, 138–41, 184, 207, 231
Mendell, N., 145, 164
Miller, N., 4, 109, 121, 184, 190
Miller, G. J., 50, 127
Mitchell, D., 163–64
Morton, R., 163–64
Morton, S., 211, 219, 222, 225–26, 230, 231
Mueller, D., 163, 166
Munley, V., 212, 226, 229
Murrell, P., 163, 166
Myerson, R. B., 43

Nakamura, K., 154
Nalebuff, B., 4
Newing, A. S., x, 13
Niemi, R., 50
Niskanen, W., 199
Nitzan, S., 3, 8, 146, 154, 163
Nunn, S., 40

Olmstead, S., 126–27, 129, 132
Oppenheimer, J., 61, 127
Ordeshook, P., 2–5, 7, 30, 41, 62, 103, 107, 109, 112–19, 121–31, 134, 136, 138–41, 145–49, 164, 184, 200, 207, 219, 231

Ostrom, T. M., 56

Packel, E. W., 5, 46, 53
Palfrey, T., 5–6, 28–37, 39, 41–42,
    107, 185, 229–31
Papageorgiou, Y. Y., 188
Pethig, R., 163
Petty, R. E., 56
Plott, C., 2, 6, 46, 50, 51, 53, 62, 99–
    101, 103–9, 112, 115–16, 120,
    127–28, 131, 133–35, 137, 140
Pommerehne, W. W., 231
Poole, K., 50
Prescott, E. C., 24, 26, 29, 39, 41

Rae, D., 101
Rawls, J., 61
Rhode, D. W., 14
Riker, W. H., 2, 5–6, 12, 14–15, 48,
    51–53, 56, 58, 62, 100, 138, 176
Romer, T., 3, 13, 53, 174, 199, 205,
    208–9, 212, 219, 224–32
Roosevelt, T., 30
Rosenthal, H., 3, 5, 9, 13, 50, 53,
    174, 199, 205, 208–9, 212, 219,
    224–32
Rothstein, P., 229, 232

Salant, S., 107, 127
Samuelson, L., 148, 155, 163–64
Sawyer, J., 191
Schofield, N., 4, 50, 53, 61, 99, 101
Schwartz, T., 103
Sen, A., 163
Shaked, A., 184

Shepsle, K., 3–6, 9, 13, 27–28, 31–
    35, 37–38, 42–43, 50–52, 100,
    179, 185, 191–92, 204, 207, 231
Singer, H., 181
Slotznick, B., 128–32, 135
Slutsky, S., 20, 42, 182–83
Smith, R., 48
Smith, J. A., 58
Smithies, A., 1, 17, 41, 184
Straffin, P. D., 42
Sugden, R., 193–94, 195
Suppes, P., 153–55

Taylor, M., 101
Thisse, J., ix, 188
Tullock, g., 181
Tversky, A., 61

Visscher, M., 24, 26, 29, 39, 41
von dem Hagen, O., 163

Wallace, G., 30
Weber, S., 193–95
Weibull, J., 148, 160–62, 164
Weingast, B., 4
Weingast, B. W., 13, 50, 52, 100, 207,
    231
Wilson, R., 3, 43, 132, 134, 136–37
Winer, M., 3, 124, 125–26, 128–31
Wittman, D., 6, 7, 27, 163, 166
Wright, S. G., 15
Wright, J., 50

Yinger, J., 164

Zimmerman, H., 163–64

Subject Index

Abstention
  Due to Alienation, 2, 30
  Due to Indifference, 2, 146, 152
Admissable Set, 121
Agenda
  Amendment, 4
  Control of, 6, 46
  Endogenous, 5, 132
  General, 3, 13, 36, 100, 103, 132, 134, 179, 199, 204, 207
  Manipulation as a Heresthetic Device, 53
  In McKelvey Theorem, 46, 53
  Setter, 9, 103, 199, 203–13, 215–30
Alternative Space, 57–58
Amendment
  Germane, 54
  "Killer", 52
  Sequential, 51
American Party, 30
Annapolis Convention, 59
Anti-Federalists, 58–60
Approval Voting, 8–9, 180, 188–89

Backward Induction, 25, 37, 204
Banks Model, 211–12, 215–216
Bargaining Set, 3, 127, 138
Bayesian Equilibrium, 43
Benthamite Social Welfare Function, 162
Best Response Strategies, 38–39
Binary Luce Model, 8, 38–39, 153–55
Borda Rule, 180
Budget Reversion Level, Endogenous, 9
Bull Moose Party, 30

Closed Rule, 204, 205

Competitive Solution, 3, 104, 124–27, 130, 138
Condorcet
  Competition, 180, 189
  Paradox, x
  Majority, x
  Point, 101, 104, 114–16
  Procedures, 8, 189–90
  Winner, 52–53, 100–4, 107–14, 119–21, 137, 189
Congress
  United States, 81–82, 141, 155
  Elections, 14
Constitution
  United States, 47, 58, 60
  Convention, 59
Copeland Winner, 90
Core, 7, 99, 101–3, 107–11, 124–29, 131–32, 134, 137–38
Cournot-Nash Hypothesis, 21, 22, 29
Credibility, 55

Democratic Party, 73, 74, 76, 82, 180, 188
Department of Defense, 48
Dixiecrats, 30
Duopoly, 16
Duverger's Law, 14, 31
Dynamic Stability, 5

Electoral Qualification, 50
Equal Rights Amendment, 58–60

Federal Reserve, 82
Federalists, 58, 60
Filibuster, 51

Game Theory, 2
Gerrymander, 50

Heartland, 129–30
House of Representatives, United States, 13, 81

Ideologies, 56
Inflation Game, 94
Influence Parties, 27, 39
Information
  Complete, 51
  Incomplete, 5
Interest Groups, 158–60

K-Equilibrium, 32

Legislatures, Models of, 12
Limit Equilibrium, 29–30, 33, 35

Massachusetts Miracle, 40
Minimax
  Conjecture, 21, 24–25
  Set, 46, 121
  Strategy, 123
  Strategy Solution, 5
Minimum Wage, 57
Mixed Strategy Equilibrium, 121–23
Multidimensional Scaling, 4

Nash Equilibrium, 42, 102, 114, 147, 187, 191, 219
Nash Social Welfare Function, 8, 154
Neo-Institutionalism, 3, 9
Non-Spatial Candidate Characteristics, 156–57, 159

Open Rule, 52, 205
Outcome Space, 57

Pareto Set, 4
Party Formation, 14
Pigovian Welfare-Optimizing Tax
  Relation to Medial Voter, 230

Platform, 68
Plausible Beliefs, 38–39
Pliny The Younger, 53
Plott Equilibrium, 50
Plurality Rule, 8, 52, 90, 147–48, 180, 183–84, 190–91, 195–96
Policy Implementation Model, 67
Poll, 4, 145
Populist Party, 30
Powell Amendment, 52
Principal-Agent Model, 66
Principle of Minimum Differentiation, 17–21, 29, 188
Pure Strategy Equilibrium, 121

Quota System, 194–95

Rank Maximizing, 32, 35, 39
Rank Order, 186
Rational Expectations, 4
Rawlsian Minimax Strategy, 61
Registration, Voter, 76
Republican, 73, 82–83, 180, 188
Retrospective Voting, 82, 119, 177
Revolution, 47
Roberts Rules of Order, 140

Satisficing, 42
Scoring Rules, 8, 180, 186–88, 191
Senate, United States, 48–49, 72
Separation of Powers, 50
Sequential Equilibrium, 43
Sequential Referenda, 9
Seventeenth Amendment to the U.S. Constitution, 52
Social Democratic—Liberal Alliance (Great Britain), 30
Socialist Party, 30
Sophisticated Voting
  See Strategic Voting
Stackelberg Game, 41–42
Strategy Space, 67
Strategic Voting, 46, 52, 103, 180, 199, 219–23
Structure-Induced Equilibrium, 50
Support Group, 27

Tax Share, 170
Threat Point, 80

Uncovered Set, 4, 90, 104, 121, 123, 184

Unanimity, 131–32
Unemployment, 57

V-Set, 3, 124–25
Veil of Ignorance, 127, 138

Vote Trading, 61
Vote-Share Maximization, 183

Wallacites, 30
Whigs, 51

Yolk, 90

www.ingramcontent.com/pod-product-compliance
Ingram Content Group UK Ltd.
Pitfield, Milton Keynes, MK11 3LW, UK
UKHW010039140625
459647UK00012BA/1475